IRISH

IRISH

THE REMARKABLE SAGA OF A NATION AND A CITY

JOHN BURROWES

MAINSTREAM
PUBLISHING

EDINBURGH AND LONDON

Contents

For all those who had to flee 'across the ditch',
and in particular Thomas William Burrowes,
born Sligo 1868, died Glasgow 1918.

'The guilty one is not he who commits the sin,
but the one who causes the darkness.'

'There is always more misery among the lower classes
than there is humanity in the higher.'

Victor Hugo, *Les Miserables*

Preface

It was the much-respected Glasgow historian, the late Charles A. Oakley, who wrote: 'There is no subject which writers and speakers about Glasgow are less willing to tackle than that of the Irish in Scotland.' That perhaps helps explain why a book like this has not been done before. I appreciate Charles Oakley's words far more now, after having worked on this book for the last two years. In commenting as he did, Oakley was well aware that even if a writer or speaker on the subject were not coming from a particular viewpoint, he or she would in all probability still be accused of partiality. Oakley must also have been aware of the reluctance which (surprisingly to me) still exists among some to be identified with their Irish background. A few very prominent people preferred not to speak about or have their Irish roots aired in this book.

Belonging to neither of the two opposed religious camps of the Glasgow Irish, although having Irish antecedents, hopefully I am not guilty of the kind of biased tendencies which Mr Oakley considered to be one of the hazards of writing a book like this. No writer, of course, can be without an opinion and after the long research in which I have been involved for *Irish*, I have no doubt that my own viewpoint on such matters will have altered somewhat along the road. If that is the case, then I sincerely trust that it is in the direction of a fuller understanding of events in the past and their effects on the present. I have endeavoured to tell the remarkable story of the coming of the Irish to Scotland, and in particular to Glasgow, in the most impartial and dispassionate fashion possible.

I have also made a sincere effort to refrain (as much as I could) from being judgemental. It is all too easy to fall into that trap when writing about Ireland and perhaps such judgements are best left to the historian and the academic. I have no pretension to be either, the objective of this book being to lend some humanity to the history of that quite phenomenal mass movement of people who were cast out of Ireland in numbers even greater than had been the Children of Israel from their homeland. The Children of Ireland were to know suffering of biblical proportions in their flight from a country ravished by famine, arbitrarily misgoverned to the point of vindictiveness, and racked by sectarian violence.

The Great Famine of 1845–51 was to inflict on the Irish misery and degradation so abject that, in proportionate terms, it was unequalled anywhere else in the world. More than two million were wiped from the face of their land, either dying from starvation or fever, or fleeing to whatever country would accept them.

The Glasgow Irish came from these grim circumstances and in my telling the story for the first time in such terms, I have concentrated on the most significant and momentous of the events leading up to and during the main movement of the Irish people out of their homeland, particularly focusing on those who were to settle in and around Scotland's biggest city. This is not the customary chronological account of those who normally record such historical events. There are no long lists of dates and figures with accompanied annotations and references. Instead my objective has been to seek out and relate some of the most eventful, moving and remarkable of the human dramas which were to occur throughout that unique period in history, dramatically affecting the city of Glasgow as well as many other parts of Scotland. While these stories are often filled with tragedy and the worst of human suffering, they bear the hallmarks of the Irish: their unrivalled adaptability and supreme optimism combined with incredible courage and fearless fortitude. Such were the factors that have seen them achieve, and continue to do so, the great things they have. The Glasgow Irish have contributed so much to the city.

Few cities outside of the New World have known so many incomers as has Glasgow. Many waves of migrants have settled in Scotland's biggest city, each new ethnic community contributing its own individual flavour to the heady cocktail which constitutes that rather unique blend of people, the Glaswegians. But none were to affect the mix of the population of the city as much as those from Ireland. Their arrival, from the latter part of the eighteenth century and throughout the century after that, was to be the most significant of chapters in the long, colourful and eventful history of the city.

Of course, many of the people from Ireland who came to Scotland went on to settle in other parts of the country, principally throughout Lanarkshire, the Lothians and Fife. But no place would identify with them more than Glasgow. Nowhere else would receive such an inundation of them. Glasgow was their main port of disembarkation. For most of them it was to be their first, and indeed permanent, home, as well as that of their descendants.

Often when people think of the Irish they think of the Catholic Irish. But there were also Protestant Irish among the multitude fleeing the starvation and deprivation of Ireland, just as ready and willing to brave the sea-crossing in tiny and perilously overcrowded little steamships. At one time these were so numerous they were referred to as the 'floating bridge' between the two countries. As the passengers' religion was not recorded, there are no accurate figures of the numbers of each faith to arrive. However, the proportion of Protestants among the arrivals is usually estimated at between a quarter and a third. Like other Irish, the Protestants came to Scotland mainly for economic reasons, although many were also fleeing the sectarian violence that had plagued the two communities for centuries.

The majority of those who fled the abject poverty to which they had been reduced during and following the Great Famine had previously lived the most basic of rural existences. They were a breed of people who for centuries had known little more than the hard end of working life. They arrived in their biggest numbers at a time when Scotland was about to experience one of the most dramatic developments in its history, the Industrial Revolution. The success of that Revolution depended on labour on a scale that Scots themselves, by virtue of their numbers, could not provide. The fact that the Industrial Revolution did gather pace in Scotland, and that Glasgow and central Scotland were to become the workshop of the Empire, was in no small measure due to that huge reservoir of labour which arrived from Ireland. Without that special breed of readily mobile and accommodating worker, the new harbours, canals, railways, roads and hydro-electric schemes would not have been completed on the same scale. Without them, Scotland would be a smaller and less accomplished nation and Glasgow would never have become the city we know today.

Acknowledgements

My sincerest gratitude goes to a great number of people who at the first instance were most willing with their help and counsel, among them Liam McColgan, of the Scottish Ex-Boxers Club; Pat Woods (Celtic historian); Ian Wilson, Grand Master, Loyal Orange Lodge; Kate Cunningham, Celtic FC; the Church of Scotland Press Office; Rev. Alan McDonald, St Andrews; Paul Drury; Russell Kyle; Jack Irvine; Tom Brown; John Millar; Rev. Alastair Rammage; Heatherbank Museum of Social Work, Caledonia University; Diana Law, Manchester United FC; Dr Elinor Kelly, Glasgow University; Harry Conroy, Pat Crerand, John McCormack and Michael Kelly, C.B.E., various offices at Glasgow and Strathclyde Universities and, as always, the ever-helpful staff, especially in the Glasgow Room, of the Mitchell Library. I am also indebted to my son Kyle for his valued and much-appreciated assistance, particularly his introduction and guidance during my pathfinding days negotiating the wondrous and labyrinthine highways of the Internet. And to all those who at the suggestion that such a work was in progress and when invited to assist, considered it more prudent not to be involved – I do understand!

– CHAPTER 1 –

Salvation on a Coffin Ship

Had it been possible they would have walked all the way there. Mothers, fathers, children, grandparents, would have thought nothing of walking to the ends of the earth to escape the death and devastation to which their country had been reduced by the Great Famine. But to get to that haven of refuge where they could survive, they had to go by ship. Such was their desperation, they didn't care what kind of ship, neither did they care that most of them were to be treated by shipowners and masters not as human beings but as mere cargo. Cargo in which there were fortunes to be made, just as there had been with the slaves. They were taken across the wildest of seas in the humblest of vessels. Livestock dealers would have ensured their export cattle weren't crowded in the way these humans were on some of the crossings to the Clyde. But even taking your chance on a perilous voyage on one of the vessels

17

they called 'coffin ships' was preferable to certain
death by starvation or the prospect of a lifetime of
drudgery.

In the late evenings of fine summer days, the Irish families in
Greenock would often wander up the steep slopes of a hill
behind the town. The hill would later be known as Lyle Hill, a
tribute to the enterprising local family who, together with the
Tates from Lancashire, gave the world its sugar. The walk was
one of the few diversions in their hard-working lives. In those
pleasant late hours up there on the crest of the high hill, they
would linger and enjoy the company of others from their
homeland, and take in the view before them. It was one of the
most spectacular sights in the country, a magnificent panorama
of the Firth of Clyde, where sea meets river and lochs finger into
the woods and hills of the Cowal Peninsula, and the backdrop is
of jagged mountains that stretch all the way north as far as the
eye can see. But there was more to the view than that glorious
sweeping scene in the mid-nineteenth century. Also to be seen
were numerous little boats, sailing up from the south-west, each
of them crammed with human cargo, all heading for Glasgow.

The Irish in Greenock had been among the earliest of the
settlers to come over. It was something of a bonus to be Irish if
you wanted work in the town's sugar-refining works, the bosses
reckoning no one could withstand the terrible heat inside the
big processing plants better. They would have known all about
the hazards of that voyage over the channel from Ireland but
what they saw from the brow of that hill defied all credibility.
Ship after ship had been coming up from the south-west for
weeks, each of them wallowing deep in the water with their
over-burdened cargo of humans. But the sight that shocked the
onlookers so much was what they saw on the decks of those

little steamships, chug-chugging so slowly up the deep navigational channel of this sheltered stretch of the Clyde. No ships on which they had sailed had ever appeared like these ones. Looking down on them from a distance, all that could be clearly discerned was the pink tinge of the enormous deck cargo each of the tiny ships was carrying. It was puzzling, until one man produced a short brass telescope he called his spyglass and cried out 'Mother of Jesus' when it defined the scene more clearly. Others exclaimed in disbelief, some of them wailing and crying at the sight the little spyglass revealed to them. For the deck cargo was human beings, so tightly packed together that the pink tinge they saw from the distance was their faces, crammed closely together on the ships' decks. They were to become known as 'the ships of heads and faces'.

What could be seen from that hill above Greenock in those years was the flight from the Great Famine, Ireland's very own holocaust. In its wake the Irish experienced the days of the Great Migration, their very own diaspora.

The scale of the exodus from Ireland was as incredible as the sight of those little ships from the summit of Lyle Hill. For an appreciation of the numbers who landed from the Clyde in those years, consider the official log of the ships loaded with those desperate immigrants which arrived in Glasgow during just ten days of August 1847, the second year of the Great Famine. That year was the pinnacle of the suffering endured in that calamity, and shipload after shipload of Irish were sailing up the Firth of Clyde in numbers that had never been witnessed before or since. Note how many of the passengers for 1847 – around a third – journeyed on one particular vessel, the SS *Londonderry*, about which you will read considerably more later in this chapter. The log reads:

6 August 1847. Port of embarkation, Derry. Ship's name, SS *Shamrock*. Number of passengers, 1,233.

7 August. Port of embarkation, Belfast. Ship's name, SS *Aurora*. Number of passengers, 705.

8 August. Port of embarkation, Derry. Ship's name, SS *Londonderry*. Number of passengers, 454.

9 August. Port of embarkation, Belfast. By steamer to Ardrossan and railway to Glasgow. Number of passengers, 741.

10 August. Port of embarkation, Belfast. Ship's name, SS *Aurora*. Number of passengers, 1,000.

11 August. Port of embarkation, Derry. Ship's name, SS *Londonderry*. Number of passengers, 1,778.

12 August. Port of embarkation, Belfast. Ship's name, SS *Tartar*. Number of passengers, 717.

14 August. Port of embarkation, Derry. Ship's name, SS *Londonderry*. Number of passengers, 746.

14 August. Port of embarkation, Derry. Ship's name, SS *Shamrock*. Number of passengers, 1,130.

14 August. Port of embarkation, Belfast. Ship's name, SS *Aurora*. Number of passengers, 940.

17 August. Port of embarkation, Belfast. Ship's name, SS *Aurora*. Number of passengers, 531.

18 August. Port of embarkation, Derry. Ship's name, SS *Londonderry*. Number of passengers, 1,105.

Just 10 days in August and another 11,080 new immigrants from Ireland had arrived in the city. And that's not counting those who would have come by other routes, such as via Liverpool or on the crossing to Portpatrick, either trudging or coaching the rest of the way to Glasgow. The next ten days would have brought a similar number of hungry new citizens. In a 12-week period that summer, at the very height of the migration deluge, Glasgow was swollen by more than 33,000 newcomers. That number approximates to the population of big Scottish towns like Dumfries or Stirling, Irvine or Motherwell. Just think of that in today's terms – every single person from, say, Stirling, arriving in Glasgow in the period of a few weeks . . . And in the following few weeks, the equivalent of everyone from Motherwell would arrive. Each of them had to be housed somewhere. Each of them had to be provided for by one of their group securing work of some kind. Each of them depended on the burgeoning city's over-stressed resources: its water supply, its meagre cleansing arrangements, and its medical centres. And virtually all of them were in such a state of wretched poverty that their first port of call when they straggled along Broomielaw quayside was the offices of the City Parochial Board (the Parish) to plead for some temporary relief. The tax known as the poor rate levied on Glaswegians soared by a third in order to cater for the overwhelming numbers seeking such assistance.

The lands over the water, in both the New and Old Worlds, had been the only answer. The government in London had been as devastating a blight on the people of Ireland as the *phytophthora infestans* had been on the potatoes. The Irish had loved their native country, despite the privations, despite the grasping landlords, despite what their rulers in Westminster decreed for them. But even when the nineteenth century had reached its mid-point and the authorities were saying the potato disease was over and the harvests would be good from now on, it wouldn't mean an end to the hard times. It wouldn't mean an end to the fevers and diseases so many of them suffered. It wouldn't mean an end to their primitive living conditions, or the fact that they were the poorest and most under-privileged of

Europe's peasants. With or without famines, every day was a struggle for the Irish masses.

Now even the charity that had been coming from overseas to aid those who had suffered from the famine had dried up. Help had not been inconsiderable, the news of the tragedy affecting the compassionate in many far-flung parts of the world. Quakers, together with Protestants and Catholics throughout Britain had raised considerable sums. Queen Victoria herself had been a generous donor, handing over what would be today's equivalent of around £70,000. Such was the pity for the victims of the famine that there had even been the most touching, albeit the most unlikely gesture of all: a generous collection from workers and *sepoy* (native) soldiers in India. A classic yardstick in demonstrating just how poor and unfortunate the Irish were.

The years during and immediately after the famine were to leave Ireland in a state of post-traumatic shock. The population had shrunk to around six and a half million. That meant that the island had suffered the dramatic loss of around two and a half million people, even more if the usual natural growth in birth rate were taken into account. Just under a million had died from hunger. In the five years of the famine, a million and a half left the country, most of them for America. Pause a moment to consider that incredible number of people – approximately two and a half million – in relation to Scotland. It would represent every living soul in the city of Glasgow and the surrounding area . . . all of them gone! Not a single person left in the entire city or its satellite new and old towns. All of them either having died or fled the country. It is virtually inconceivable, but it happened in Ireland. That's the measure of the devastation the Great Famine had brought to them.

The New World, of course, had been the more attractive destination for those who chose to flee, but there was to be a place for them in the Old World too, and the ship to Glasgow was to become one of the most popular escape routes out of the devastated country. The days of the Great Migration were to lead to better lives for millions of Irish people, but there was to be no easy transition. For the Irish diaspora was yet another part of the great tragedy. While it promised so much hope, it was to lead to countless more deaths. Tens of thousands would experience the most inhumane of treatment en route to their new horizons. Thousands would even die in the attempt to start afresh. The only easy part of their adventure to new territories, it seemed, was the actual decision to leave their native land. With their minds set, the first moves were relatively simple.

Unlike those on mainland Europe who were likewise forced to leave their homelands in other times, they were not faced with a mammoth trek, often lasting weeks, to the nearest port. Ireland was a small country, so many of them would walk all the way to places they could sail from, such as Sligo, Cork, Londonderry, Limerick, Dublin and Belfast.

Those with a few pennies would perhaps make part of the journey to the seaport on the '*bian*'. The *bians* were the coaches of Ireland's first major transport service. They could carry up to 20 passengers in open-deck cars, their engine being either a sturdy gelding or hardy mare. Genuine one-horse power! The *bians* got their strange name from the man who founded the coaching service, an Italian migrant called Charles Bianconi. It's said that as a young man growing up near Como in northern Italy Charles had an affair with the daughter of a wealthy landowner. For some reason, probably because he was not sufficiently affluent, he had not been Daddy's choice and was given a traditional Italian warning – emigrate or else. He chose the former and Ireland got its *bians*.

Many didn't have to make a decision about which country

they would be heading for – landlords often paid for whole estates of workers to be transported to America and Canada, and in one four-year period more than 22,000 such migrants were to leave their homeland. This seemed most generous of these gentry fellows, but philanthropy wasn't exactly their prime motive. Saving cash was, for each individual's fare of around £4.50 was roughly the price it cost to keep them for a year. And once the estates were cleared of people, the land would become more profitable, soaring in value. Acreages could be converted into huge grazing tracts, cows and sheep making them much more money than potato plot-holders and labourers ever did. One wealthy landowner had 1,400 of his workforce emigrate over a period of some years. It cost him £3.50 per head for the operation and resulted in a much-improved property in financial terms. The more heartless estate owners would only pay the most basic transportation costs for their workers, little caring what kind of vessels unscrupulous shippers would provide for them. Some were even known to tell those heading off that food and clothing would be supplied on the trip, when in fact they would have paid for neither.

Whether by walking, even though it took a day or two, or by the *bian*, that very first stage of the migration was invariably to prove the easiest part of the long journey. After that it was up to chance. If you could afford it, especially if you already had relatives there who could help with the fare, America or Canada would be the choice of destination. The word was that the best chances for the future were to be found in the New World. Those planning to go there would be warned about the perils of the journey. Crossing the high seas in old sailing ships was fraught with many dangers, and the vicious storms and mountainous waves of the mid-winter Atlantic were not to be the worst of the hazards facing the poor migrants. Grasping shipowners and soulless ship captains and crews were engaged in one of the grimmest and most cruel chapters in the history of sea transportation, equalled only by the highly profitable business it was now replacing – slave trading.

The ships themselves little resembled those generally conjured up by the days of sail – glorious multi-masted clippers, elegant Onedin-line tall ships or ornate galleons with their high poop decks ever so gracefully slicing the waves powered by acres of white billowing sails. The emigrant traders were in stark contrast to these. Many were the most miserable-looking little tubs, which you would have been fearful of boarding to cross the Firth of Clyde, never mind the Atlantic.

It wasn't until 1838 that steamships began to be used for the Atlantic trade, the first voyage being that of the SS *Sirius* which sailed from Cork to New York in that year. The fact that they were powered by steam made little difference to their size; the little *Sirius* weighed a mere 260 tons and was able to carry around 200 to 300 passengers. Put it alongside that most perennial of paddle steamers, the *Waverley*, and it makes the Clyde's favourite ship look like the *QE2* by comparison. The *Waverley* weighs more than 690 tons – more than two and a half times that of the bold *Sirius* – and is able to comfortably carry more than 800 passengers.

Such was the demand of the emigrants for transport, there weren't sufficient available vessels from Britain, let alone Ireland, to cope with the trade. Boats of varying descriptions had to be chartered from other parts of Europe. Many of these ships were freight-carrying vessels cheaply converted for the bulk transportation of passengers, who would be housed for the long journey in stinking and overcrowded dormitories. The bedding of the cramped berths in which they spent most of their time in these sea-going dosshouses would not have been changed or aired from the previous voyage, or the one before that, and even further back. The only time passengers' quarters would receive any form of cleansing was when the ship was approaching the quarantine station at its destination port in order to obtain a clean bill of health.

Provisions for the voyage would usually be doled out along institutional lines, with a strictly measured (to the ounce) allowance per head, per day. Rations usually consisted of low-quality meal and the mariners' dreaded salt beef, so heavily salted it drove those who ate it mad for water, and those who didn't weak from lack of vitamins. Damned if they ate it, damned if they didn't.

But there were worse vessels – the Coffin Ships. Conditions in these were so vile that thousands were to die on the journey, their bodies callously tossed to the predators of the sea. Many of these ships were old cargo vessels that had spent their entire sailing existence thus far transporting loads of lumber, grain or flax seed to Europe from the vast forests of North America and Canada. The shipowners needed some kind of ballast for the return journey across the Atlantic and the new trade in people was to be a godsend for them. The migrants paid them money to be crammed into the foul cargo holds of their leaky, creaky old sailing ships. Not for them the luxury of the normal passenger ship with its cabins, bunk beds and stewards to serve them food from the galleys, nor even the crowded dormitories or the cramped berths of the regular passenger vessels. The lower end of the migrant trade bore no resemblance whatsoever to such journeys. Most of the Irish emigrants would spend six miserable weeks huddled together in the ship's damp and dingy holds, some of them no bigger than a modern freight container, and as functional and cheering. There were no beds, no chairs, no furnishings or comforts of any kind. Their only light would come from a couple of blackened oil lamps, their only heat, apart from that generated by their own bodies, from a small stove on which they would also warm what food they had. Their toilet facilities were usually open buckets, although some captains ordered that the women use the crew's primitive deck closets. On the stormiest nights, the hatches would be battened down and the migrants would lie in the fearful darkness, clustered together, many of them delirious with fever, others suffering acute sea-sickness, all of them terrified at the incessant creaking of the ship's timbers, the raging winds and the pounding waves. The stench from those who were sick and from the unemptied toilet buckets inside those small, dank holds can only be imagined.

Some humanitarians had become so concerned about the many reported horrors of the Coffin Ships that they accompanied some of the unfortunate migrants on their voyages to new lands in order to publicise the wickedness of this stratum of the migrant trade. One who travelled across the Atlantic in 1847 wrote about his experiences on board a small brigantine which made the journey with 110 passengers crammed into its tiny hold:

> There had been fever among some of the passengers but the captain refused them any medications from his stores. He turned away a delegation who wanted to air their complaints to him and when the men had then decided they would have to break into the ship's stores to get vital medicine, the captain had turned a gun on them. During the height of one storm, water had crashed down from the decks on top of them, soaking everyone.

One such ship, carrying a cargo of estate workers, their fares paid by their landlords, lost 136 passengers on the voyage, either through fever, other disease due to malnutrition, or simply as a result of the insufferable conditions on board. Another lost 93. In one of the most notorious crossings, 46 passengers died of starvation alone. In all these cases, the corpses were thrown overboard. On other ships, workers in the ports where the ships landed would be paid bonus money in order to clear the corpses from the holds of the newly arrived vessels, using boat hooks to drag them out from the hellholes in which they had died.

Almost half of the migrants crossing the Atlantic at the height of the famine flight would go to Canada, but not by choice – it cost less. Accommodation in the cheapest steerage class was about half the price of ships going to the United States. Once in Canada, many thought they could eventually trek south to join compatriots who had settled in New England or New York. So many were to head there that at times there was a virtual armada of immigrants in the Atlantic, all sailing westwards at the same time. On one such occasion, the Canadian authorities had been notified to expect some 34 ships carrying 10,636 new settlers.

Because those destined for Canada had been the poorest of the voyagers, they were also the ones in the worst state of health, resulting in a horrific death toll. Migrants died not only during the long sea crossing (it took between five and six weeks at the time), but also in the quarantine centres in which the fevered and diseased would be detained before being admitted to the dominion. Many of them would have contracted their illness, usually typhus, on board the ship on which they travelled. It spread with deadly rapidity in the congested conditions. Tens of thousands of the sick were dumped in what was nothing better than a concentration camp, located on Grosse Island in the mighty St Lawrence River, about 30 miles from Quebec. Grosse Ile, as it was known, was the Canadian Ellis Island, neither of them the kind of place where they hoisted 'Welcome Stranger' signs for arrivals. For an estimated 5,424 of those unfortunate wretches who had survived the most hellish of sea journeys, Grosse Ile would be all they would ever see of their New World. They succumbed to the sickness with which they had landed. Their bodies lie in the huge burial ground on the island, the biggest mass grave of its kind, bigger even than any resulting from the Great Famine in Ireland itself. The thousands who died there are commemorated by a 40-foot-high Celtic cross positioned on the highest part of the island so that it can be seen by every passing ship. It's reckoned, however, that outwith Grosse Ile some four times that number died soon after their arrival. Hundreds of their children were left orphans, many being adopted by local Canadian families.

There was another dimension to the horrors of crossing the Atlantic in the Coffin Ships, and that was the experience of the thousands who began their journeys by crossing from Dublin to Liverpool in order to catch one of the numerous boats sailing almost every day from the English port for Canada and America. Many of them had the most lurid of tales to relate of their varied experiences at the English port. Waiting for the flood of migrants as they passed through the burgeoning Mersey city were the full Dickensian panoply of crooks, cheats, charlatans, swindlers, scoundrels and all sorts of conniving rascals. The migrants were a huge and booming trade, and this lot were in for a share of it – all at the migrants' cost.

'Oi, mister!' they would shout, emphasising their strident Liverpudlian accent to make it sound even more Irish than it already did. 'Oi, mister, I'll dollar yer Oirish coin for ye cheaper than the banks will.' 'Oi, mister, look at me bargain tickets for

New York.' 'Oi, mister, I've cheap lodgings for ye.' 'Oi, mister, I'll guide you to a great place.' While the bewildered new arrivals were distracted by the authorities, others, foxy-eyed and slippery-handed, were ready to empty their inviting pockets, filch their unattended baggage and anything else they could get their thieving mitts on.

The dollars they were selling, of course, would often be lesser-value Confederate money (the American Civil War was still to come) or even more spurious currency. Those 'New York' tickets were as doubtful as the dollars were and would result in whoever invested in them being turned back at the gate of the ship's purser, or finding themselves aboard a vessel going instead to Boston or Baltimore, sometimes even New Orleans. Even the legitimate ticket agents were up to that trick, often booking eager customers on passages to ports many hundreds of miles from New York, with the glib assurance that their destination was 'just nearby', an explanation gladly accepted by the desperate and naive migrants, who till now had never travelled further than Michael up-the-road's potato patch. As for those 'Oi, mister, cheap lodgings', that was one of the surest lures to invite a family to dens of the worst kind of vagabonds. The lucky ones were those to whom the robbers would permit the return of the luggage they hijacked from them, for a price that is. The unlucky ones were those that were left with nothing. Even the safer lodging houses were fraught with peril. Being the most basic and ill-kept of lodgings, they were often one of the main sources of typhus and other diseases. As a result, many tragically succumbed to illness at sea and never saw their promised land. Migrants were compelled to use the boarding houses, however, as port regulations forbade the boarding of the ships until just before they were due to sail.

Liverpool in the mid-nineteenth century was no easy city for the impoverished transients, but nevertheless it became the focal point of the Irish migrant trade. It had cornered the market for transatlantic shipping, so much so that by the mid-nineteenth century some 90 per cent of the Irish heading for New York boarded ships on the Mersey. At one time such trade had avoided the port because fares had been more expensive there, but shrewd shipowners, realising the potential of the seemingly endless new business slashed their prices (as well as their standards) and by the time the migrant flight was at its height it could offer the cheapest rates and the biggest number of sailings to the New World. At this time there were more than 4,000 migrants passing through the port every week, a loss to Ireland of more than a quarter of a million people a year. The equivalent of the entire population of modern cities like Aberdeen or Dundee was wiped from the map of Ireland in a single year.

By comparison to those heading out over the Atlantic, the ones that chose Glasgow as their destination would have a comparatively easy journey, although not without its perils and privations. There had been regular sailings to Glasgow from Dublin and Belfast for many years prior to the Great Famine. Because of the success of these routes, services were increased until there were twice-weekly sailings from Dublin, while from Belfast there was a twice-daily service. Many of the ships engaged in these crossings were among the smallest and unlikeliest of sea-going vessels. Steam was being introduced to shipping at the time and owners were quick to see its potential, principally for the coastal trade. When the famine exodus came, these little steamships were to fulfil all the potential which had been predicted of them, despite their appearance. They were virtually the first descendants of steam pioneer Henry Bell's *Comet*, the first commercial steamship in Britain, and indeed the first efficient steamship in Europe.

Bell had launched the little *Comet* on the Clyde in 1811. It weighed a mere 25 tons and was about 40 feet long, akin to the dimensions of the lifeboats carried by the big cruise liners of modern times, bearing in mind it was also minus a couple of centuries of technology.

These first-generation steamships had been used initially as riverboats, scores of them fussily puffing up and down the Clyde from Partick to Bowling and Port Glasgow. They had a variety of functions: carrying passengers, or small loads of freight, or ferrying supplies to and from bigger vessels. Their Captains Courageous ventured further down the Clyde with them once the harsh winter months were over, and with the lure of Ireland on the horizon when they chugged south of Girvan and the Ailsa Craig, why shouldn't they go the 14 miles extra and pick up trade there as well. There had always been plenty of it, particularly in summer, when the seasonal migrants would come over. There was brisk business too in bringing across the fattened cattle and sheep. The shippers could always rely on the lively and regular trade of those Irish agricultural labourers for whom Scotland was a great attraction; at harvest time they could earn themselves wages at around five to six times what they received in Ireland. They would pour over in their thousands for the various harvests, from hay to corn, wheat to barley, turnip to potato to berries, and the Agricultural Revolution which was to modernise Scottish farming would never have been so effective without these adaptable and hard-working itinerants with their scythes and sickles, rakes and forks. When necessary, they could speak the Scots farmers' tongue, and knew a graip from a graik, a shuil and a scartle from a snakefork and a spail, and a wassock and weedock from a wylie. All of these harvest tools and equipment.

It was because of these harvesters, on which the little ships of the steamboat fleet had thrived, that there was a ready-made service available for the migrants fleeing the desolation and disorder the Great Famine had brought to their country. The choice of Glasgow as a destination was in the main a financial decision. It cost a few pounds to go to America or Canada, that is if the landlord wasn't paying the passage, but only a fraction of that for the half-day's journey over to Scotland. The great competition among the coastal shipowners had brought about considerable reductions in their charges. In the years before the famine it had cost around £1 per head for a family sharing a cabin, less than half that for the cheapest accommodation below decks. This was known as steerage, and took its name from the compartment space around the ship's steering equipment. These fares were to come down over the years and when the famine rush was at its peak, cabin fares had been reduced to around two shillings, steerage space about half that amount. Eventually you could do the crossing for as little as around two pence, that is if the weather was half decent and you were fit – or fearless! – enough to remain on deck for the nine to twelve hours it would take for the journey. There was little choice for the thousands who were to make that tuppenny trip to what for most of them would be better days. Such was their destitution that those two pennies would have represented their entire life savings. It was well worth giving their all to flee the misery they had experienced for so much of their lives. They would have learned from kinsmen who had already made the crossing that there were many difficulties over the channel too, and on the Coffin Ships, but at least there was some hope for them and their children if they departed, and there was little of that in Ulster or Munster.

The small steamboats which had performed such an admirable service in carrying the seasonal harvesters on their return journeys over the years were now to be the ideal way to meet the new demand of those fleeing the famine and its aftermath.

Up the Clyde they poured, the little ships literally packed to their gunnels, so crowded that some passengers even sat on the vessels' paddle boxes, the safety housing covering the churning side paddles which drove the ship. On the open main deck the migrants were packed shoulder to shoulder; there were so many of them they had to crush together, all standing firmly upright, not one of them having the room to sit or lie down. The small ships were loaded so heavily they visibly wallowed under their weight. Some captains, irresponsible to the point of ruthlessness, would carry as many as 1,500 on one single crossing. To give an idea of just how overcrowded these insignificant craft were, and again using the *Waverley* for comparison, consider the fact that these meagre migrant tubs were about half the size, if that, and less than half the weight of the Clyde paddler. Yet they were carrying many more passengers than the law permitted the *Waverley*.

The progress of the immigrant trade and the incredible numbers crowding the inadequate vessels was one of the main topics of the day among Glasgow citizens, viewing as they would the incredible sight of the over-burdened ships sailing up the busy waterway of the Clyde. Glasgow newspapers regularly featured special reports on the phenomenon. In the summer of 1842 in particular there had been a wave of Irish coming over, a combination of immigrants and seasonal workers, packing the meagre steamers to an extent that had never been witnessed before. This really was the time of the boat people, the puny vessels on which they travelled thronged to such an alarming extent it was a wonder that they could even float, let alone tackle the crossing of the Irish Channel. Reporters from the *Glasgow*

Courier (one of our long-extinct journals) monitored the situation one week in the middle of August that year. Literally thousands had poured up the Clyde that week. The *Courier* sent reporters to the Broomielaw after a report from Belfast about one of the ships, the SS *Aurora*, having been so inundated with passengers it had to sail, sardine-packed as usual, despite leaving hundreds behind on the quayside.

As the *Courier* put it:

> On Monday night an immense number of Irish reapers, around 1,400, sought passage from Belfast to Glasgow on board the steamer *Aurora* which, although an excellent and capacious vessel, was unable to accommodate them all and in consequence about 200 of these poor creatures were compelled to remain behind. They besieged the police office night asylum but they could not all be taken in. When the *Aurora* arrived in Glasgow it was crowded in every part. The whole length and breadth of the steerage presented a mass of human beings literally packed together and not a few of them had taken positions on the quarter deck, in fact, the appearance of that vessel was that of a shipload of heads and faces.

Astonishingly, in the wake of the *Aurora* there were other steamers that were even more mobbed. Just two days after the *Aurora* the SS *Rover* from Londonderry arrived. Journalists were there to see it slowly drift up past the Anderston and Lancefield quays to Broomielaw. They couldn't believe any ship could have been more crammed than the SS *Aurora*, that 'shipload of heads and faces'. But the SS *Rover* was carrying about 1,500 passengers, so tightly jammed together on the main deck, shoulder to shoulder, rail to rail, that they had overcrowded on to the quarter deck, normally used by crewmen for operating the ship. They were also on top of the ship's paddle boxes. They were huddled together on the flimsy roof of the cook's galley. They filled the gangways. And they were even clinging to the ropes and cables used to stay the masts. Had there been any kind of emergency at sea, no one could have moved anywhere on that ship. They had sailed like that all the way from Ireland!

One factor, the reporters noted, which had probably ensured the ship's safe arrival was the fact that all on board were sober. Previously on such crossings there had been an added alcohol factor which, understandably in such conditions, had brought problems. As the *Courier* reporter noted, the current sobriety on board the ships had been 'an instance in the progress of temperance'. The report went on that it had been decided in the interests of safety, to 'deprive the bhoys' of the drink they had been asking on board the packed paddle steamers for such crossings. 'When they had their slips [carry-outs] they were a pugnacious lot, but without them there was no drunkenness and they were as easily managed and as peaceable as a boat full of lambs.'

Each week would bring its own flotilla of Irish in this Dunkirk of the Great Famine. They would come from Belfast, Derry and Sligo, in little ships with names such as the *Shamrock*, the *Tartar*, the *Aurora*, the *Antelope*, the *Arab*, the *Rover* and the *Londonderry*. As mentioned earlier in this chapter, attention was soon to be focused on the latter, a regular visitor to the Clyde with its shiploads of incomers. The *Londonderry* was one of the vessels which had been put into competition with the new and speedy crossings that had been opened up from Ardrossan, the Ayrshire port having now been linked to Glasgow with steam trains, and the very latest of steam trains at that, boasting 'covered carriages'. For around 13 pence you could do the Derry to Glasgow trip, which offered below-decks steerage accommodation on the ship and rail fare in one of those covered carriages. To beat the competition, the steamship *Londonderry* boasted steerage accommodation which was not only 'exceptionally spacious' but also had the luxury of heating, and for those who could afford it, there were comfortable cabins and even state rooms. Into the bargain, it was one of the fastest ships on any of the crossings. It wasn't any larger than the others, though, again being less than half the tonnage of the *Waverley*. As well as being a regular on the Derry to Broomielaw run, the *Londonderry* was familiar on many of the other crossings, including Sligo to Glasgow and Sligo to Liverpool.

It was on one of these latter trips that this ill-omened and wantonly overcrowded boat was to take its place in the history of cross-channel shipping, in a tragic episode that has been condemned as one of the worst-ever crimes at sea. It was like a marine 'Black Hole of Calcutta', involving the deaths of 72 innocent travellers fleeing the deprivations of the Great Famine.

They had loaded the *Londonderry* up in Sligo harbour early that bitterly cold and stormy winter morning of Friday, 1 December 1848, with a full complement bound for Liverpool. Many of the passengers, of course, would have been going on to Glasgow from there, as well as to America and Canada. Some were heading for the homes of friends in Liverpool, and other places in England and Scotland. They would take any available ship just to get away from the hell they had been experiencing in Ireland. Understandably, considerable numbers of those boarding would have been fraught about what might be in store for them, not only in Liverpool (about which they would have been well warned), but also on the perilous voyage across the Atlantic.

They would have taken one last look at their homeland as they filed up the *Londonderry*'s narrow gangplank, but as it was just after six o'clock in the morning and still dark, there was little more than the dimly lit Sligo quayside to take in for that final memory. Had it been a little later, they would have seen for themselves the deteriorating condition of the weather, the fierce winds scudding the big banks of mist across the face of Benbulbin, obscuring its flat summit along with the peaks of the neighbouring Dartry Mountains.

Once on board they would have taken up their places in the various quarters depending on the value of their tickets. A few would be in the spacious cabins, mainly in the forward part of the ship, but most would go down the narrow gangway into the steerage compartment, which the owners had boasted was both accommodating and heated, crowding in until every available space had been filled. Only the ones who would be travelling in the lowest class of all, on deck with the bullocks, pigs and sheep and other cargo, would see in the very first light of dawn the big white horses angrily frothing out in the open sea.

Everyone realised the kind of voyage they were in for not long after the eight o'clock sailing time. As they passed the lighthouse at Rosses Point and sailed into Sligo Bay, gateway to the Atlantic, the little ship seemed to pause and then shudder as though smacking into some solid object. The first of the giant waves crashed in on her as she cleared the waters of the bay, veering to starboard for the most awful part of the voyage, heading north on a course parallel to the Donegal coastline.

Sailing in that northerly direction, there's nothing on the port side of a ship except America and two and a half thousand miles of one of the world's fiercest oceans. After a few more hours into the voyage, the ship was in that area of the huge ocean where it meets the north-westerly part of Ireland, and it was thereabouts the SS *Londonderry* was hit with the worst of the seas. The little ship was no match for such waves, although its meagre steam engine did give it sufficient momentum to keep it on a relentless, dead-slow course. The deck cargo, both humans and animals, had already been soaked, but as the storm intensified the waves were breaking right over the ship with such ferocity they would all have been washed overboard had crewmen not quickly cleared the decks of the drenched passengers, hurriedly herding them below to the ship's hold. Like the *Londonderry* itself, the hold was of the humblest dimensions, just a little over 20 feet long and with six and a half feet headroom. Into that space they corralled the 200 terrified deck passengers, a good number of them family groups, many of the women and children screaming as they struggled for space in the dark confines of the horrendous black hole, the men shouting protests about the crush. Fearing that water might flood below decks, an officer had ordered the hatches battened down and, apparently, in a fit of pique at the continued screams and shouts from the passengers below, had then ordered the batten planking to be covered with tarpaulins. This not only made the jam-packed hold absolutely watertight, but also airtight.

What went on in that dismal, dark and airless ship's hold throughout the long hours of that stormy night can only be imagined. The tarpaulins had curtailed the noise of the screams all right, but not merely because it was shutting them out. The noise had diminished because the passengers were no longer screaming. Many of them were no longer living, and those with any energy remaining were using it to gasp what little air was left to breathe. Because the storm was still raging that morning, the ship was to change course and head for Londonderry, the port after which it had been named. It was only when it had made its exit from the boiling ocean after rounding the long finger of

Malin Head on the Inishowen Peninsula, the most northerly point in all Ireland, and entered the calm and safe waters of Lough Foyle that the crew first realised something awful had happened deep inside the bowels of their ship. They had anchored in the lough just offshore from the town of Moville for the remainder of the night and only then had the order been given to strip the tarpaulins from the battened hatches. When the first of these had been taken off and a hatch opened, the crewmen performing the task had looked at each other in disbelief before quickly cupping their hands over their noses as a cloud, described later as being steam, rose out of the hold accompanied by the most fearful of stenches. There were no shouts now. No screams. No knocking. No raised voices of protest. No pleas for help. Just silence: the most sinister and chilling of silences. For more than a third of the 200 passengers who had been forced below were lying there dead. The others were either dying or too feeble and shocked to even speak.

When the emigrant ship eventually sailed down the remainder of the lough early that morning and docked in Londonderry, they brought the victims out and one by one laid them out in neat rows on the quayside. Customs and port officials were quick to spread the word that a terrible tragedy had occurred on board the ship and police and magistrates from the town were summoned.

So too were reporters from the local newspaper, the *Londonderry Journal*, who were to be given the first accounts of the biggest single disaster there had ever been in their district. They were given a glimpse of the scale of that disaster when they first boarded the ship on the Londonderry quay. The body of a young child lay on the quarter deck, its face a dark livid mask. When they went into the little engine room they discovered the bodies of three adults, one of them similarly marked, the other two with some blood on their faces. That was before they were to come upon the most dreadful sight – what lay in the ship's hold. It presented them with the 'most hideous spectacle of mortality' and was accompanied by such a stench 'it made close inspection impossible'.

In order to quickly ascertain what had happened, and before witnesses dispersed, an inquest was hurriedly convened on one of the victims as representative of all who had died on the fateful voyage, and through the questioning by magistrates of survivors the full story of that dreadful night on board the SS *Londonderry* was to emerge. The victim chosen for the inquest was a young girl named as Anne McLaughlin, aged eight. Little Anne had left the humble family home in Ballina, out west over the Ox Mountains, together with her mother, her five sisters and one brother, for the trek to Sligo the day before the *Londonderry* had been due to sail. Despite the hardships they had known, the children were sad to leave home but were cheered at the prospects of meeting up with their father and brother who had settled in England. The last letter they had received told them everything would be fine for them in their new country. There was work enough to provide good and regular meals for all of them, and that was something they hadn't known for years.

It was Mary, Anne's bigger sister, who was to tell what she could remember of that horrendous night after sailing from Sligo. First of all they had asked Mary her age, but she replied that she didn't know, although she thought she might be between 12 and 14. Because there were so many of them, her family could only afford the deck fares on the ship and they were all crouched together there as night approached and the fiercest of storms broke around them. They had been at sea for around eight hours when at about four o'clock in the afternoon they had been ordered down below to the steerage compartment. Mary recalled how warm it had quickly become down there; her mother had begun clamouring for water. Mary had gone several times to the bottom of the companion ladder where there had been some water, but every time she managed to get a cupful it had been snatched from her hands as she tried to find her way back through the densely packed crowd. Eventually she had lost contact with her mother and stayed with her little sister Anne, holding her hand. Anne became feverish with the heat, panicked and started tearing at her sister's hair with her hands. There was lots of shouting going on about robbers being among them, and some men were flailing at others with sticks. She knew her mother had kept their money, and it included a £20 note which she had sewn into her jacket for safety. She had seen her mother being hit by the men with sticks, as well as some other women. Anne had been frightened by this and kept asking if she was going to be taken to the robbers. It was then Mary had tried to get to the companion ladder again for water and had lost the hand of her little sister, who by now was getting very weak. That was the last she had seen of her. Mary's mother, her sister Anne and three other sisters all died during the night.

Michael Brannan, a young man, had also been a deck passenger and with his mother and three sisters was ordered below along with the rest of them. He was to give the most graphic and horrifying account of what had happened that night below decks. When told to go below, Michael had held back and was the very last passenger to be cleared from the deck, waves by then crashing right over the storm-tossed vessel. The crew had been shouting angrily at the passengers and abusing them, one of them calling Brannan an Irish bastard. When eventually he had gone below, the first thing that struck him was how warm it was. It had been absolutely crowded below decks, so much so there was no room to sit anywhere and, along with some others,

Michael was forced to remain standing in the middle of the crammed compartment. There was nothing on which to hold for support and every time the ship rolled in the storm they would be sent lurching over one another into those who were sitting. It was then that the crew had started closing the hatches covering them. The passengers remonstrated with them, to no avail. There was by now considerable panic below, with men lashing out with sticks, although he didn't think they were robbers. One of Michael's sisters had then gone berserk, mainly because of the heat, and had hit his mother on the face. An old man beside him kept shouting for the captain: 'For God's sake, come down and save us.' By this time, such was the pitching of the ship that Brannan had fallen over. Everyone was rolling about, the living and the dead tangled together on the floor. At one point he had become intertwined with the others on the floor and such was the crush of bodies around him, he could not extricate his legs from the limbs and torsos of those pressed tightly against him. Eventually, with considerable effort, he managed to wriggle his legs free and, remembering the direction of the companion ladder, made for it. Clinging on to the ladder when he reached it, however, were three men.

By this time the tarpaulins had been put over the hatches and tied with coils of rope. Despite the men draped on the stair he managed to work his way up only to find that at the top of the steps there was a dead bullock blocking any further progress. Eventually, he did find a way out by climbing up over some sacks of mussels, part of the general cargo being carried, and at the top of these had found a way out on to the deck. The first crewman he had spoken to 'damned him', telling him to get back below, but he ignored him and continued to make his way forward. The ship had been rolling so badly at this point, with giant waves continuously breaking over the decks, that he had to tie some chains around his arms and secure himself to the superstructure in order not to be washed overboard. Seizing a moment between the waves, he later freed himself from the chains and made a dash for the bridge, where he found the first mate, telling him of the plight of the passengers in the hold.

'But he didn't believe me,' Brannan said. He persisted, however, and eventually the officer got an oil lamp and the two of them returned to the hatches over the hold. When they tried to enter, a sudden wave of foul air rose from below which immediately doused the lamp, the noxious cloud instantly condensing in the night air. Brannan described it as being 'like that coming from a boiling pot'. He broke down at this point of the interview, but managed to say that he had been able to rescue his mother and two of his sisters, but his other sister had died sometime during the night.

Other witnesses were also to tell of their experiences. One woman spoke about the bullocks and pigs which got loose and struggled about in the dark among the passengers making the most terrible noises. Michael Feely, from Manorhamilton, County Leitrim, had been lucky enough to afford a cabin in a forward part of the ship but heard the terrible shouts during the night from the passengers. People were offering their life savings for someone to bring them water, but when he asked a crewman what was happening he was told: 'It's only Irishmen murdering each other.' The captain had appeared just as indifferent to the suffering as his crew, saying to one witness as they lay at anchor in Lough Foyle that night that he only had six crewmen and if people were dying he couldn't help it – 'They will just have to help themselves.'

When they had finished separating the dead from the half-dead that morning on the quayside, they were to count 72 corpses. No figures were ever registered of those who died later as a result of the hellish experience on the ship from Sligo. A comparison between that night on board the emigrant ship and the horrific legend of the Black Hole of Calcutta seems an appropriate equation. But in fact what happened on that hellish voyage along the Irish coast was far worse than what had actually transpired at Calcutta where fewer people were involved and considerably fewer deaths occurred. Nothing had ever equalled that night on the SS *Londonderry*.

– CHAPTER 2 –

The Irish Holocaust

It was the greatest disaster ever to occur on any part of that geographical area known as the British Isles. It affected the lives of millions. It was worse than any world catastrophe of recent years, worse even than those horrific television images of calamities in Africa which have so shocked the world. As one witness of the day was to write on being confronted with the misery and suffering of one community: 'The scenes which presented themselves were such as no tongue or pen can convey any idea of.'

They died at work in the fields, they dropped dead by the roadside, they passed away in their sleep in their homes. Entire villages were found where everyone had died, virtually overnight. In proportional terms, the Great Famine of Ireland was the most ravaging national tragedy ever recorded. It was to virtually wipe out half the population of the entire island, either through death or migration. In the first year following the Great Famine, the census recorded six and a half million living in Ireland. Fifty years later, just after the turn of the new century, it had dropped to an incredible low of just over three million. More than a million were to escape on the fleets of private shipping companies, who were to make fortunes from the trade, just as they had from carrying slaves to America. Of the million who fled on the Coffin Ships, around half were to settle in mainland UK. Tens of thousands of them were to come up the Clyde in the most incredible of immigrant invasions, an influx only equalled by that in New York at the height of its migrant days. It was those people, the survivors of the most harrowing of experiences, the most wretched of times, who were to become the backbone of the community which was to change the city for ever – the Glasgow Irish.

The greatest single reason why Glasgow was to be invaded by so many people from Ireland has its origins in what was to be unearthed in a remote country field in Belgium. The discovery was made in 1845 and was to cause death and havoc across Europe, but nothing on the scale of the misery it would generate in Ireland. Just why or from where this scourge originated no one is really sure.

It came in on the wind, they say, perhaps secreted in the raindrops of one of the climatic low-pressure systems of that moist and sunless early summer of 1845 – tiny microbes, mysterious particles of nature's freaks. They had first noticed it over in that field near Courtrai, or as the locals would say

Kortrijk, in the West Flanders region of Belgium. One morning, a farmer had been out checking his fine potato crop. The long and substantial drills of them in his fields had been perfectly fine the day before, the plants bushy, erect and healthily green, the flower on them having come and gone, meaning the tubers under the soil would soon be ready for lifting. But in a corner of one field that morning the farmer noticed that a group of the plants had turned a peculiar brown colour and, instead of standing firmly upright, were sagging and sickly-looking. When he knelt down beside one of the limp-looking plants, he could see a powdery fungus on the leaves. Then he scattered the mound of earth from around the decaying stalk to expose the tubers. There was a strong odour, confirming his worst fears. It was the dreaded potato disease. There was a variety of such crop maladies and they had experienced two of them before; the English had called them the 'curl' and the 'taint'. What this one would come to be known as was immaterial to the farmer. What he did know was that by all appearances it was some kind of hideous rot and was threatening his crop and his livelihood.

The disease spread fast after that fateful discovery, much faster than any other they had known before in their potato fields. Virtually within days it swept over the rest of Flanders and into the neighbouring Netherlands, continuing its deadly progress north through the cultivated fields of the Scandinavian countries. In the opposite direction it was carried with the wind and the rain into France, reaching down to the most southerly provinces, and by early autumn they were experiencing it in Switzerland and Poland. It had become so rampant that it had blown over the Channel into Ireland and into Scotland too.

There were long debates among botanists and scientists on what exactly this agricultural epidemic was before they agreed that the infestation was the one known as *phytophthora infestans*. More simply the farmers knew it as potato blight, an agricultural pestilence equivalent to the Black Death of humankind. They already knew of it in America; it was suspected that the disease arrived there on the ships bringing guano fertiliser, the bird-dropping manure, from Peru. Many of the seed potatoes that farmers in the British Isles used for planting came from the States, and this probably facilitated the great leap of the disease over the Atlantic.

Apart from the poorest of peasants of Flanders and the Netherlands, for whom the potato was the staple of their diet (they flavoured them with vinegar), nowhere was the potato blight so devastating as it was in Ireland. For no race of people anywhere relied so much on one single item of foodstuff for their subsistence than did the impoverished of Ireland on the potato. It had been God's own gift to the poor toilers of the soil. It grew vigorously in even the thinnest of earth. It stored well after being harvested, and they would fill the entire loft spaces of their cramped cabin or cottage dwellings with enough of them to tide them over the winter. Families with their tiny plots, the landless labourers, could grow enough of them on which to live the year round. So many of them did, that more than one and a half million out of a population of eight and a half million – nearly one in every five – existed on potatoes and virtually nothing else. They were the main, and one and only, course of every meal of every day. Adult male labourers would eat an average of 14 lb of them every day; roughly 70 potatoes. Their children would each have around 5 lb pounds, about 25 potatoes. No matter how improbable it may seem, how revoltingly tedious it must have been, those potatoes, together with the nutrients from some milk or buttermilk, was a diet on which the hard-working Irish peasant could well survive and even thrive. On that diet, Irish country dwellers had become an even more well-proportioned race than their rural brothers across the water in England and were better nourished than their counterparts in many other European countries.

The potato blight arrived in Ireland in early September 1845, and appeared first in the eastern counties (such as Carlow, Kildare and Kilkenny) quickly fanning south to Waterford, Wexford and Wicklow before progressing westwards to Cork, Kerry and Tipperary. There was no immediate sign of panic from the authorities, or for that matter the farmers. There had already been an excellent result the previous month from the early potato harvest and hopefully the main potato liftings in October and November would not suffer too badly. It was not to be. The first-affected eastern areas were severely afflicted, the blight quickly taking root in the plants and rapidly ravishing them. What potatoes were saved there and from the less-affected western areas were quickly stored, either in the usual straw-thatched field pits or housed. This was to delay the full impact of the disease that year, for it was only when these potatoes were taken from storage for consumption that it was discovered that although they had looked healthy enough when lifted, they were in fact infected. The blight had worked on them while in storage and a disturbing percentage of them were found to be discoloured and pulpy.

For the next four years, Ireland was confronted with the worst tragedy it had ever seen. They called it the Great Famine. It was a disaster of a magnitude only equalled on a scale in countries with huge populations, like India or China, where rice crop failures and ensuing famines wiped out millions. But not even in these most populous of nations had there ever been such a per capita impact as was now threatening Ireland. What would replace the staple diet on which they had survived since the colonialists had introduced the humble potato to their country more than a century before? How could they live without it? What would provide the rent now? What else could they eat? Unless their prayers were answered, they were facing catastrophe.

In 1845, Ireland was one of the most populous countries in Europe. It had experienced a sensational population explosion in the preceding 100 years. In 1750, when there had been a census, there had been little more than two and a half million people on the island, about half of Scotland's present population. When the potato blight was first discovered in eastern Ireland that autumn of 1845, however, the population had soared to its highest ever – eight and a half million. It was the fastest increase of any country in Western Europe and ironically many were to attribute that incredible expansion to the very substance which was now threatening them with famine and starvation – the potato. That was a simple and singular (although not exactly accurate) answer. There had been other factors: a considerable fall in the death rate, an improved all-round diet and better transport. Nevertheless, the potato had doubtless contributed to an improvement in the way of life of the Irish peasant class since being introduced by the English colonialists in the previous century. It had been much more reliable to grow than grain and no other crop required such a small plot for cultivation in order to sustain a family. This had facilitated the establishing of more young families in the countryside and in consequence there was a considerable lowering of the average marriage age. The potato, even though it was such a major part of their daily nutrition, had also improved the diet of the poor. Seven million tons of them were being grown every year and by 1845, when those first diseased plants were discovered, more than four and a half of Ireland's eight and a half million population relied on the potato as the major part of their diet. Nearly two million of them had no other significant source of food than those precious tubers, the poor consuming in total three-quarters of all the potatoes grown in the country.

Many had predicted there would be disaster of a kind when the blight swept through the eastern counties of Ireland during the autumn of 1845, but as yet there was no general acceptance of that possibility. Much of the crop had already been taken in and there had been an excellent grain crop that year, resulting in comparatively few food shortages. Considerable emphasis must be placed on the use of that word 'comparatively', however, for near-famine conditions were beginning to be reported in many outlying rural areas. Potato farmers relied on retaining a certain portion of the crop as seed potatoes for the following year's growth and it was later discovered when the store pits and storehouses were opened up that these too had been decimated by dormant blight.

So what would 1846, the following year, bring them? They already knew there would not be sufficient plantable seed potatoes to provide them with their normal harvest, but would the blight return again? Surprisingly, however, sufficient seed potatoes were found to make adequate plantings and it was reckoned that the 1846 crop would only be marginally down. Cheered by this news, optimists suggested that the blight would vanish between the growing seasons. But that was not being realistic, others warned, saying there could be lean times ahead. The pessimists pointed out that the blight had by now devastated the Belgian small farmers; they had lost seven-eighths of their entire crop, the Dutch two-thirds, and they were suffering severe famine conditions and a considerable death toll.

They had been lucky so far in Ireland, having lost only about a third of the crop that year. The following year, it was predicted, there would be the direst of consequences: crops would be threatened and thousands would go hungry. But even those pessimists were wrong, few of them foreseeing just how severe and how widespread the potato disease would be in the summer of 1846.

On a Sunday morning in October 1846 the gravity of the famine took on a new dimension. Denis Kennedy was a labourer on a public works scheme on the Caheragh road just outside the little village of Skibbereen, in the furthest south-west, where he lived. He was owed two weeks' wages for his labour and without it he had gone without food. They found his body that morning by the roadside, where he had collapsed on his way to work. The cause of his death, the coroner found, was 'want of sufficient sustenance'. In other words, Denis had died of starvation. He was one of the first recorded victims of the famine. Shortly afterwards another Caheragh road worker, Jeremiah Hegarty, was also found dead by the roadside. Jeremiah had had some barley in his dwelling, but his landlord had confiscated it. Like Denis Kennedy, he had been owed unpaid wages. Days later, another man, Daniel Hayes, from the parish of Lorha, was found dead, again by the roadside. The coroner was told he had been living on the refuse of vegetables and had gone out the morning they found him dead on a quest to find some food. He had lain down by the roadside in despair. Within days similar stories were in every local newspaper daily. Soon the deaths were being reported in their dozens, then by the score, and within weeks there would be hundreds, within months there were thousands.

Some of the stories made the grimmest of reading. A mother with her three little children was found drowned in a ditch by the roadside at Webbsborough, near Cork, one Sunday in November 1846, just a month after those first labourers. It was stated by police that the four had been seen in the neighbourhood for some days in a state of 'very great destitution'. They were last seen sitting together by the roadside and the ditch, although the mother, aged about 30, appeared to be unconscious. Then they were all found dead, the bodies presenting 'a truly heartrending spectacle, partially covered with filthy rags saturated with mud, and frozen, having been exposed to the inclemency of the weather'. The hand of one child and part of the foot of another had been devoured by rats. A post-mortem of the bodies was to reveal that there had only been a trace of food consumed by the mother in the day preceding her death. The nine-year-old child's stomach contained only a very small quantity of half-digested potatoes. The coroner's jury found that their death had been caused by drowning and that they were in a state of hunger, 'but how they came into the water whether by accident or design on the part of the mother, we have no evidence to show'.

The crop failure of the sole food commodity on which millions survived was to be on a scale the like of which was unprecedented in the history of modern Europe. The spores and fungus of the disease had spread relentlessly, devouring whole fields, entire crops. The blight first of all formed on the leaves of the potato plant, then crept down the stalk to the roots and into the potatoes themselves. By the time the infection had reached the tubers under the soil, the tips of the plant's leaves would be so rotted they would fall off like fine ash and be carried away with the wind or driving rain, immediately affecting other plants onto which they drifted. The advance of the disease was measured at just over seven miles a day, or across an entire county every two days, until it had travelled throughout the whole country.

The monstrous agricultural plague was to change the very face of the landscape. A third of all cultivated land in Ireland had over the years been given over to potato growing, which meant that mile after mile, as far as the eye could see, instead of being a lush and healthy green, had taken on the brownish-black hue of the limp, rotting and diseased potato plants.

Even though they were under the soil, the stench of the blackened, infected potatoes was everywhere. It was described by one gentleman farmer of the times as 'intolerable', and so bad that you could smell the rotting crop long before you caught sight of it. Worse, more and more people were starving to death.

In normal times, with good husbandry, farmers had been getting almost eight tons of potatoes per acre. When they began lifting the crop of 1846, they considered themselves lucky if they could salvage a third of a ton from an acre. And even that third of a ton would consist of some barely edible potatoes, others with such stunted growth they were little bigger than children's marbles. It was to be worse, much, much worse than even the grimmest of forecasts. With it being the only source of food for many, the onset of starvation was to be almost immediate that summer of 1846. After people had quickly devoured what little edible crop they might have had or had finished what may have been left over from the previous year's store, they first of all resorted to grubbing around in their fields to rescue the least diseased of the blighted potatoes in order to consume them.

Word quickly spread that provided you cut out the diseased parts, the bits that had degenerated into a grey and blackish pulp, then it was safe enough to eat the remainder. But you had to eat them quickly, for even within a day or two any healthy portion remaining in the potato would quickly discolour and rot. At all costs you should avoid them when the stench from them was really bad, although you could break them up and convert what was left into starch, then mix that with flour or meal and bake it for bread.

As things became more desperate, they even began experimenting with various ways of trying to eat diseased potatoes. Some tried cooking them the usual way in water, then when it reached boiling point throwing the water (which usually had a strong smell) away, bringing them once more to the boil in fresh water. If there was no strong smell after this they would try eating them, if not, they would change the water once more.

Others added salt herring to the stinking rotten potatoes, mashing the two together. The strong-tasting fish helped to disguise any strange flavour of the potatoes. As an alternative to the herring, turnips and onions were sometimes mixed with the discoloured potato mash. But neither the herrings, turnips and onions, nor what putrid potatoes were passable enough to even contemplate for consumption, were enough to feed the people. Nor were the few available alternatives, such as meal and maize. Instead, Ireland was to descend into its nightmare years; years of the utmost suffering when the number of deaths horrifically soared to such a scale that they were being tallied in their thousands, and then in their tens of thousands, and beyond that in their hundreds of thousands. No country in Europe had ever known its like before or, thankfully, since. It was the worst disaster of its kind in history.

The famine wreaked chaos throughout the entire rural society of Ireland. While over in Scotland and England farming techniques had advanced to a stage where they were the most efficient in the world, the average Irish landholder still survived on the merest patches of soil. The majority of small farmers lived off properties of less than ten acres and more than 135,000 survived on the tiniest of holdings of less than one acre. The relationship between the small farmers and the cottiers, the smallest of the landholders, who rented their small potato plots, and those at the very bottom of the rural pile, the landless agricultural labourers, was to be thrown into turmoil. The labourers were a very substantial class, constituting with their dependants a quarter of the nation's eight and a half million population. For years they had survived by working for the small farmers on average incomes of about £13 a year. The equivalent of around £600 today. As well as their wage, they would be given some privileges, perhaps a cabin for themselves and their family, and a little piece of ground, often no bigger than a suburban back garden, for their potatoes. Now, because of the blight, the farmers were without an income from their crops and could not afford to pay the labourers. Nor were the cottiers able to afford the rents for their potato plots, the farmers now demanding that they be paid in advance because of the likelihood of there being no crop.

The rural classes fragmented and the entire agricultural system degenerated by the day. Hundreds of thousands of slaughtered pigs could not be replaced because they too had depended on the potato as a large part of their diet. The loss of their pigs was to deprive thousands more of their little cabin homes, for the income from a single pig was often sufficient to pay the rent for a humble shack. Even the sheep flocks had to be drastically thinned, farmers being unable to protect them from the nighttime rustlers who were now marauding their properties in the search for food.

There were now the most alarming reports coming forward by the day on the deteriorating state of the country, and the disastrous effects of the famine. Whole communities were being decimated by starvation; there were fearsome reports of travellers in more remote parts of the country coming upon hamlets, and even some bigger villages, where the entire population had died, many of them still unburied and lying dead in their homes.

Village after village in the worst hit areas, such as in the south and far west, lay in a weird and ghostly silence. Those who had not fled to the ports in order to emigrate somewhere were dead, or in a state of near death. A Cork magistrate on a visit to the village of Skibbereen, on the outskirts of which poor Denis Kennedy and Jeremiah Hegarty had died, would be horrified at what he was to come across when he visited some of the houses, or hovels, as he described them in his report. He was to record, 'the scenes which presented themselves were such as no tongue or pen can convey'. In one such house he found a family of 'six famished and ghastly skeletons, to all appearance dead, huddled in a corner on some filthy straw, their sole covering which seemed a ragged horsecloth, their wretched legs hanging about naked above the knees'.

The rural population of Ireland was reduced to a miserable and wretched state virtually unequalled anywhere in the world. The French traveller, writer and sociologist, Gustave de Beaumont, had not long returned from an extensive journey across America when he visited the worst of the stricken areas. Despite his experiences among the most deprived, even he had seen nothing like it. He wrote:

> I have seen the Indian in his forests and the Negro in his chains and thought, as I contemplated their pitiable condition, that I saw the very extreme of human wretchedness, but I did not then know the condition of unfortunate Ireland. Like the Indian, the Irish man is poor and naked, but he lives in the midst of a society where luxury is eagerly sought, and where wealth is honoured.
>
> Irish poverty has a special and exceptional character, which renders its definition difficult,

because it can be compared with no other indigence. Irish misery forms a type by itself of which neither the model nor the imitation can be found anywhere else . . . the history of the poor is the history of Ireland.

The Irish had endured many hardships in the past – those abysmal wet summers with their never-ending rain, the rain that was their best friend and their worst enemy. They would have the poorest of crops those summers and in the winters that followed there would be periods of great hunger. They knew that same hunger when diseases had affected their livestock, even though that might just be the solitary pig, on which the family's nutrition for the year so heavily depended. But never had they known anything like the Great Starvation with which they were now confronted.

Malnutrition can be the most hellish of conditions. At first its victims suffer the awful agonies of hunger pangs and a voracious longing for sustenance, any kind of sustenance, to quell the demands of the weakening body. But that is merely the beginning. It only takes a few days after those first cravings for the systematic progression of physical decline to set in, a tormenting wasting process which dominoes around the human frame as the body functions deteriorate one by one, each linked to the other, each bringing its own disorder and its own special agony.

The absence of the various vitamins, acids and chemicals on which life depends begins taking effect. Skin rashes, brain dysfunction, tongue and mouth irritation and diarrhoea come as a result of niacin deficiency. Marasmus, or wasting, immediately retards the growth of children. Lack of vitamin C brings about hair damage and bleeding under the skin, gum disease and in severe cases convulsions. The nervous system starts to break down through lack of vitamin B12, and loss of night vision and destruction of the cornea comes with the deficiency of vitamin A. The absence of vitamin D induces rickets, the bone-bending disease in children, and osteomalacia in adults, a softening of the bones.

The heart begins to reduce in size, which in turn decreases the amount of blood being pumped around the body, resulting in slower breathing. Lung capacity is reduced through the breakdown of the respiratory system and, combined with the degeneration of the muscular system, this induces a low capacity for exercise or work. The nervous system becomes further impaired, with the onset of apathy and irritability, although strangely the intellect remains intact, making those suffering their decline cruelly aware of their individual agony. By now, the destruction of the body is in full process, with anaemia and low temperatures, immune deficiency, fluid accumulation in the skin, accentuated shrinkage of all the vital organs, and so it goes on, each stage another in the downward spiral towards death.

All famines are accompanied by the grimmest of companions, a deadly collection of fevers and diseases. In Ireland there was typhus, which swelled the faces and attacked the brain; relapsing fever, with its recurring bouts of exhaustion and abnormal temperatures; famine dropsy, causing the limbs and body to swell frighteningly; scurvy, dysentery and cholera, which often led to blindness. There were early reports that over 1,000 young children had already lost their sight. These varied fevers became so widespread it's estimated that at least a million and a half became infected, ten times more dying of one of them than of actual starvation itself. Such diseases raged through whole parishes, leaving so many dead that there were not enough coffins to bury all the corpses; little wonder when you appreciate the enormity of the death toll for just one year, 1847, more than 250,000 succumbing to fever and almost 28,000 to starvation.

Undertakers were in short supply, as were hospitals, there being only 39 infirmaries in the entire country, which for the period equalled just one clinic for every third of a million people. Funeral directors could not be expected to cope with this mountain of death. Various alternative methods had to be deployed in order to dispose of the dead – some villages had their corpses wrapped in straw for burial, others used the novel trap-door burial box, the ingenious re-usable coffin. The victim would be placed in one of these contraptions, which to all appearances was a normal-looking coffin. There was one vital difference, however. The base of the box in which the corpse lay was hinged so that when the coffin was lowered, a catch was released when it reached the bottom of the grave, allowing it to be smartly raised again without its contents, ready for use once more. The use of the trap-door coffin had first been noted in the parish of Kilmoe, the Cork newspaper reporting that they were now in such a sad state of affairs that one coffin to one dead body was a luxury and using this method for taking bodies to the graveyard was 'no mere fiction but appalling reality'. Even the trap-door coffin didn't suffice in the worst of places where, such was the number of dead and shortage of both coffins and labour to bury the victims, huge pits had to be opened up for mass burials. Up to 36 corpses were interred in such a pit at Cork. Most pathetic of all were the little villages where the victims were left where they had died, some by the roadside, others in their own homes, there being no one left in their community in sufficient health to bury them.

Perhaps because of its remoteness – it was the furthest-flung part of the country – the area around Skibbereen, where the very first victims of the famine had been discovered, was to become associated with the very worst horrors of the tragedy more than perhaps any other community. One reporter wrote after visiting one of the little hamlets there that the people were reduced to living on seaweed and what cattle they could steal.

> On Sunday night they broke into the food store and stole all that was in it. There were thirteen burials in the Schull churchyard yesterday; not one of them had got a coffin. It is cruel to insist that these wretched skeletons go miles to and from work to earn a few pence [a reference to the forced labour in public works schemes]; it would be much wiser to give them a little food and permit them to remain within doors.

It was also from Skibbereen on 18 January 1847 that the *Cork Examiner* newspaper ran a story with the headline 'Deaths! Deaths! Deaths!', describing just one day in the village. The story was based on the grim findings of Joseph Driscoll, of Schull, the poor-rate collector. He had gone to Rissbrine, in the vicinity, to collect rates. On knocking at the first house, belonging to a man called Regan, there was no reply. He had pushed in the door and was astonished to find three dead men in the house. He had also told the paper's reporter that a woman named Neill had been lying dead in her house since the sixth of that month, that is for more than ten days. On the Tuesday of that week, three of her children had died and the father was also a corpse. On the Sunday a man had been found nearby, having dropped dead on the roadside the previous night returning from work. Another man was found dead in a field and a great part of his body had been eaten by dogs. His corpse was so mutilated it could not be identified. There had been another two deaths that week, one at the police barracks, another in the Union Hall on the same day. 'So you see what a state this once plentiful country is now reduced to; and the general opinion is that matters are not at the worst.'

So what did the government of the day about the situation? That question is perhaps the most controversial part of the story of those sad and tragic years. There is no dispute about what actually happened during the Great Famine: the potato crop was ruined, substitute food could not be provided in sufficient quantities, the agricultural system was disrupted, rural society was in disarray, thousands were cleared from the land, the poorhouses were filled and millions were affected by hunger. These things all happened. There are no easy or definitive answers to the equation about what the government did or didn't do to help. In a society with the history of Ireland, value-free judgement is rare. One of the areas where that difficulty is highlighted is when the specific question is asked – just what did the government do to try to alleviate the suffering? There is a saying among Irish nationalists that 'Providence sent the potato blight; but England made the famine'. Few would disagree with the comment of John Mitchel, one of their more famous brothers, that the famine had been a genocide perpetrated by the British. But it is not only nationalists who feel that way – the famous English historian A.J.P. Taylor wrote that the governing class of his country had the blood of two million Irish people on its hands. And to give substance to such points of view, there's no shortage of statistics which reveal that right through the years of the famine, that is from 1845 to 1850, there was an abundance of other foodstuffs in Ireland, much of which were exported throughout the five years when those hundreds of thousands were dying. Quite clearly, what in fact did happen through British rule is deeply concerning. There was food on hand, either in storage or from harvests, or readily accessible from other countries, yet it was not made available to the hunger-stricken hordes.

Ireland at the time of the famine was part of the United Kingdom and had been for some 45 years prior to the outbreak of the famine, following a succession of bloody rebellions. It had been as a result of these uprisings that in 1800 the Act of Union was passed by Parliament to make Ireland an integral part of Britain, admitting 100 representatives from the island to be Members of Parliament. As part of the United Kingdom, it was to be ruled just as any other part of the nation, that is by the laws and policies of Westminster.

When in the early autumn of 1845 the first reports of the failure of the potato crops reached the office of the Prime Minister, at the time the Tory Sir Robert Peel, there was no overwhelming concern. Peel had always taken the view that Irishmen and exaggeration went hand in hand and that matters might not be as serious as they were being made out. He was fully aware, however, that every year much of the Irish population experienced near starvation conditions for a period and if there was any likelihood of this being exacerbated it could be serious. He therefore ordered weekly reports to be compiled on the state of the potato crop. As these grew more ominous by the week he decided that some action had to be taken and supplies of maize were ordered for shipment to Ireland from America. A relief commission was established in Dublin and taxes were removed on grain, lowering the price of bread. These measures seemed most appropriate, even quite admirable, particularly if the government was to continue with its caring ways. But there was a limit dictated by political policies. It was an unshakable belief of Peel and his Conservative government that there should be no interference in market forces, that well-aired theme of a much more recent Tory administration. His government, he insisted, stood for the rights of property and free competition and there would be no question of abandoning such principles. Not even if people should starve and die.

There were other factors. Certain attitudes prevailed at the time about the Irish. Politicians, writers and commentators regularly made outbursts of the most disparaging kind about Ireland and its people which went mainly unchallenged. Magazine cartoonists depicted Irishmen with apelike appearances; the London *Times* referred to Ireland as a 'nation of beggars', two of their defects being 'indolence and improvidence'; prominent figures such as Thomas Carlyle, the Scottish essayist, described the Irish as 'the worst evil'; Engels, one of the founding fathers of Communism, commented on their 'filth and drunkenness'. Even the Prime Minister commented that 'the Irish have been taught many bad lessons and few good ones'.

The maize that had been so promptly ordered from America by Prime Minister Sir Robert Peel was issued to the hungry from April 1846. It did seem to be a most humanitarian gesture, but sending American maize to Ireland was the equivalent of dropping peanut butter sandwiches to starving Afghans or packets of popcorn to famished Ethiopians – it just wasn't their food. When potatoes have been your staple, and virtually only, diet for decades, the sudden switch to meals of a bright yellow, powdery substance presents complications. After consuming their ration of maize, many still felt hungry and weak, others were to suffer gastric pains and severe bowel problems, and some became quite ill following the switch in diet. The government responded by adding oatmeal to the maize meal to make it more palatable and issued pamphlets on how to cook the new foodstuff. It was an audacious gesture, but it did seem to alleviate many of the initial problems in the somewhat drastic changeover in eating regime.

The distribution of maize from the depots was to be strongly opposed, however, when the government put a senior civil servant in charge of all relief in Ireland. As it turned out, the new official was to have even stronger views on market forces than the Prime Minister himself, and because of these beliefs there was to be a marked lack of response to the tragic events unfolding in Ireland. Charles Edward Trevelyan was a career civil servant who had spent years in India as a colonial administrator and was now, as the Permanent Head of the Treasury, in charge of all relief measures in another, older colony – Ireland. And yes, Trevelyan is the one in 'Fields of Athenry'! Whether the fans realise it or not, his name comes in at the third line of the poignant Celtic Football Club hymn, 'The Fields of Athenry', the words going, as any of their fans will tell you:

> By a lonely prison wall, I heard a young girl callin',
> Michael, they have taken you away,
> For you have stole Trevelyan's corn.

Trevelyan had all the right ingredients for the great figure of vilification he was to become. He was English and Protestant, and evangelical at that. He was often to be seen, and unmistakably heard, reading long passages from the Bible in loud and resonant tones. Trevelyan was described, among many other things, as a man bereft of compassion and obdurate – and this was the man they had put in charge of welfare. His apparent indifference and disdain for the suffering of the poor was quickly to be demonstrated when he expressed his concern about the distribution of the cheap maize Peel had secured. He decreed that it must not go to the people who normally suffered from lack of food every year – and that was countless thousands – but only to those who had become starved by the lack of potatoes. One can only speculate on how in all reality he intended to apply the logic of that ruling! As the insensitive Trevelyan had anticipated, however, there was the predictable rush on the grain depots for food during the summer of 1846 when there were wide-scale reports of the potato blight now having spread throughout the island. To put an end to this he ordered that the grain depots be closed, thus forcing the poor and hungry to depend on the open market for their sustenance. Which is why Michael and the others stole Trevelyan's precious corn and ended up, as 'Athenry' goes, in those prison ships in the bay.

Earlier that summer, there had been a change of government. Peel was replaced by the Whig, Lord John Russell, another staunch and unbending supporter of market forces, who was to fully endorse the rigid policies of Trevelyan. In the very first week of the new government assuming power, Trevelyan was to cancel a cargo of maize which had been ordered for famine relief. Any maize destined for the country should only come in the regular mode, that is through the market, a move which was to be fully supported by the new Prime Minister, who affirmed that neither he nor any members of his cabinet were in favour of interfering in the grain market. Conditions were to degenerate alarmingly with the almost complete failure of the potato harvest that year until, at the end of 1846, Trevelyan gave the order that the grain depots be opened again, but the meal was only to be sold at market prices plus a levy. If they were to give free handouts, he warned, they would have 'the whole country on us'.

Despite the opening of meal depots in the worst-stricken parts of the country, there still wasn't sufficient food available to make up for the loss of the potato. Starving citizens attacked the depots and carts transporting any foodstuffs to ward off their hunger.

There were riots in various parts of the country, and the military were called out to guard food stores and transportation. Such was the desperation of the worst affected that dead bodies were found whose mouths were smeared with green from the grass they had been trying to eat. Others took to living on weeds, the roots of ferns, the bark from trees, the berries from bushes, and what edible-like detritus was to be found on the seashore. Hundreds trying to escape death from starvation were to die from the poisonous effects of the obnoxious alternatives they had been consuming. A man arrested for stealing a sheep told the court that he had only done so because he had found his frenzied wife trying to eat the flesh of their dead daughter.

Yet still they were exporting grain and other food grown in the country, and still they were maintaining that the government's unshakable policy should prevail. There would be no interference with the market forces of supply and demand, otherwise the natural flow by which supplies reached the market would be threatened. Harming the grain trade could have consequences that would affect the people as a whole for years to come, and if the people were given food, it was argued, it would have a serious effect on market prices. In turn that would force merchants to withhold food from the market altogether, which would make it even worse for the hungry. On these principles, the government loudly proclaimed, they were not for turning. It wasn't that the politicians were immoral; it was the result of their ineffective policies that was immoral. Trevelyan and the Whig government had been convinced that by non-interference, Ireland would right itself. They considered that while their solutions may be painful, they would be the best for the majority in the end. But it was not to be, and it was policies such as these, not the actual shortage of food, which were to cause the horrendous death toll of the Great Famine.

Following that disastrous potato harvest of 1846, a period of unmitigated, unparalleled misery was to descend upon Ireland. The country that always confronted travellers with its abject poverty and the basic living conditions of its huge peasant class was now faced with the unimaginable. Because they were no longer able to afford the rents for their cabins and the garden-size plots of land on which they had grown potatoes, tens of thousands were to be evicted, the evictions continuing throughout the five years of the famine and going on for some years afterwards. They were facilitated by a clause in the Poor Law prohibiting all those with more than a quarter of an acre of land from claiming relief. This meant that the lowly cottiers could only obtain relief by surrendering their little plots, the landlords ensuring they wouldn't return by demolishing the flimsy, windowless shacks which had been their abodes. The bailiffs and police were always willing to encourage any recalcitrants who were slow in leaving.

In total, some three-quarters of a million were cleared from the pathetic little homes they called cabins. That euphemistic description belied what these pitiful shelters were really like. They ranked alongside the most primitive of housing accommodation to be found anywhere in Europe. This was the rural equivalent of the Glaswegian's tenement single-end, but even that is no real comparison. The old tenements were made of stouter stuff and at least offered decent shelter from the elements, plus the added warmth of the other houses closely surrounding them. The Irish cabins were made of dried mud, just like the humpies inside an African kraal except they had to withstand the inclemency of the Irish climate. Their mud walls would often dissolve back to their original wet and slimy condition. So too would the earth sods they had for roofs, leaving only the straw to vainly combat what the heavens sent down on them. Some had chimneys of a sort, but they were merely a crude hole cut in the roof. Just as frequently, however, they would rely on the aperture they used as a door to let the smoke from their turf fires escape. Inside their single room would be the entire family and invariably also old Gran and Pa, children, parents and grandparents all crushed together for warmth round the fire, which acted as cooker and central heating. And also sharing the room would be the family pig, clarty as always. As Beaumont, the Frenchman, put it:

> . . . the only thriving inhabitant of the place, for he lives in filth. The presence of the pig in an Irish hovel may at first seem an indication of misery; on the contrary, it is a sign of comparative comfort. Indigence is still more extreme in a hovel where no pig is found!

After eviction from their cabins, they crowded along country lanes with what few possessions they could carry, like refugees fleeing an invading army. Their enemies were the oppressive landlords or farmers for whom they had worked and a government over the water which had failed to achieve the proper management of their country. Salvation for them now would be the workhouse or what pittance they might collect from labouring in the public works schemes, one of the government-inspired 'remedies'.

The Westminster Parliament heard regular reports on the plight of the hunger-stricken. Daniel O'Connell, the Cork MP and one of the greatest of Irish patriots, warned that unless England came to the rescue of his country, a quarter of its people would perish. Confronted with such a number of homeless and destitute, the government did respond with the Destitute Persons' Act, commonly known as the Soup Kitchen Act. Others too came in with soup kitchens – a variety of religious charities, including the Quakers, were in the forefront. Being mainly non-Catholic organisations, they were obviously treated with great suspicion by the established Roman Catholic Church. Nevertheless, food was food, whether it was coming from the government or the Protestants. Some of the latter, acting in a most un-Christian way, were to demand that those pleading for whatever their kitchens could provide (and, as often as not, it was merely the most god-awful of watery soups and a handful of breadcrumbs) would only receive such sustenance if they were to condemn their Church of Rome and all it stood for.

Some were to stand on their principles – more appropriately, perhaps, collapse or even die for them. Others, and who could have blamed them, would have said the devil was their friend for a cup of the rotten soup. They called both the givers and the takers of such relief 'the soupers', the latter also being known as 'jumpers', meaning they would jump back and forwards in their religious faith according to who was providing the food.

The government was also to introduce massive public works projects throughout the country, although the final cost of these was to be met out of increased local taxation, not central funds. Tens of thousands – almost a quarter of a million, in fact – were to be employed in such schemes, their slave-rate wages barely enough to keep them and their families.

It was work suitable only for the fittest and those who had known life on the hard end of the pick and shovel. Payment for the assignments on which they laboured was on a basis of completing the task allocated them each day. If they could finish what the gaffers said they should, they would get the full rate for the job, around five pence a day. If they could do even better than what had been set for them in their task, they would be paid even more, the most competent earning up to seven and a half pence a day.

Those who could only manage a portion of the work allotment set for them would make proportionately less, perhaps only earning around four pence for their long day's graft.

For the destitute who were not able-bodied enough to do such work, the sick and infirm, the widows and orphans, there was only one last and dreadful resort – the workhouse. There were around 130 of these fearful institutions scattered throughout the country, capable of accommodating somewhere in the region of 100,000 people. Prior to the outbreak of famine, the workhouses had been already half full of those for whom they were meant, the aged and the handicapped. But now there were more than two million in a state of dire poverty and the workhouses were besieged by the most desperate of the poor, pleading for some kind of shelter. Because of the pressure for places in them, their capacity was to be increased by almost two-thirds, but even that was far short of what was required by those with nothing. Most were appallingly overcrowded, practically concentration camps for the poor. In one case there were 1,800 souls crammed into a workhouse built to house 800. In another, also meant for 800, 2,800 were squeezed into the grimy stone building. Perhaps the average death rate of 12 per cent gives some indication of just how grim life was inside these fearful places. Some had even worse records than that, such as the one with nearly 2,000 inmates, almost a quarter of whom died within two months of admission.

Conditions inside the workhouses, as can be imagined, were appalling to the extreme. They resembled penitentiaries, with separate yards and dormitories for men and women. To relieve the pressure of the overcrowding in them, the fit men were ordered into working gangs and employed in stone breaking, reducing boulders into workable material for building. If they refused such duties their relief was stopped. Others were put to a variety of labours inside the workhouse; these were designed to be as harsh and tedious as possible to discourage people from seeking refuge in them. One of the more common of these exhausting and oppressive chores was turning the huge capstan of the mill wheel which supplied the energy to grind corn. This medieval form of labour, although torture is a more appropriate term, involved a team of about 40 men divided into 20 pairs, one pair to a spoke of the gigantic wheel, monotonously walking in a circle for hours on end to keep the wheel in motion.

The agonising years of the Great Famine dragged on as though the hell was never to end. It was to last longer even than the First World War and as long as the Second. The deaths of the innocents who starved in Ireland were proportionately as great as in the countries who suffered worst in each of these wars. This was Ireland's greatest war; a war of a people against incompetence, intransigence. A war in which reports from the frontline, which could be anywhere, everywhere, on the island, made gruesome reading. In one of the despatches in 1849, the Irish correspondent for the London *Times*, who reported extensively on the tragedy, included in one special report a letter written by a Protestant rector in Ballinrobe, County Mayo, to the Prime Minister. The clergyman was describing just one aspect of how the famine had affected his parish. The letter made the most fearful of reading. It told the story of a body being washed up from a shipwreck on the shore of a neighbouring parish. The corpse had been found by a man wandering along the beach, who had been on the outer limits of starvation. When he came across the body, in a form of delirium he pounced on the corpse and in the clergyman's words, 'the starving man extracted the heart and liver, and that was the maddening feast on which he regaled himself and his perishing family'.

The minister went on to tell the Prime Minister of another

story, again typical of the state to which the people had been reduced. It was of a poor forlorn girl living in a nearby parish who, on hearing that her mother was afflicted with cholera, had hastened to her house in the hope of nursing her back to health. She was too late, for her mother was already dead, but, as the letter went on to say, 'with a deep religious and filial devotion, desiring at least a decent interment for her dear departed parent, was driven to the shocking necessity of carrying the corpse upon her own back for three long miles to this parish so that she might make her wants known, and simply obtain a coffin from the relieving officer. Need I tell you, my Lord, the dismal sequel? She herself died of cholera the next day.'

Alexander Somerville of the *Manchester Examiner* wrote a series of dispatches from Ireland during the worst years of the famine. One of the most extraordinary of these told the tale of seven men he had come across working in a three-acre field growing oats. It was late in the afternoon when he saw them, and they appeared to him to be working somewhat indifferently, all seven of them apparently doing less than one man's work. Fascinated at such an unusual spectacle – it was unheard of for rural workers such as these to be so casual about their labours – he watched them unseen for some time. He noticed some of them leaning for long periods on their work implements while others appeared to be staggering among the furrows of the cultivated field. It became obvious to him that they were suffering from sheer weakness and hunger. Then he saw one of the men leave the field and crawl through a gap in the hedge and onto the rough road running alongside. When the man got through the hedge it was obvious he was having extreme difficulty getting off his hands and knees to regain his feet. He had all the appearances of a very elderly man and when he finally did get back up, he stumbled off unsteadily in the direction of the nearby village. Somerville followed him, as he wanted to speak to the enfeebled worker, who, it turned out when he eventually caught up with him, was not nearly as old as he had first appeared, less than 40 years of age. 'He had all the appearance of what would have been a strong man if there had been flesh on his body,' wrote Somerville. The man was a ghastly sight, bowed, his cheeks sunken, his skeletal hands clutching the handle of a shovel which he used as support in order to stand up. When he finally mustered the strength to speak to the journalist, it was as if it was his last gasp of life.

The man told Somerville it was hunger which was making him so weak. He said he had to get home before he collapsed. His family consisted of his wife and six children and they had consumed no food at all the previous day. That morning all they had had between them before he had left for work had been a handful of yellow meal cooked as a porridge. He had eaten nothing since. 'Sure, this hunger will be the death of all of us,' the man said feebly. His parting words to the writer were: 'God have mercy upon me and my poor family.'

Later, the man from the Manchester paper went to see the family and was shocked at the sight of them. They were skeletons, all of them, he was to write. A mother skeleton and baby skeleton; a tall boy skeleton, four female child skeletons and the tall father a skeleton, unable through his weakness to work any longer, and if he had been able, he still could not get food for them.

Similar harrowing reports were carried in the Irish newspapers, some of them stories of a horror far beyond the range of normal belief. Yet such things were really happening among a people reduced to the lowest depths of human existence. Reports of inquests into the more ordinary deaths from starvation were so commonplace in the newspapers by now that they were read only for the detail of the victim's name. They appeared in every newspaper, every day, column after column of them. The most common ones were reported in the briefest of terms. One, in the *Kerry Examiner*, of John Botend, of Ballireanig, to the west of Dingle, read simply that he was 'a poor labouring man' who fell on the new road on which he had been working 'and expired immediately after being carried to his residence'. The verdict was 'he came by his death from hunger and cold'. Untold hundreds had an identical death to that of the poor labouring man.

Another report, this time in the *Mayo Constitution* newspaper, described how a 'poor man named Williams from the neighbourhood of Foxford, left his residence for the purpose of seeking admission into the Swinford Poorhouse; when he had proceeded about halfway he sank exhausted from hunger, and after having been conveyed into a neighbouring house he expired'. The poorhouse at Swinford was reported to be housing some 200 paupers more than for which it was intended.

The Cronin family lived at a place called The Windmill, about a mile from the town of Youghal, near Cork. The main newspaper of the area was the *Cork Examiner* and it reported on the deaths of a family of three under the headline 'Awful State of Destitution in the Neighbourhood of Youghal'. The inquest on the Cronins revealed that the family consisted of the parents, Michael and Margaret, and their son Patrick. They had all shared the same bed in their tiny home, a rough wooden shack. Mrs Cronin and her son Patrick had died first and Michael Cronin, who lay in the bed beside them, had been reduced to such a weak and helpless state that he had been unable to help his wife and son in what the newspaper described as 'their last struggle . . . nor even make their case known to the neighbours'. Michael Cronin, on seeing his wife and young son lying dead beside him, had himself slumped into the final unconsciousness.

The same newspaper also reported that day another case which it described as 'of a still more horrible nature'. It related to a man named Thomas Miller, who came from Ring, a village on the wild and remote southernmost coast of Cork, opposite Cable Island. He had travelled from his home with his wife to Youghal where they both had called at an apothecary's shop and offered for sale the dead body of a male child aged seven years. The police were immediately informed and the couple were arrested. When they were questioned, they calmly explained that the little boy had been a nephew and had died in their house from starvation. They had brought his body to Youghal in the naive hope of getting enough money for it to feed themselves and their hungry children. They had told the police of the frightful condition to which they had been reduced, and how they had agreed to kill and eat the family cat but had only refrained from doing so at the last minute because they feared it might poison them. The inquest simply returned a verdict on the dead child as one of 'death by starvation'.

Still the inquests kept coming, each week bringing another which reached into new realms of the bizarre. One such inquest had been held in Nenagh, County Tipperary, into the death of Edward Hogan, a carpenter, who had been found dead, as the local newspaper reported, 'under circumstances of aggravated horror'. The story had begun in the usual fashion. Hogan had been a man of great physical strength but had been disabled by fever and had gone to a place called Dolla to get relief. It had been a cold and wet day and the relieving officer had not turned up to alleviate the suffering of those waiting for the merest morsel of food or some watery soup. Hogan had then stopped by the police station where one of the constables had got permission to have him put up in a neighbouring barn. The concerned policeman had gone to find him some food and on his return was shocked to find Hogan on the verge of insanity, with a sod of turf firmly grasped in his two hands and on which he was trying to gnaw. He was found dead the following morning.

The entire country, it seemed, was teeming with paupers, men, women and children with no homes, no possessions, no money, the very poorest of the poor. The 130-odd workhouses in the country were to become full to capacity, many of them closing their doors to any further intake, no matter how desperate supplicants might be. Among these had been the ones at Bantry, Killarney and Skibbereen. The latter was built to house 800 and had to slam its doors shut after being crammed to the limit with more than 1,340 inmates. Such were the numbers of these most wretched of the poor, it was expected that their numbers would increase four-fold in the weeks following the Skibbereen workhouse's closure.

Despite the plight of the country, they were still returning shiploads of paupers from England, mainly from Liverpool, but also from Glasgow. These were the ones who had not been able to satisfy the authorities that they were entitled (by length of residence) to obtain relief. Boatloads of them had been dumped back on the quays at Dublin, as one of the city newspapers was to put it, 'having been grabbed up by the humane officials of generous England and thrust on board a steamer, without provision for the voyage, or shelter against the inclemency of the weather, and the exposure of a wild night on an open deck . . . If the wretches died on the voyage it was only one of those casualties which daily happen.'

It was a famine of a scale which had no previous benchmark. Its catastrophic impact on the little island nation had never been known before or since. If a yardstick is required, it might have been a gesture from India. There would have been a certain empathy, of course, from the people of the subcontinent for those suffering such a calamity as this. They were accustomed to frequent periods of starvation and deprivation, but they realised that the people of Ireland were victims of a cataclysmic disaster. A Bombay Relief Committee was organised in order to raise funds to help the poor and needy of the Great Famine, and they were to report in May 1847 that the 'very liberal subscription of the natives is most gratifying'. The committee went on to report that *sepoy*s, the Indian soldiers in the service of the British, had subscribed to the fund as freely as had the same grade, rank and file of the European regiments, as also had local civilian employees in various departments of service as well as local princes. The Bombay Relief Committee's report concluded: 'These mutual acts of kindness and fellow feeling tend to strengthen the attachment both of the mother country and her dependencies, and are among the best pledges of its perseverance.'

The poor people of Ireland had never been in such a desperate state. Relying on public works schemes and soup kitchens, sleeping in ditches, begging for handouts of rough meal, pleading to be admitted to the workhouse and, in the most extreme cases, resorting to cannibalism. Their Ireland had become the world of Victor Hugo's *Les Miserables*. But thankfully for tens of thousands, there was an escape route; a way of fleeing their accursed homeland. Emigration gave hope of a better life for them and their families. For those who could afford it, about £4.50 was the going rate for the westward journey over the Atlantic to the United States. Many got themselves cheap or even free passages for indentured work on the farms of Australia and Canada. But if you could muster two pennies for each of your family, then the popular and quickest route of all was the boat to Glasgow where, as the song went, they could have their 'dreams and songs to sing'.

Around the fields of Athenry and countless other places throughout the land, it had never been so lonely.

– CHAPTER 3 –

Welcome to Paradise!

There were no reception committees for the new arrivals. There were no social services, no obligation for the city council to provide accommodation for them. There was no Salvation Army, Women's Voluntary Service or any other agency to offer guidance or point them in the right direction to find housing of some kind. There were no social security offices where they might register and perhaps be given some relief, and no food tokens either. There were no surplus council houses which might be utilised, no night shelters – no day shelters. They were not even eligible for the poorhouse. Anyway, they daren't ask anyone for aid because that meant being involved with the authorities, which incurred the risk of being bundled back on the next ship to Belfast, as thousands were. Yet such were the conditions they had left back in Ireland, they were coming to a much better world. Welcome to paradise!

It wasn't to be the easiest of transitions for the Irish. They had left their old country with nothing and until they could find work and a wage, only old kinship would stand between them and further starvation. There were no asylum seekers' hostels, no government allowances, no charitable helping hands – just hope and determination that they would make it, as most of those who had come before them had, in their new adopted land.

The number of migrants flocking to Glasgow in the nineteenth century was so staggering that it was to drastically change the entire face of the city. It would never be the same again. Until the incomers poured in, Glasgow had been a rather pleasant place, by all accounts even one of the most handsome cities in Britain. With hardly any exception, the great travel writers of the day lavished the highest of praise on the city. One wrote that 'it seems a much sweeter and more delightful place than Edinburgh', backed up by another who commented that 'in Glasgow the streets and houses are more neat and clean than those of Edinburgh', while yet another compared the city to Oxford, 'its streets are very broad and pleasant'. The seasoned traveller Tobias Smollett, a popular eighteenth-century Scottish novelist, was enraptured by Glasgow, describing it as 'one of the prettiest towns in Europe' and 'without doubt the most flourishing in Great Britain'. Even the legendary author Daniel Defoe, also a distinguished travel writer, was considerably taken with what he experienced during a visit in the early eighteenth century. In fact, the great author became somewhat ecstatic in his admiration of the city, considering it 'the most delightful of places'.

Defoe went on:

> It was the emporium of the West of Scotland, its principal streets not only the fairest for breadth, but

the finest built that I have ever seen in one city together
. . . 'tis one of the cleanliest, most beautiful and best-
built cities in Britain.

Judging by the views of so many others, Defoe's praise was not hyperbole. However, if he and the city's other admirers could have seen it just over 100 years later, at the time when the biggest influx of immigrants was taking place, they would have been writing significantly different reviews. Within a lifetime Glasgow was to become a vastly different place, much of it degenerating into areas of the worst slum conditions in all of Europe. Its most central living areas became vile, stinking, disease-ridden hellholes.

Glasgow was to suffer for being the city which grew too fast, a victim of its own success as the greatest powerhouse of the Industrial Revolution. That great industrial transformation needed those for whom Glasgow was a haven from poverty and persecution, from starvation, rapacious landowners and religious pogroms.

'Give me your tired, your poor, your huddled masses yearning to breathe free,' proudly proclaims the inscription on the most wonderful of monuments, the Statue of Liberty. Glasgow had been putting that sentiment into practice for well over a century before the liberty lady raised her glorious and lofty head and her flaming, welcoming torch over the entrance to New York harbour. The tired, the poor, the huddled masses had flooded to Glasgow from the Highlands, from the Lowlands, and from England too. There was no better place for those starving and destitute people of Ireland, whose country had become the saddest and most tragic place in Europe.

Glasgow was a boomtime city, burgeoning out in every direction from those few city-centre streets along which Defoe and those other writers had so enjoyably wandered. In one incredible period, the years between 1811 and 1836, the inflow of migrants was to double the population of the city, an absolutely staggering statistic, particularly when compared to the comparative dribble (and the reaction to) of those refugees who arrived, mainly from Eastern Europe, in the latter years of the twentieth century. In order to meet the needs of the tidal wave of migration into the city, there was a period of housebuilding the like of which the city had never known before. Builders were throwing up tenements everywhere. What a beanfeast it was for them! No one, it seemed, cared how they built their tenement blocks, or where they put them. They looked solid enough from the outside, but there was no shortage of jerrybuilding on the inside of what were to be the slums of the near future. The new tenement blocks were carved up into the smallest of apartments, a large number of them being the pervasive single-end: the toiletless, kitchenless, one-roomed family home. A census at the time revealed that 100,000 of the city's residents lived in such scant and humble accommodation. Some builders even cut their costs by altering the method of installing windows, which normally opened and closed in those days with a system of weights and sash cords, requiring some fine joinery skills as well as time to fit. So they abolished the weights and sashes and made them fixed windows instead. That was just one of their cost-cutting tricks.

As for building sites, anywhere seemed good enough. If there was sufficient space in the backyard of the tenement block which they had just completed, then they would put another one there as well. It is certainly no exaggeration to say that the enormous change which the city underwent occurred with such haste that it happened in the period of a lifetime. When the elderly historian who wrote under the pen-name 'Senex' retired at the age of 88, he was to note in his farewell speech that almost every building standing in the city had been erected in the span of his own lifetime.

For thousands, however, not even the construction of these white freestone and red sandstone tenements, the city's future new slums, would be a solution to their living problems. Being the poorest of the poor, most of the new arrivals couldn't afford the rent for a single-end in the newer tenements, or even one in the older of the near-city-centre districts such as Garscube Road and Cowcaddens, areas not quite as bad as the very worst, but nevertheless old slum territories – a count of 174 houses in Cowcaddens, for instance, revealing that between them they only had six outside lavatories and three middens. Yet landlords in such areas were charging – and getting – as much as 38 pence a month for single-roomed hovels. In today's terms, that 38 pence would be the equivalent of about £17, but the real measure of the sum is the fact that it was far beyond the means of many, particularly the new arrivals. It was people such as these, and there were thousands of them, that had to make do with the oldest, most dilapidated buildings. These were the most decrepit dwellings, loathsome, crumbling edifices of unknown antiquity, the kind of place Dickens so graphically described in his classic *Bleak House*. By all accounts, the streets of Glasgow were more mean than even the one in which the legendary Bleak House itself stood, the one its illustrious author described as 'an eyesore and a heartsore . . . in a street of perishing blind houses with their eyes stoned out . . . without so much as a window-frame . . . chimneys sinking in . . . the stone steps in every door, the very crutches on which the ruins are propped, decaying'. The poorest areas of Glasgow had hundreds of houses like that.

Just how bad these conditions were is perhaps best illustrated by a variety of reports on one area of the inner city which was to give concerned officials the utmost of anxiety. It was known simply at the time as District 14. Today it fringes on the trendy Merchant City and is specifically those streets in and around the Bridgegate (or Briggait) area, just south of Glasgow Cross. Its boundaries are Stockwell Street and Saltmarket, Trongate and the River Clyde. It was Glasgow's very own Hell's Kitchen and throughout the nineteenth century the mere mention of the name District 14 evoked the most sinister of connotations. There was nothing else like it in the city, nothing like it anywhere else in Britain, or Europe for that matter. That was the judgement of the reporters who travelled to these places and saw the worst they had to offer.

District 14 was a human cesspit, a concentration camp of filth and disease. Accounts of it, and other areas like it, make the most harrowing but vital of reading, in order to fully appreciate what the early Irish migrants of the 1800s experienced. The following is a selection of some of these studies, all of them first-hand accounts by experienced individuals.

At the time, Glasgow had an active Philosophical Society, a grouping of the city's more enlightened gentlemen whose range of interests encompassed the rational investigation of all forms of being and discipline. District 14 had come to its attention and a full report had been requested by the Society as a study for its members. In 1889, at an evening meeting in their city-centre rooms, the philosophers were presented with the long-awaited report. They were shocked at some of the details they heard that night.

In the compilation of the report, District 14 was to be contrasted with the Blythswood district, at the other side of the city as it was then, but only about 20 minutes away by foot. Heaven and hell were nearby neighbours in the Glasgow of the time. Blythswood (the area around Blythswood Square) was at the time the city's prime suburb, the home of some of the city's wealthiest merchants and leading professional gentlemen, and no doubt some of the very same philosophers who with their families lived there in some of the most handsome and spacious terraced homes in the city, many with the most splendid views out over the southern moorlands. The statistics revealed in the Philosophical Society's report showed that Blythswood had the lowest number of people per room per house, the largest proportion of large-sized houses, the lowest death rate, the lowest birth rate per 1,000 born in Glasgow, and the lowest proportion of Irish-born residents in the city.

In contrast, District 14, merely a few acres in size (an acre is approximately the size of a football pitch), had a population of 7,150 living in 1,308 houses. Within the district were 63 of the 99 common lodging houses of the city, all of them the most hideous of living quarters, of a standard prior to the creation of the model lodging house. District 14 had more deaths in a year than births, with 232 dying against 218 being born. The death rate among children under the age of one was one in four. Twenty-five per cent of all children were born out of wedlock, no other district in the city approaching that illegitimacy figure. Although there were more than 1,300 houses, there were only 100 water closets in the whole district. In the St Margaret's Place block, just behind where Paddy's Market is today, there were 655 tenants. The average death rate among them was 50 per 1,000, or one in 20. There were four public houses and seven food shops. The philosophers were said to be most dismayed at their findings.

District 14 was to be the main feature in one of the finest pieces of journalism of the day. The *Daily Mail*, known at the time as the *North British Daily Mail*, had become so concerned about the horrors of life in the slum areas throughout Britain that it undertook to conduct a major investigation of just how bad conditions were in such areas. The paper appointed a special investigation team, known as the *Mail*'s Special Commissioners and composed of doctors, engineers, police and sanitary officials. For four months in 1868 and 1870 the team toured the worst areas of Britain, compiling reports in order to force the government to take action. The *Mail*'s Commissioners visited London, Liverpool, Manchester, Bristol and Glasgow, everywhere from Gallowgate to Bethnal Green. It was in Glasgow, in District 14, that they were to come across the worst misery and deprivation of anywhere they had visited. One of the investigating team gave the most graphic of the first-hand reports published about the poverty in Glasgow at the time. What the *Mail*'s Commissioners saw and reported is not for the fainthearted. In their own words, 'some of what you might read may be a shock to rarefied sensibilities'.

Their report begins with their initial reaction on seeing the area, of the houses crowded together, built back-to-back and constructed in many instances with no definite ground plan. Courts and passages had no free access to air and the sunshine could not penetrate backyards because of the height of the surrounding walls. Open middens and privies were in a state of filth and abomination so bad they would be 'utterly impossible' to describe: 'Even if the scavenging department were to act in the most vigorous and thorough manner, such is the arrangement of the middens and privies it would be impossible to keep them clean for a day.' The closets (dry toilets) were cleaned at night by the 'night man' who 'wheeled the stuff out in wheelbarrows through the closes to the street where it is shovelled onto carts, filling the air even more with stinking smells'.

The report goes on to give an eyewitness account of how one

of the Commissioners reacted on entering one of the tenement blocks and visiting the houses in them:

> Now we enter one of these poisoned dens, for we can call them nothing else. Selecting one of the many staircases which surround you, then ascend. Here let there be strong stomachs and bold hearts; grope your way up the dimly lighted stairs worn by innumerable footsteps with the sewage of the houses in some instances slowly trickling down in all its odious repulsiveness. You reach the landing, you enter a passage with a couple of dwellings on either side. The passage is crossed by another landing, right and left, the whole forming a T.
>
> There is no provision for ventilation or light – a dark and unwholesome dungeon. Along the passage and there's two or three houses on either side making in all eight to a dozen dwellings on the landing. Knock at a door. You enter briskly but suddenly fall back. Is there anyone living here? Can human life sustain itself here? Do not draw back. You have your inspection to complete so get on with it. Well, what do you see? The floor is covered with men, women and children huddled up promiscuously in corners of the room on tressed beds or no beds at all or in closet beds with doors which, where you enter, were carefully shut to exclude even a suspicion of fresh air, were such a thing possible here. Rags, scraps of blankets and old clothing, grey with dirt and crawling with vermin, are wound in frowsy coils around the limbs of little children and of grown-up men and women. A twisted mass of humanity and dirt too horrible to contemplate.

But this is not all. See the walls glistening with a moist flow of condensed vapour and filth from the reeking mass of life and dirt that surrounds you. You can scrape it off, a pasty mass. See every crevice in the window stuffed with rags in order to exclude the obnoxious air from outside, while the panes are coated with a blue, misty, iridescent film, like the oxidising of filth on putrid gutters. There's a small bench in a corner, an apology for a table. See it covered with dirty plates, broken victuals, bones and scraps of herring and potato peelings. Strewn around the floor are unclean cooking utensils in close proximity to the reeking night tub, all lending their quota to the general nosegay.

Survey all this and when you have, inhale the atmosphere and when you reach the limit of human endurance, rush to the open air and thank God you have not to live in such a den. This is no fancy picture. Let those who doubt its reality visit the Bridgegate.

Although they were to go on to tour the worst slum areas in the major English cities, the *Mail*'s Commissioners found nothing to equal their experience of District 14 in Glasgow. The city's medical officer of health at the time was well aware of the horrors so many of the new arrivals from Ireland faced. In one of his reports for the period he confirmed everything the visiting *Daily Mail* Commissioners had discovered, going on to give yet another vivid account of the conditions endured by Irish and native Scots alike:

The streets or lanes and alleys in which the poor lived were filthy beyond measure. The houses in the disease-haunted areas are ruinous, ill constructed and to an incredible extent destitute of furniture. In many there is not an article of bedding and the body clothes of the inhabitants are of the most revolting description. In fact there are hundreds in the city who never enjoy the luxury of the meanest kind of bed and who if they attempted to take off their clothes would have difficulty in putting them on again. The lodging houses are the medium through which the migrants find their way to the fever hospital and it is remarkable how many of the inmates of that hospital come from lodging houses and have not been six months in the city.

High Street, Saltmarket, Briggait are all sanitary evils. Narrow closes, only four to five feet in width, leading into the houses which are so high daylight never reaches much of the property. Large midden sheds are underneath the houses in the immediate vicinity of the windows and doors of human dwellings. For years the population of many thousands has been added to Glasgow by immigrants without a single house being built to receive them. The overcrowding and wretchedness of those years has brought typhus with it, a disease that not long ago was rare in the large cities of Scotland, and wherever typhus prevails so too does cholera.

Typhus outbreaks did become prevalent. In one there were 44 cases of typhus in one single close in the High Street. Many of the impoverished wretches would break windows on a Saturday night in order to be taken to the police station where they would at least get some shelter.

The spate of epidemic diseases had accordingly raised the mortality rate far above the level of corresponding towns in England or on the continent. In specific reference to the Irish newcomers, the medical officer added that while he acknowledged their arrival had not been without its problems, 'no matter how bad their new conditions were they were greatly more favourable than they had ever enjoyed before'.

Alexander Brown, who had a printing business in Argyle Street, made regular trips round District 14 during its most notorious period of overcrowding, when it suffered all the allied ailments of such conditions, such as disease, drunkenness and crime. It was during that period, in the wake of the Great Famine, that Brown methodically noted what he had found on those visits, his published accounts equalling the forceful words of the *Daily Mail*'s investigators. Brown describes one of his observations as he walks down the Bridgegate. The street was crowded with people of all ages 'lounging about in idle groups preferring the open air of the street to the vitiated atmosphere of these pestilential dwellings'. He noted that most people he saw were in filthy rags, having made only the 'feeblest attempts at face-washing'. A friend who accompanied him on this particular walk was so utterly amazed at the sight of the decrepit buildings and impoverished residents that Brown was to write he appeared as if under the influence of some mysterious spell. 'How do they live?' the friend had asked. 'How do the poor creatures live?'

The two went into a few closes in the street and knocked on some of the doors, encountering people who had fled the horrors of the Great Famine. They visited eight or so families. Each of their homes consisted of just one apartment, measuring about 8 feet by 12 feet, each with an average of four or five residents; their bedding was in a corner of the room, mostly a pile of straw, and the bedclothes were a few old rags. In only two of the houses was there any form of furniture, that being a chair or a stool. One little room in the attic was the home of an Irish couple and their child. The woman was dying from consumption, her husband invalided through injury at work, doubtless one of the many navvies who had paid the penalty for the absence of work safety regulations.

Further along the street they came upon a young Irish lad. He was barefoot, his clothes were in tatters and the three buttons of his waistcoat did their best to hide his dirty little shirt. He asked the two men if they would buy some of the matches he was selling. They asked his name and he replied that it was Johnny, he didn't know his age, though it was probably seven or eight. His father had been called Paddy, but he was dead. He told them he had two brothers and a sister, but their mother couldn't help them as she was 'owre auld to dae onything'. One of his brothers sold old newspapers, his sister sold fire kindlers, and the other brother sat at home with the mother. They asked if the priest gave them any help. The boy replied: 'No. He asks if we're well; my mither says yes; then he bids as guid morning and walks out again.' When asked how they survived, he said they did so by what they could sell, such as his matches and his sister's kindlers.

The waif with the matches walked on, searching for other customers whose pennies, together with those made by his brother and sister, would hopefully see them survive for another day. Others from Ireland who had come to Glasgow for their salvation were doing even worse. Circumstances had reduced them to basic survival on the streets. You would sometimes see families hiding from the elements in the scantiest of shelters, often in lanes or the old wynds, perhaps in a close mouth. They were the poorest-looking wretches, in the most threadbare of rags. They would be a considerable contrast to the homeless in the city at the beginning of the twenty-first century, the city-centre squatters with their placards and mandatory dog. In contrast, their faces carried a haunted, hunted look of dejection; they required no signs signifying they were hungry and homeless, no sympathetic dog. The very sight of them, even from afar, said it all.

One of the most striking descriptions of the pitiful state of these unfortunate new citizens of Glasgow is by journalist Peter Mackenzie, one of the most caring and campaigning writers of the day. One of Mackenzie's proudest achievements was helping establish the city's very first soup kitchen, the only form of sustenance available to those who had been reduced to life on the streets. Writing in his newspaper, the *Old Reformers' Gazette*, he was to recount a moving experience he'd had of coming across such an impoverished family.

It was a cold, mid-winter Sunday afternoon in the 1860s; he was returning in the early afternoon with his family from the lunchtime service at St Enoch Church when they came across what he was to describe as 'a most dismal sight . . . sufficient to touch the heart of a stone'. A bitter wind was whipping up the falling snow, blowing it into their faces and making it difficult to see ahead. There was ice on the rough pavement and they were walking slowly because of this and the driving snow. They had just reached the corner of St Enoch Square and Argyle Street when they encountered:

> . . . seven young helpless children, the oldest apparently under the age of ten, huddled together on the cold pavement with a bare, shivering mother, miserably clad, sitting beside them, whose countenance solemnly indicated that she was in the

last stage of consumption. In vain she was trying to suckle an infant at her breast. The children were sobbing and shivering, benumbed with cold and almost in a state of nudity, all without shirts, shoes or stockings. Standing beside them was their other parent, the father, whose mute and dejected countenance attested the mental and bodily misery he was enduring.

Despite the blizzard howling around them, the Mackenzie family stopped in their tracks at the sight of the family and made inquiries about them. It was with no great surprise that the Mackenzies learned they were Irish, they being the principal victims of such misfortune. It turned out they had come there to try and gain admittance to the nearby house of refuge, but even that hope had been dashed. The hospice was crowded 'to suffocation and mainly with Irish', Mackenzie wrote. Not one other soul, no matter how impoverished and needy, could be admitted. The fact that the refuge had been crammed to capacity with so many other Irish roused the writer's general feelings on the subject. He criticised Irish landlords who, to 'save their own pockets from pauper assessments, were shipping off whole cargoes of their population by steamer to Glasgow to live or die as beggars amongst us in Scotland'. Warming to the subject, he went on to comment on the current move in Ireland to repeal the union with Britain. 'Repeal the Union, they say. Yes, we say, repeal the Union and see what the Irish themselves would make of it!'

His feelings on that controversy did not colour his sentiments for the family before him. Mackenzie reached in his pockets and gave the father a half crown, no small offering for the day, being the equivalent of around £4.50. Mackenzie described the father's reaction:

The Irishman had looked at the money in amazement. 'Ah, your honour,' he said. 'God bless your honour (an Irishman with all his faults has often much politeness about him), but what is this lump of money to me, sir, when I can't procure a bit of bread or a mouthful of warm soup on this blessed day for my poor, dying wife and starving children?' He dropped to his knee, kissed the half crown and threw his tattered coat over the shoulders of his dying wife and baby uttering the words, 'Christ Jesus, for his Mother's sake, have mercy on us.'

Mackenzie's family were so appalled at the distressing scene that they decided they had to do something more than merely hand over some money, even such a handsome sum as half a crown. While his family waited, Mackenzie hurried off on his own along Argyle Street to the Central Police Office, at the time sited in Albion Street. There he met Sergeant John Walker, who was the orderly officer of the day, a man who had seen considerable service with the army, principally in India. As it turned out, Sergeant Walker was also one of life's Good Samaritans and as soon as he heard Mackenzie's story about the family, despite the fact that such events were not a rarity, he immediately hurried with the journalist back to St Enoch Square. There he lifted the woman from the pavement and threw his greatcoat over the children. He then blew his whistle to summon other policemen and had them escort the family to the police office for some warmth. But it was too late for the impoverished mother who, despite the warmth and comfort offered in the station, collapsed and died along with her youngest child, the tiny baby on her breast.

Mackenzie's poignant experience was to have, as he described it, 'some extraordinary results'. Police Sergeant Walker had been as moved by the incident as he was and complained bitterly to him about those he called 'the bigots of the city'. The term 'bigot' in the mid-nineteenth century had a different connotation than today. Sergeant Walker's use of the word was a reference to the 'never-on-a-Sunday' Presbyterians who for years had been objecting to any form of aid for the poor on Sundays, necessities such as soup kitchens and the like, because they maintained it would be sinful and amount to Sabbath desecration.

Inspired by the policeman's wrath, Mackenzie launched a campaign in his newspaper for Sunday soup kitchens, 'not only for the Irish but for the Scotch poor as well'. Almost immediately his appeal helped raise over £100, today's equivalent of nearly £4,000. At the same time, a site was procured nearby the Roman Catholic St Andrew's Cathedral in Clyde Street, which had been completed some 30 years previously. Mackenzie sought volunteers to staff it and was able to spread his enthusiasm at the prospect of a soup kitchen among the officers of the 74th Regiment, stationed in Glasgow at the time. They arranged for three sergeants and twelve men to help with the setting up of the kitchen and its cooking facilities. They cooked the soup on a Saturday night for doling out on the Sunday.

Despite his contempt for the Sabbatarians who had so deplored Christian aid, they were still a major force in the city and in order not to offend them too much, Mackenzie arranged the opening hours of the new soup kitchen to be between those of the church services. Even then, churchgoers vehemently protested about the work of the soup kitchen, calling all those who had anything to do with them the worst insults they could muster and labelling them 'atheists, infidels and sinners'.

Fortunately, the name-calling was to little avail. The Clyde Street soup kitchen became a huge success, and the Glasgow newspapers of the day hailed it for its humanitarian work. The *Constitution*, one of the old broadsheets, sent a staff reporter along to the opening day. The journalist was obviously moved by the experience and wrote:

> Such a mass of misery and rags and trembling, famishing people, down to the merest of infants, we never saw before. All the objects of pity we daily see on the streets and whose deplorable cases we have frequently noticed were there . . . naked children having their cries suppressed by their famishing parents. By two o'clock they had fed some 800.

The reporter from the *Argus* newspaper was every bit as touched, leading his column with: 'The scene the soup kitchen presented brought tears to the eyes of those who witnessed it.'

The Clyde Street soup kitchen was soon to become something of a Glasgow institution, to the extent that Mackenzie noted that it had become a tourist attraction for what he termed 'the higher classes'. He was to write in his newspaper column that it had even become quite common for them to be heard saying to one another: 'Oh, it is going to be a fine day. Let's go and see Mackenzie and the soldiers feeding the poor!' It received the highest accolades; some church ministers at last realised the fine Christian deed that was being done in their midst and gave it their complete blessing. More money also poured in and they were able to afford awnings to offer some shelter from the worst of the elements to those who so greatly depended on the vital nourishment from the Clyde Street soup kitchen.

That countless families were to be confronted with conditions such as this – and worse – and survive them, raise children and through their labours earn a living sufficient to improve their lot, must rank as one of the greatest tributes to the human spirit. But despite their individual efforts, there were those who, no matter how they tried, failed to better their circumstances. Like most of the others, they would arrive from Ireland in a state of near destitution, the few coppers they paid for the sea crossing being the sum total of their wealth. However, for a variety of reasons, among them ill health, advanced age, meagre wages and harsh rents, they remained as penniless as the day they arrived. Such circumstances saw hundreds reduced to begging, while scores of abandoned and orphaned children desperately seeking sufficient succour to stay alive wandered the city. These were the most pathetic of urchins who required no canine companions to jerk the heartstrings as they uttered yet another 'spare some change'. These youngsters reeked of destitution. They were a heart-rending sight with their sad, pinched faces and the pitiful, sodden rags, pinned and strung together, which covered their undernourished bodies.

A variety of institutions were able, albeit in a Dickensian fashion, to look after some of them. There was, for instance, the Mossbank Industrial School at Hogganfield, Millerston, established in order to 'lay hold of and educate neglected and destitute children who, having no parents, or worse, whose parents living themselves in vice and profligacy, leave their offspring to grow up in ignorance or become vagrants and criminals'. The school did, in fact, do noble work among such waifs, teaching hundreds of boys trades and girls domestic duties. There was another school in Greenhead Street, by Glasgow Green, for the 'education and industrial training of destitute boys'. Two others in Govan, one for boys, the other for girls, also took in neglected and abandoned children, training them for placement in work across the Atlantic in Canada. There was the House of Refuge and Night Asylum in North Frederick Street, the Night Asylum for the Houseless and the House of Industry for Indigent Females, in the same street, and the Glasgow Home for Deserted Mothers in Renfrew Street. All did their own little bit to alleviate the desperation and suffering being endured by so many. For those whose circumstances didn't match the category for which these institutions had been established, there was always a chance they might be taken into the care and security of that ultimate redoubt of the impoverished – the poorhouse.

– CHAPTER 4 –

Poorest of the Poor

It was like the last pit stop in a lifetime where the odds had always been against them. All of their lives had been spent on the bottom rungs of existence. They had spent a lifetime with the poor, but then that had been the way of it for them. There was almost a degree of acceptance in such a lowly subsistence. But not when they got to that final pit stop, for that was when they were officially categorised, given the stamp of the ultimate degree in humiliation – Dweller of the Poorhouse.

There were poorhouses and various other similar institutions dotted all over Scotland, nine of them in Lanarkshire alone. The biggest of them was in Glasgow, where thousands were housed, hundreds of them from Ireland. It was the punishment for not being able to find the resources to maintain your life, the paupers' penitentiary. The reality of life in such places was drudgery and degradation. Until fairly recently, men and women were sentenced to the most horrific living conditions, the most utterly wretched of existences. With the exception of some of the old buildings of the Southern General Hospital, which was the original Govan Poorhouse, and the high boundary wall of the biggest poorhouse of them all, Barnhill in Springburn, virtually all traces of them have thankfully been expunged. They should never, however, be forgotten.

Here is a list of just some of the poorhouse residents, picked at random, but all of them Glasgow Irish: James Arbuthnott, Bridget Armstrong, Ann Begley, Henry Blair, Robert Bogie, John Bogle, Hannah Boyce, Neil Boyd, John Boyle, Margaret Boyle, Mary Brawley, Elizabeth Burnes, James Cairney, Bridget Cairns, Hannah Cairns, Sarah Calahan, Mary Calder, Edward Calnus, Mary Campbell, David Carruthers, Robert Carson, Patrick Colligan, Michael Connachan, Bernard Docherty, Mary Finies, Daniel Green, James Lafferty, Charles Lappin, Hugh Lochrie, John Lynch, Neil McCormack, Mary McGinty, William McGuigan, Mary McGuinness, Amelia Mooney, Henry Mulholland, Helen Scullion and Joseph Sloan.

As their names indicate, those unfortunates were from both sides of the Catholic and Protestant divide of that country. What they had in common was that they were all residents of one of the most well-known institutions in Glasgow, Barnhill. And there they called them inmates, not residents. Before they were given a place they were scrutinised, questioned and tested. Barnhill was about the lowest rung there was in the ladder of life at the time. It was the biggest poorhouse in the city, probably the biggest in the whole of Britain. In England such places were called workhouses.

The Irish inmates mentioned above arrived in the wake of the Great Famine. All of them had occupations listed alongside their names, jobs which paid the lowest wages, ranging from mason's labourer to fishwife, potter to washerwoman, domestic to caulker. Most of them were elderly, many in their 70s, a few, like Hannah Boyce and Mary Finies, in their 80s. Others, like Mary Campbell, David Carruthers, Robert Carson and Colin Gibson, were just in their 20s. Mary Crawford was only 14. James Forrest was ten, little Daniel Green just five. No inmates are listed as having anything more known about them. Name, age, occupation and place of birth – that was all that was ever recorded, but then who needed to know more? They were Irish and such was the flood of them pouring out of their native country that shipowners were even bringing them over free of charge, using them as cargo ships' ballast, the vital deadweight used to stabilise unloaded vessels. Mercenary captains and cut-price shipping company owners had discovered it was cheaper to load and unload living ballast such as the cargo they simply called 'Irish' than it was to carry stone, sand or shingle. You could pack the Irish in the cargo holds in no time and they didn't require dock labourers or quayside derricks to get them on and off the ships. They were the cheapest and most easily facilitated of ballast cargoes. Shipowners were thriving on them. Who cared about personal details?

The names above were in the Glasgow poorhouse at around the same time as a group of men in the east end of the city were thinking about starting up the sporting organisation we know today as Celtic Football Club, 1887. That's as recent as the days of many of our great-grandparents. All of them were Irish-born. All the inmates of Barnhill would have been destitute when they arrived. All of them would at some stage in their struggle to sever the bonds of destitution have failed and in desperation turned to the authorities of their adopted city for help.

In a sense, they might be considered the lucky ones. Others like them applied for places in the poorhouse only to find themselves classified as paupers, arrested, detained in custody and then, without any form of appeal, deported back to Ireland. Hundreds were regularly sent back like that. It was just one of the measures to which overwhelmed authorities had to resort while trying to cope with the incredible inpouring of immigrants. The staggering increase in the numbers of destitute on the city streets had devalued the very treatment and help they so badly required. In a two-month period around that time more than 26,000 new arrivals, all of them impoverished, many of them completely destitute, had travelled up the Clyde. As one writer put it, the city's streets were literally swarming with Irish. Fortunes were being made out of the trade by Belfast and Glasgow shipowners, mainly the latter, who had never experienced such a demand for their little ships. These owners had become so powerful that when the authorities in Glasgow made moves to quarantine the ships in order to prevent new outbreaks of fever coming into the city, the shipowners had them blocked. The city agreed that an inspection of newly arrived passengers would suffice. As a result there was yet another major fever epidemic, nearly 10,000 cases being reported, half of them Irish. The outbreak was so bad that two of the city's main infirmaries had to erect outdoor sheds to cater for the huge number of victims.

Glasgow city officials were engulfed with pleas for help. Traditionally the poor had been looked after by the Church (the Church of Scotland, that is). But the Church had problems of its own – big problems that culminated with that historic event known as the Disruption in 1843, in which 400 ministers split from the establishment kirk and formed the Free Church of Scotland. Because of this, the Church was thrust into such hard and lean times due to the drastic reduction in collections that it was considered they could no longer meet the financial demands involved in helping those in need. Principles had taken precedence over the poor, some might observe. However, even if the Disruption hadn't happened, they still couldn't have coped with the astonishing numbers of people desperately in need of succour.

The authorities had to act. The Poor Laws were revised and the care of those in great need was taken over by local communities through the Parochial Board, or, in the colloquial, 'the Parish'. The Parish was the social security system of the day, although in a considerably smaller form. The new Poor Laws were aimed at helping those most in need, but they came packaged with new regulations, new conditions. Relations and attitudes between officials and those they looked after were formalised. There would be no abuse of the new rules. Procedures would be followed strictly according to those rules and only those the rule book decreed should be helped would in fact be helped. In order to get relief in Glasgow, supplicants now had to apply to the local Parochial Board, which had offices in John Street and Cochrane Street. Such relief came in a variety of forms: a small pension, medical treatment, perhaps qualifying for free clothing or a pauper's burial for a parent, or being admitted to the poorhouse. All applicants had to undergo a strict investigation. They would be visited by an inspector of the poor who went into every aspect of the state of the finances of the family concerned. Their residential qualifications would be checked first, it being the responsibility of the inspector to determine which parish should be responsible for the person claiming relief. If, for instance, you came from Kilmarnock and tried to get some relief in Glasgow, you would be summarily redirected back to the Ayrshire town for help. Unless you could prove you had lived in the city for the previous seven years, there would be no help forthcoming. If you satisfied such residential rules, the officials would then inquire into other aspects of your application. If you looked able-bodied, you should be working so there would be no help for you. Even if you weren't completely able-bodied and they considered you were capable of earning a living, there would be no help. If you had relatives that were capable of working you would also be considered ineligible.

The most shocking of surprises awaited many of the Irish claimants who had gone to 'the Parish', until the word got around, that is. Not only were they being refused any form of help, but hundreds were to find themselves taken into custody and held there until there was a sufficient batch of them before being issued vouchers to cover their one-way fare back to Ireland on the next ship. To make sure they didn't jump ship and sell their vouchers to those looking for a cheap return ticket to the land of their birth, officers would guard them till the ship sailed. The shipping companies, incidentally, did a deal with the authorities, only charging them half-price for the deportation trade, obviously one of those two-way favours to be reciprocated when they needed a kind turn, like not having their ships quarantined!

When the various provisions were being made for the new Poor Laws in Glasgow, it was decided they would be administered by the city's four parishes at the time: City, Barony, Govan and the Gorbals.

With the exception of the Gorbals, poorhouses were established in the parishes. As can be imagined, they were not to be the most salubrious of establishments. In the one in Parliamentary Road, known as the City Poorhouse, there was accommodation for 1,500, making it one of the biggest in Britain. Despite its size, there were only two baths for the male inmates, and there was just one day a week when they were allowed to bathe. This meant that when it was weekly wash day, the men had to line up before the two tubs, and it would take from seven in the morning till seven at night before all had been bathed. There were consistent reports emanating from the Parliamentary Road poorhouse about its general substandard conditions, such as overcrowding, the inadequate separation of the sick from the able-bodied, insufficient open-air exercise facilities and poor sanitary arrangements. These were so basic that water closets were being doubled as sculleries and pantries. That being the case, the state of the kitchens and other culinary arrangements are best left to the imagination.

Although the City Poorhouse was rated as one of the biggest institutions of its kind in Britain, Barnhill was even bigger and better known in Glasgow at the time. Everyone knew the name 'Barnhill' in those Victorian days. It was synonymous with having reached the end of the road. The very name became part of the Glasgow patois. When chiding someone, people would often say, 'You'll end up in Barnhill if you carry on like that.' If describing a down-and-out they would say, 'They look like something out of Barnhill.' Children would be scolded with the threat of being sent to Barnhill, and the like. The stigma associated with such a place lingered into much later years when they changed its name to Foresthall and it was no longer deemed an official poorhouse, although it still accepted the homeless and the destitute.

Barnhill looked every bit the grim institution of its reputation in the days when so many, including many Glasgow Irish, were forced by circumstances to become its residents. The Barnhill Poorhouse was in Springburn, not far from the local railway station which shares its name, and situated on an ample, 33-acre site bounded by Petershill Road, Avonspark Street and Edgefauld Road. From a distance its varied buildings, standing apart as they did from the rest of the district, gave it an almost pastoral appearance, surrounded as it was by sweeping lawns and parkland with laburnum and rowan trees. Closer up, however, its soot-blackened barrack-like structures took on a more sombre, gloomy image, once described as a cross between the Bastille and Colditz. My own memory of it (as Foresthall Hospital it wasn't demolished until the late 1980s) was that if it didn't remind you of Peterhead Prison, it certainly did of Barlinnie.

Attitudes were said to be less harsh in Scotland towards the poor than they were in England. If that was the case, then judging by life in the Barnhill Poorhouse, conditions in the English workhouses must have been truly grim. In fact, such was the reputation of the poorhouses in Scotland that in 1887 (the same year Celtic FC had its inaugural meeting), more than 1,400 refused the opportunity of a place in one of them. They would have applied to the parish in the hope of getting some financial assistance or even a clothing grant, and turning down the offer of the poorhouse would mean they'd be refused relief of any kind. But even that, they considered, was better than having to live at Barnhill or the one in Parliamentary Road. Perhaps the Glasgow Irish accepted life in the poorhouse more cheerfully, knowing as they did the infinitely worse horrors of the dreaded Irish workhouses.

Life in a place like Barnhill had few pleasures. Completed in 1854, the Barnhill Poorhouse could accommodate up to 2,000 inmates. The original buildings were along typical institutional lines, constructed in the form of a quadrangle with four central courtyards which were utilised in the same fashion as they would have been in a prison, that is for the inmates' recreation or the daily walkabout. Extensions were later added at the rear of the main buildings to accommodate another category of society's unfortunates, those they preferred to keep out of sight – the mentally handicapped. They weren't known by that term, of course, in Barnhillspeak. All their windows had stout iron bars, exactly like Barlinnie Prison not far up the road. The poor, the Irish, the idiots, the insane! It was society's way in those latter years of the nineteenth century – Barnhill was the place for them all!

The jail-like appearance of the institution was enhanced by the four big exercise yards inside the quadrangle of the main building. These were for each of the four strictly segregated groups of inmates: men and boys, women and girls. The four groups were rigidly confined to their own yard under threat of punishment. They were easily spotted if they wandered since all inmates had to wear a tartan scarf as part of their compulsory poorhouse uniform, each of the four segregated groups having their own individually coloured tartan.

If applicants for a place in the Barnhill Poorhouse passed the residency test – meaning they had lived in that parish for the required number of years – they would first of all be sent for a period of examination in the Barnhill Testhouse. Being poor and satisfying the residency qualifications were not sufficient grounds for getting a place at Barnhill. You had to show them not only were you poor, but you were also compliant. That was why they had to undergo the carefully monitored assessment period at the testhouse, the main purpose of which was to find out if they were in any way awkward or difficult types, to ascertain just how hard they could and would work, and the form of work to which they were best suited. The scrutiny of the applicants by the manager of the testhouse (known as the testmaster) was also aimed at deterring superfluous claims. This applied to those who were considered to be 'dissolute', including the work-shy and those who would not comply with poorhouse discipline. A mark of the times was that the 'dissolute' also included mothers of illegitimate children.

In order to eliminate such people, life in the testhouse was a more severe, sterner form of existence than in the routine areas of the poorhouse. They were made to work harder and do a more rigorous form of labour, such as stone breaking, and were given a harsher diet. If they survived the arduous testhouse examinations, they would be admitted to full-time poorhouse residency and be given a summary of the principal regulations and conditions by which they had to abide. Visitors were strictly controlled and inmates were only permitted to leave the building with the permission of the management. Their clothes would be taken from them on admission and either destroyed or kept, usually the former, and they would be issued with the Barnhill regulation clothing, either in dark-grey herringbone tweed or black moleskin for men and women, with the coloured scarf of their segregated dormitories, together with a bowl, a plate and a spoon. Welcome to the club! They were now official inmates of the poorhouse.

Poorhouse might have been the name, but workhouse was the ethic. The inmates worked in the gardens; in the laundry; in the mill, where they ground flour; in the yard, where they broke stone; in the sheds, where they chopped timber into bundles of firewood; and in the halls, where they grafted in that most dreaded of penitentiary labour, picking oakum. Oakum is a fluffy, wool-like material painfully and laboriously obtained by handpicking the fibres of old ships' rope until it is reduced to a heap, this being the vital substance used for sealing the wooden planks on ships' decking. As it was always old ships' rope which they used, it would be tarred and stiff, meaning that the picking process was not only painfully difficult but that it also inflicted horrific sores on the fingers of the workers. When nineteenth-century prison inmates were sentenced to periods of hard labour, picking oakum was invariably one of their most reviled penal drudgeries.

Stone breaking was another of the Barnhill work tasks. Each inmate would be allocated sufficient quarry boulders which they were expected to break down with heavy sledgehammers into small pieces of stone of a type suitable for road-building. Each man was expected to produce five hundredweight of such stone per day. If their duties were in the woodsheds, they would have to chop and tie some 350 bundles of firewood a day. The women likewise were set a variety of tasks, one of the most labour-intensive being in the laundry, where the prescribed work quota per woman was washing 60 sheets or 50 shirts a day. If you couldn't complete the allocations, the management had a simple remedy – you got less for your dinner. New inmates working on such routines would have to spend at least six weeks at them before becoming eligible for their families to receive relief money. If at any time they refused the work or became difficult, they were put on a bread-and-water diet and sent to a punishment cell, Barnhill having five of them. As Barnhill was largely self-supporting, there were plenty of other duties involved in maintaining the existence of the institution, such as cultivating the vegetable and fruit garden, working in the clothing shop and boot repairers, or engaging in the general maintenance of the grounds and buildings.

Life at Barnhill, apart from the hard labour of daily routine for men and boys, women and girls, was virtually that of an open prison. Everything the inmates did was governed by institutional regulations, whether that be work or leisure.

However, they worked from six in the morning till seven at night, so there was precious little time left of the day to even think about leisure or pleasure. They even had to work for three hours every morning before being allowed to the dining halls for breakfast. Inmates were given a half-day off on Saturday, work finishing at 2 p.m., and the Sabbath was strictly observed.

There were even regulations for having a smoke. That was only permitted for two specified periods in the morning and a further two in the afternoon, and only allowed in the men's sitting halls or the exercise yard, euphemistically termed the 'airing court'. Women didn't smoke. And, as the regulations stated: 'Any inmate found smoking at other times will be guilty of a breach of discipline and shall be liable to punishment, either by forfeiture of his allowance of tobacco or by confinement to a cell, or both.' Such punishment varied and could mean a bread-and-water diet, a reduced diet, or the withdrawal of luxury items from an offender's meals. These luxury items, incidentally, were milk and buttermilk!

In the ritualised and decorous way of Victorian life, the staff at Barnhill were under orders to be seen to be good and proper people, which doubtless many of them were in the age of the poorhouse. For their guidance in the daily running of the institution, they too were given regulations by which they were expected to abide. They were solemnly reminded by these that:

> To ensure proper management and discipline in the institution, it is absolutely necessary that the officials and tradesmen should be exemplary in their conduct, speech and work. Undue familiarity between officials and inmates is always detrimental to discipline.
>
> The manner in which duty by the officials is performed has an elevating or lowering effect on the

inmates, who are ever observant and ready to detect any failing in its fulfilment. Treat the inmates with kindness and humanity, at the same time maintaining order and discipline. Do not receive any visitors. Do not allow any familiarity on the part of an inmate towards you. Use the utmost alacrity and vigilance to the inmates. Do not receive directly or indirectly any fee or present from any inmate or person visiting the house.

There were also new rules introduced for the burial of the dead, this being principally due to some scathing comments in the Glasgow newspapers about the treatment of those in the Barnhill Poorhouse. Because no records have been kept, little is known about the style or whereabouts of the burial place for that most final rite of the resident, the pauper's funeral. Presumably the bodies would have been spirited away, more than likely in the hours of darkness, to unmarked graves in the nearby Sighthill cemetery, the humble pinewood coffin being returned for re-use to the poorhouse after the tarpaulin-wrapped body it had carried was finally interred. They kept two dozen of these much-used coffins in a storeroom at Barnhill. The newspapers had been complaining about the burials and the fact that bodies were taken to the cemetery by porters from Barnhill carrying them on trestles and with no minister in attendance. In 1851, following these stories, it was decided that the Springburn institution should purchase a horse and cart to be used as a hearse. In yet another charitable gesture, the governors also announced that, in future, burials at Sighthill would be attended by the chaplain and if any of the inmates wished to attend, they should be issued with an Inverness cape to protect them from the elements.

Irish

James Arbuthnott, Bridget Armstrong, Ann Begley, Henry Blair, Robert Bogie, John Bogle, Hannah Boyce, Neil Boyd, John Boyle, Margaret Boyle, Mary Brawley, Elizabeth Burnes, James Cairney, Bridget Cairns, Hannah Cairns, Sarah Calahan, Mary Calder, Edward Calnus, Mary Campbell, David Carruthers, Robert Carson, Patrick Colligan, Michael Connachan, Bernard Docherty, Mary Finies, Daniel Green, James Lafferty, Charles Lappin, Hugh Lochrie, John Lynch, Neil McCormack, Mary McGinty, William McGuigan, Mary McGuinness, Amelia Mooney, Henry Mulholland, Helen Scullion and Joseph Sloan. These, and countless other Glasgow Irish poorhouse inmates would have known all about life in Barnhill, the long days of back-breaking labour, the punishment cells, the restricted diet, the staff who were not permitted to allow any familiarity, and the dreary, wearisome and seemingly never-ending routine of it all. Some of them would have died there and been carried to their final resting places on a trestle without a priest or minister to give them the last rites or a final blessing. That was their punishment for being poor.

– CHAPTER 5 –

Gawkers, Knockers and Mockers

Despite what has been recorded and written about the time, it is still difficult to fully appreciate what everyday life was like in the past. Were the rough and coarse of their day more or less rough and coarse than they are today? Were their refined and genteel the same? Did they react in the same way as people do today, or were they more ill-tempered, more judgemental and more intolerant of others? It's difficult to know just how those near ancestors of ours behaved in those days of the great migration from over the channel. Imagine you wakened tomorrow and went into the city only to be confronted with hundreds of the poorest-looking of new arrivals wandering around, lost souls wondering what tonight might bring. Imagine going to town again the next day, to find hundreds more; and hundreds more the day after that. After a week or so those hundreds

would become thousands, all pouring into your
city. How would today's citizens react to such a
situation? Would they be more or less nasty in
their judgement? More or less tolerant? More or
less discerning? More or less discriminating?
Perhaps the reader should meditate on that.

They didn't have the welcome sign out on the Broomielaw, or
anywhere else for that matter. What was happening as a result of
the endless line of little ships which kept coming up the Clyde
would change Glasgow and, in fact, would change Scotland for
ever. And few, if any, at the time would have offered the opinion
that these changes would be for the good. The cautious
considered what was happening a disturbing development,
something that may cause a few problems. The more wary
considered it a terrible state of affairs. The concerned viewed it
as deplorable. And those who thought of it along the lines of a
national catastrophe had no shortage of supporters. They called
it the immigrant flood, and it was a flood of Amazonian
dimensions. Still the little ships kept coming, so full that they
were known as 'the ships of heads and faces', so many they called
them the floating bridge.

The Glasgow newspapers of the time carried regular features
on the impact the migration was having on the city, as well as the
continued suffering the most impoverished of the immigrants
were experiencing. This story from the *Herald* gives a vivid
picture as well as an account of one group's solution to their
housing problem:

> The streets of Glasgow are at present literally swarming
> with vagrants from the sister country and the misery
> which many of these poor creatures endure can

scarcely be less than what they have fled from or been driven from at home. Many of them are absolutely without the means of procuring lodging of even the meanest description and are obliged, consequently, to make their bed frequently with a stone for a pillow. Others, however, have managed to find shelter in various ways and with an ingenuity which is given birth by necessity. A rather remarkable case of this kind was discovered in Gorbals. A number of them had taken possession of an old granary and malthouse in Buchan Street and the colony continued increasing until there were more than 50 of them.

Then fever broke out and the authorities did all they could with money and medicines, some being admitted to the fever hospital. But despite all that, the numbers continued to swell at the place. The agent of the railway company who owned the store was told and when he arrived was to find one woman dead and about 30 seriously ill with fever, so ill they could not be moved. Because of the threat of the disease they expelled all those who didn't have fever and were able to walk. They were given some money and food and, with permission of the railway company agent, those who were ill were allowed to stay. Until measures can be taken for their relief the police were notified not to let any more in because of the threat of disease.

Note the overall sense of compassion, despite their numbers, and the fact that these poor souls in the Gorbals were only expelled because of the fear of fever. By way of some compensation they were offered money and food. To gauge the general reaction of native Glaswegians of the time, however, consider the more recent experience with Eastern European asylum seekers who were to be housed in the Sighthill area of the city. There were fewer than 2,000 of them and they were met with a measure of hostility that shocked the majority of Glasgow's citizens. They were shouted at, labelled with derogatory names. Some were racially assaulted. One was murdered. Yet their numbers, in comparison to what Glasgow experienced in the latter half of the nineteenth century, represented the merest of trickles, roughly equivalent to just one of the Coffin Ships from Ireland which arrived in their hundreds.

Despite the tragedy of the SS *Londonderry* and the hellish conditions they expected to endure because of the overcrowding of the ships, the migrants were sure that coming to live in Glasgow would mean a better life for them than they had experienced in Tyrone, in Mayo, in Cavan, in Antrim, Down and Donegal. So they kept coming. In one 12-day period alone, 13,000 arrived in the city. The scourge of the potato blight that had devastated their crops and the ensuing Great Famine had ravaged Ireland so much that they were to keep coming in huge numbers, a virtual tidal wave of migration, for another quarter of a century after that. Just 100 years prior to the Great Famine, around the time when Robert Burns was occasionally passing through Glasgow on his way to Edinburgh, the Catholic population of the city totalled a scant 39 – that's right, one less than a mere two score. As a reflection of prevailing attitudes at the time, there were 43 active and flourishing anti-Catholic societies campaigning against any incursion of that religion in their little city. You can imagine, then, the kind of reaction from their descendants when those ships came sailing up the Clyde. Even after the turn of the eighteenth century, there had been no significant growth in the native Catholic population. In 1805

Glasgow had but one priest, a man called Andrew Scott, and his worshippers totalled a mere 450, most of them native Scots, more than likely incomers from those parts of the Highlands and Islands which had been unaffected by the Reformation.

Even before the Great Famine, Irish eyes had been looking more fondly towards Scotland and the prospect of a better life there. Within a generation of that remarkable statistic of 39 and 43 (39 RCs, 43 anti-RC movements) there were almost 20,000 Irish Catholics resident in the city. By 1845, with the Great Famine deluge of migration still to come, the number of Irish in Glasgow (both Catholic and Protestant) had swollen to a quarter of the entire population, that being around a third of a million. Note that figure – just 50 years previously, the number of people living in Glasgow had been only about 77,500. No other city in Europe was growing that fast and to find anything comparable you had to look west to New York.

Their immediate impact on the city was to create some peculiar (although perhaps predictable) reactions from native Glaswegians. For some of the wealthy, an amusing Sunday outing involved taking a horse-and-carriage ride along the Clydeside to view the soup kitchens and the hundreds of poor Irish lining up to be fed. It was a human zoo for the beautiful people, seeing the poorest of wretches they never realised existed until now. Then a canter back to their mansions again to tell their friends about the amazing things they had seen. Others – the Glasgow 'rough' – also wanted their share in the phenomenon that was taking place in their city. It was something of a diversion for them to go along the Broomielaw quaysides to watch the latest boatload spew out its straggle of migrants. Baiting the 'Barneys' was the name of the game. They would wait for them on the opposite side of the road from the quayside, where they would taunt and abuse them. You couldn't miss these new arrivals, the future children of the dead end. They were the ultimate of rag-tag brigades, every item of apparel on them shoddy and threadbare, and invariably showing signs of bare elbows, shiny seats, stains and rips, mud and grime, tatters. Among the men, heavy, dark serge suits predominated. There were lots of moleskin trousers, double-canvas shirts and heavy, hob-nailed boots – bare feet too. Some would have old square-tailed overcoats, long out of fashion. Many wore breeches and heavy worsted stockings, string-tied above the calf of the leg. A gaudy neckerchief was ubiquitous. The womenfolk would be in long skirts and dresses, with not much colour evident; if there was, it would invariably be shades of green and brown, red being avoided because of its association with England. The lucky ones would have their luggage and everyone, including the children, would have a part in carrying some of it. Most, it seemed, had little, perhaps an old haversack slung over their back on a rope made of pleated straw or an old net bag holding together a jumble of odds and ends bundled together with some ancient clothing. Sometimes they had nothing except what they walked in. But then nothing was their lot after a life of digging and scraping, planting and reaping for their landlord.

The more of them that came, the more there was to dislike about them. Not only were they mainly Catholic and coming to a Protestant city, but they would be taking jobs away from Glaswegians. That was even worse than being Catholic. No one seemed to have a good word for them, from the uneducated to those you might expect to have known better, like the political intellectuals of the day. Friedrich Engels, the great political philosopher and collaborator with Marx, was particularly vehement in his views:

> These Irishmen who migrate for fourpence on the deck
> of a steamship on which they are often packed like

cattle, insinuate themselves everywhere. The worst dwellings are good enough for them; their clothing causes them little trouble, so long as it holds together by a single thread; shoes they know not; their food consists of potatoes and potatoes only; whatever they earn beyond these needs they spend on drink. What does such a race want with high wages? . . . Drink is the only thing which makes the Irishman's life worth having, drink and his cheery carefree temperament; so he revels in drink to the point of the most bestial drunkenness.

So spake the voice of nascent Communism.

The Church of Scotland, as mentioned before, was as vitriolic about them as socialist preacher Engels. They were a menace – not the Irish in themselves, for there were Orange Irish as well as Green Irish. And, said the Church, the Orange ones were all right. They were of the same faith, not like the other ones, the Catholic Irish. They could not be assimilated and absorbed into the Scottish race, for they remained a people by themselves, segregated by their beliefs, their customs, their traditions and above all their loyalty to their faith. Students at Glasgow University rose up in protest when a favourable reference was made by the rector to the new St Andrew's Roman Catholic cathedral, in Clyde Street, just after its opening. They didn't appreciate sentiments like that at all and howled the rector down for his statement. Even the small community of native Catholics in Glasgow were to express their disapproval of the incomers. Some of the clergy said they considered them 'dirty and superstitious'. They opposed recruiting Irish priests to the Scottish mission and their Scottish Bishop, the Rev. Andrew Scott, denounced the formation of the Glasgow Catholic

Association, established to secure the political emancipation of Catholics. They were still banned from sitting in Parliament unless they took an oath renouncing some of their fundamental religious beliefs. Bishop Scott also considered that 'his Paddies', as he called them, were a bit too enthusiastic about everything Irish.

As well as being prohibited from sitting in Parliament, Catholics had also been barred from high administrative office as well as judicial and military posts. It had been a long-running and obvious sore with them, resulting in outbursts of unrest and periods of 'troubles', these causing no little resentment in the Glasgow newspapers which, until the flare-ups, had been showing some sympathy towards their cause. The *Courier* turned on the Irish, accusing them of being 'drunken and improvident' and saying that 'the task of cleansing Ireland was impossible until illicit distilling was rooted out. This want of sobriety needs more than the exertions of the government.' The *Glasgow Herald* lost much of its sympathy for the Catholics and its columns published many petitions against emancipation proposals which would remove the restrictions from their lives. Even after the Emancipation Bill had been passed and Catholics were given the rights others enjoyed, the *Herald* still grumbled on. A long article in the paper by a contributor named John Ball some six years later was to castigate the granting of such freedom to those of 'that other religious persuasion'.

The presence of Roman Catholics in the House of Commons was obviously too much for Mr Ball, who, in his long article in the *Herald*, recalled the fact that when it was proposed Catholics could become Members of Parliament, an argument in favour had been along 'why worry' lines, as only a few would put their names up as parliamentary candidates and even fewer would be elected to the House. Alas, that was not to be and this had caused the very Protestant Mr Ball some considerable concern.

If we were warm and violent in our opposition to the admission of Papists to Parliament, then what may we not assume to ourselves now? May we not throw back with scorn and contempt the allegations of intolerance, the charges of bigotry, the allegations of wilful malice and hatred and uncharitableness with which we were loaded and assailed? We say yes, the experiment has been tried, the proof has been obtained. So far from Popery having decreased in influence in Ireland since the concession, it has increased in power, in authority and in insolence. Cathedrals have arisen where mass houses stood before; prelates have been honoured where priests were before 'allowed'; the presence in State of the wife of the Lord Lieutenant has added a new lustre to the pomp and vanities of the image worship; and we are told on very good authority that the Pope himself proposes to honour Ireland with a visit. Instead of two or three or six or ten or twenty Papists in Parliament, between thirty and forty now sit. They have already evinced their desire and disposition to legislate in favour of the Church to which they are devoted. And we see no reason unless the Protestants arouse themselves in self-defence and bar the door of the House of Commons by their votes against them, why their number should not soon be doubled or even trebled. So much for the disinclination of Catholics for Parliament!

Mr Ball expressed what so many had been thinking.

It wasn't until the immigration figures began peaking in the years immediately following the Great Famine that ordinary Glaswegians, those who had previously had no political or religious axe to either grind or wield, became more vocal in their opposition to the immigrants. Like everyone else, Ball had been affected by the hordes who had landed on this shore. Their presence, it seemed, had become overwhelming. They were everywhere. The sheer numbers of them made their very presence as visible as it was audible. Worst of all, when plain, hard-working, undemonstrative and very ordinary Mr Glasgow went for his next job, he was now finding that wages were being depressed. Bosses could pick and choose more than they ever could before. There was more labour on the market than there had ever been in the past, and it was cheap. Before, when he and his mates were having problems with the bosses, they could always organise a strike in an effort to win their case. Now, not only were their wages being threatened, so too was their strike weapon, for there were plenty of strike-breakers for hire – Irishmen. Strike-breaking wasn't really their way, but when they found themselves marginalised in the jobs market, desperation drove them to it.

Mr Glasgow was discovering other things about the newcomers. It seemed they were more interested in their Church and what was happening back in Ireland than their fellow Scots workers and events which were happening right here in Glasgow and Scotland. What about the drunks? And as soon as they got themselves a wage, it seemed, they were out drinking it. Wasn't it bad enough having all those inebriated native Glaswegians without swelling their ranks with Irish ones as well?

There was an unexpected twist to the problem, growing now in these post-Great Famine years to alarming proportions. It had seemed to many that if you said the word 'Irish' and followed it with 'immigrant', the next response would be 'Catholic'. But

Protestant Irish too were coming in very sizeable numbers. They were arriving virtually in proportionate terms to their Catholic Irish brothers and sisters. Because religion wasn't stated on census returns of the immigrants at the time, the precise number of Protestant Irish who came over was never accurately known. The consensus among historians who have done considerable research on the subject puts the Protestant numbers at between a quarter and a third and at one period as many as 45 per cent of the total inflow. The Irish Catholics and Protestants were both to arrive in Glasgow with age-old perspectives, and these were expressed in age-old ways. Scotland wasn't just accepting an inundation of immigrants, it was taking in a nation, together with all its hang-ups, all its problems. Both Catholics and Protestants had come hoping for work in Scotland. But they didn't leave behind their sentiments for each other, nor did they leave their various societies, secret and otherwise, their feelings, passions, hatreds and attitudes. These were unpacked with the rest of the luggage when they arrived, and had native Glaswegians beginning to wonder just what might lie ahead for them and their city. The *Glasgow Herald* had aired the grievances of its contributor John Ball, and it also expressed disquiet and disapproval of the Orange Lodges being opened up in Glasgow and elsewhere in Scotland.

There was considerable disquiet in the city one summer weekend in 1875 over what seemed an innocent celebration for the centenary of the birth of the legendary Daniel O'Connell, the great nationalist leader, who as well as having been one of the major figures in the House of Commons, had led Catholics to their first awareness of their modern political power. The great Daniel was obviously one of the most illustrious of Irishmen, but not all Irishmen saw it that way and Glasgow was to suffer for it in one of the worst riots of its kind the city has ever experienced.

CHAPTER 6

The Battle of Partick Cross

That so many people of one race could move more or less peacefully to another country where, among other things, the religion was diametrically opposed to that of the majority of their own, must surely be a tribute to the Scots' understanding, forbearance and tolerance. Many unkind things have been said about the lack of such qualities in Glasgow and Central Scotland, yet when compared with other nations where there have been similar displacements, they have certainly prevailed in Scotland. The ingredients for violence were all there, but it was never to erupt. Yet there were moments of open hostility, times of tension and trepidation when the bubble almost burst, but didn't.

One such moment came one warm summer weekend in August 1875. The inpouring of the immigrants was still at its height, even though it was more than 20 years since the ending of the

Great Famine. There was much huffing and puffing about 'them', those with nothing who kept coming from over the water; fisticuffs from time to time, but nothing much more. But then, for a variety of reasons, there were a few days in August 1875 when all that understanding, forbearance and tolerance were put to their most severe test in what might be remembered as the Battle of Partick.

It was, in a way, the I-told-you-so happening of the latter part of the century. It was perhaps inevitable that a riot would one day break out. It was predicted that when it did, there would be lots more of them, each worse than the one before. Who knew what the future held? Church of Scotland ministers had been warning everyone of the menace of the Irish race. Glasgow had been so inundated with them, they said, that it was no longer a Scottish city. It would lead to nothing but trouble; the future of Glasgow with all these Irish around did not look good.

The doomsday people must have felt no small measure of smugness that warm and dusty (the roads and pavements were not so completely asphalted then) summer weekend in August 1875. Friday the 6th had marked the centenary of the birth of Daniel O'Connell of Kerry, one of the greatest of Irishmen. Born into an aristocratic family who lived in Cahersiveen in County Kerry, O'Connell had been educated at some of Europe's finest Catholic colleges, places such as St Omer and Douai, becoming a lawyer in London and going on to be one of the most famous barristers in Ireland, before turning to politics and dedicating his life to fighting for religious tolerance, democracy and the needs of the Irish people. O'Connell had been the leading voice in the campaign for the repeal of the Act of Union between Britain and Ireland and for Catholic emancipation, the removal of all discriminations against Catholic Irish, such as being barred from becoming Members of Parliament. His success in the latter enabled him to be elected as

MP for Kerry and to become one of the major figures in the British House of Commons, active in a variety of major non-Irish campaigns, such as the abolition of slavery, prison and law reform, free trade and Jewish emancipation. Obviously he was a man well worthy of commemoration, particularly on this August weekend, the centenary of his birth.

News about the forthcoming celebration had taken a comparatively minor place in the newspapers in the days preceding the event, occupying no more space than the salmon fisherman at Troon who had just caught an 11-foot-long shark which, so the story said, had a six-foot girth; or another story about the spate of thefts and robberies that had been taking place at Queen Street Station, so many of them that a special force of detectives was being stationed there to catch the culprits. However, the story most were talking about that week was that of the man in a Holytown pub who auctioned his wife off and when a navvy offered five shillings for her, he accepted and walked out of the pub with the money! The news about the O'Connell celebration was that thousands were expected to take part in the event, first of all gathering in Glasgow Green and then staging a procession through parts of the city accompanied by bands and various dignitaries, finally congregating in a rally near Pollokshaws in commemoration of their great hero.

That was the plan. Alas, the big celebration day was not exactly to turn out like that. Right from the start there was to be dissension between Irish Catholic and Irish Protestant but this time there were also arguments between Irish Catholic and Irish Catholic. There had been some rumblings between them in the weeks prior to the anticipated celebration day, originating in the nature of the commemoration proceedings. One faction wished to make it a great political occasion on which they could vent their frustration at the continued detention of Irish political prisoners, demanding they be given an amnesty, and to renew their calls for the repeal of the Act of Union. All of which was sacrilege to the opposing faction, who wished the day to be one of a much more reverent nature, conducted purely in the memory of the legendary O'Connell. By the Saturday, however, the day of the event, they were nowhere near to resolving their differences and although they would still, as originally intended, all congregate at Glasgow Green, it would be in two separate places.

As the *Daily Mail* put it:

> The Irishmen of Glasgow had resolved to make a great demonstration on Saturday in honour of the centenary of Daniel O'Connell, but the element of discord entered their ranks not many days previously and effected such a disunion among them that the indigenous inhabitants of Glasgow soil were entertained with two long processions of Irishmen and two motley pageants, one at Pollokshaws and one at East Muir.

The organising committee, which had been meeting prior to the celebration, had resolved that a feature of proceedings should be unmistakable declarations in favour of amnesty for political prisoners and self-government for Ireland. Then, according to the *Mail*, 'the priests interfered and exhorted all good Catholics not to give a political character to the demonstration'. It was that call of the priests which was to render the split in the proceedings, the churchmen very quickly being given considerable support for their stance, and despite the strenuous efforts of prominent political and workers' leaders, such as John Ferguson, to effect a reunion, it became very evident that there were two distinct factions, each bent on celebrating the centenary of O'Connell in its own way.

The fact that John Ferguson was involved was to give some considerable credence to those in favour of the breakaway faction and it is worthwhile at this point to reflect on this highly respected politician, particularly as he has been hailed as 'Glasgow's Greatest Irishman'. Such an accolade may seem somewhat surprising in view of the fact that Ferguson was a Protestant, a very common belief being that only Catholics have been great Irishmen. But this has not always been so – some of the greatest of Irish nationalists have been Protestants, not least of them the legendary Wolfe Tone, leader of the United Irishmen rebellion, who was sentenced to death for his nationalist activities.

Ferguson was from Belfast and had come to Glasgow in his early 20s at the height of the post-Great Famine migration, working first of all as the representative of a publishing company and eventually becoming a partner in the firm with an income sufficient for him to move with his family from their humble tenement house in Tradeston to a comfortable home in Lenzie. His newfound affluence, however, was not to detract from his political desires, such as his work on behalf of the Irish Home Rule movement, in which he was one of the leading and most esteemed figures in Scotland. He became recognised as Irish nationalism's most prominent advocate and even became a member of Glasgow Corporation as a Progressive and Irish Nationalist councillor. Considered something of a political firebrand in his early career, it was said of him that becoming involved as he did in Scottish politics had softened his temperament somewhat. Lord Provost Bilsland noted that when Ferguson had become a member of the council, its influence not only improved him but toned him down. Nevertheless, he was still an outspoken and tireless worker for his political causes, being credited with giving more than 1,200 platform addresses throughout the country and contributing as many published articles and letters to newspapers and magazines. His unshakable view on Home Rule was that no nation, no matter how benevolent its intentions, could rule another as well as the host country could rule itself. It was Ferguson who had tried, but with no great success, to persuade the Glasgow Irish to break out of their ethnic isolation and participate in Scottish political issues. All of which demonstrates why his presence that day was no small factor in the group opposing the clerics achieving the considerable status it did.

The word went out to the opposing groupings that while they would still all congregate at the Green at noon on the Saturday, it would be at two different spots there. The words of the *Mail* were not without a hint of bias as they predicted (wrongly as it was to turn out) how the gathering would go:

> Those in favour of flaunting the Home Rule and Amnesty flag on British soil would be the far most imposing of the two and that the sound of their drums on Glasgow Green would at the last moment prove an effectual rallying call to the malcontents who had been wheedled into submission by the oily words of the priests.

Putting aside the sentiments expressed, articles in those pre-political correctness days certainly made for provocative reading. On the day, however, the Home Rule and Amnesty supporters were not in the majority, the priests being given the biggest support, or as the *Mail* put it, 'the sequel only shows how strong the clerical influence is over the Irish mind'.

Thousands flocked to Glasgow Green for the great day. They flaunted gaudy banners and wore bright sashes with the red heart and hand worked upon them (the red hand is the symbol of ancient Ulster and does not exclusively belong to Orangemen), the national green being the prevailing colour. The Amnesty party chose for its assembly point on the Green the area known as Fleshers' Haugh, the most easterly section of the park, lying opposite Greenhead Street. It's one of the most historic sites in the entire open area, being the place where Bonnie Prince Charlie reviewed his Highland army when it came to Glasgow in 1745. For the previous three years, Fleshers' Haugh had been and still was the home ground of the new Glasgow football team, which local followers at the time were saying could have a good future. They were called Rangers Football Club.

Those who were to heed the call of their religious leaders chose for their rallying point the area around Nelson's Monument, a few hundred yards away at the opposite end of the park. The tall obelisk is a rather special tribute to Nelson, as work on it was begun just a year after the admiral's death and some 30 years before they got round to erecting the column in his honour in Trafalgar Square, London.

Overnight, however, the Amnesty supporters had some dramatic second thoughts about their proposed meeting point at the other end of the Green from Nelson's Column. It is not clear why they changed their minds, but there had obviously been some concern among them about the strength of the support the priests were anticipating. Perhaps the sight of the huge number of posters which had been put up overnight by the churchmen's followers urging 'all loyal Irish to assemble on the Green and follow their priests to Pollokshaws' had had an effect. If the clerics were going to have such a huge crowd, it could make the Amnesty supporters' lack of numbers all too obvious if their rally was held at such a distance. It would not be noticed so much if they were to meet in the vicinity of their opponents; perhaps their speakers would even persuade the others to waver and join them! No doubt there were those who merely desired to create dissension by their close presence as well as arouse the political feelings of their more peaceably disposed countrymen. Whatever their true intentions, it was decided by the Home Rulers that they would meet in much closer proximity to the others than had been originally planned.

In fact, they were all close enough to make it difficult to differentiate between the two. The thousands of spectators who had turned up with no particular desire other than to see what was going on confused matters further. It wasn't until they marched off to their separate rallying points, those with the priests to Pollokshaws, the others to East Muir, a park at Shettleston, that their respective numbers could be assessed. Before that, however, there was nothing to distinguish between the two sides as they intermingled. Many of them were dressed in grotesque costumes with high-peaked green caps and large cloaks of the same bright colour, reminding Irish spectators of the old mummers – the masked folk performers – of a bygone age.

Newspaper accounts of the scene reflected on the costumes and colour of the occasion. Said one:

> The intense nationalism of the Irish could be seen in the amount of green which was everywhere. The women wore bright green sashes as well as the men, with green ties and green ribbons on their bonnets and some had gorgeous green parasols. Many of the sashes would have cost their menfolk half a week's wages.

Others had bright green ties with a harp and 'God Save Ireland' in gold letters, more conspicuous than tasteful. The advocates of Amnesty carried long white wands and pikes with large cards on them with the word 'Amnesty', and black crepe armbands and belts.

An open carriage appeared, carrying one of the leading priests, the Rev. Fr Tracey, together with two laymen. As soon as the crowd recognised him they surrounded his carriage cheering loudly. Fr Tracey mounted the platform and addressed his followers. Looking over at the nearby Amnesty faction, he harangued the crowd about their presence, saying he was sorry about the current disunion between them. However, union might prevail if they all followed them on the march to Pollokshaws. They should not be carried away with their political feelings on such a day, he said, and should follow the banner of St Patrick to the field near where the battle of Langside had taken place and where his fellow priest, Fr Munro, would deliver an oration on O'Connell. Fr Tracey was to emphasise he was not against Amnesty, but he said that it had been wrong to let their opinions cause so much discord among them and they should all come along to Pollokshaws. 'Follow your priests – the natural leaders of the people,' he said, and then broke into Irish, '*Cead mille failthe*' (a thousand welcomes).

His speech was received overall with great enthusiasm but there were those who made other feelings known, some shouting 'We won't go' and 'We want Amnesty'. On hearing that, others were to shout back just as loud, 'His reverence' and 'Ould Ireland'.

There were similar shouts of opposition towards the Amnesty speakers and reporters noted that for a time it looked as though things might take an ominous turn. One made a comment about the fact 'that the Irishmen loved to settle all disputes by strength of arm might be rather disagreeably exemplified by a free fight before they marched from the Green'. Apparently, however, the presence of a considerable number of uniformed police was a strong deterrent in preventing such 'strength of arm' fisticuffs. By the time the various speeches had finished, it was after two o'clock and nearing time for the march to begin. The musicians were warming up and aligning themselves with the group they would be accompanying. The Amnesty section was the first to begin their march, around 2,000 of them liberally sprinkled with broad green sashes, and they were cheered off by about twice as many onlookers. Although they were due to head east for the Shettleston area, they wheeled left after leaving the Green in order to march through the city centre, going by Clyde Street and through St Enoch Square, hoisting high their 'Free the Political Prisoners' banners to show to the big crowds as they continued along Gallowgate, Bellgrove and Parkhead, on to their destination at East Muir Park. John Ferguson, together with several other political stalwarts of the day, accompanied the marchers in a number of horse-drawn waggonettes, as well as a considerable number of brass and flute bands, described by the *Daily Mail* as 'a motley crew'. The *Mail* also noted the fact that because each of the bands was playing a different tune, and because the groups were marching so close to each other, none of their tunes could be recognised, or as the paper put it, 'the element of music was not an enjoyable one'.

The usual Glasgow crackpot was there, of course, a youth in George Street trying to drive his horse and cart through the ranks of the marchers. He was summarily dealt with, however; as one reporter put it, 'he received some rough treatment from the bhoys'. By the time this procession reached the park at Shettleston, it was about 3,000 strong. There the marchers were treated to a variety of speeches, including that of a young priest called Fr Condan, who was greeted enthusiastically when he got up to speak about O'Connell. He exhorted them to shut out all dissension from their ranks and to be combined in their attempts to obtain their rights, 'so that amid the united shouts of the Irish nation the walls of the British constitution should fall down'. These were just the kind of words the big crowd wanted to hear – his remarks were greeted with loud cheers.

John Ferguson was listened to with the reverence he usually received and made the point that he couldn't ignore the fact there had been 'a slight difference of opinion' over the manner in which they celebrated the great occasion but he hoped for friendship amongst all the Irish men of Glasgow. When he mentioned, at this point, the name of Fr Munro, someone in the crowd bawled loudly, 'We don't want him.' On the subject of Home Rule, Ferguson stressed the need to be free of the union with England, which, he said, had been conceived in iniquity and had brought nothing but disaster and ruin upon Ireland. 'After 70 years it has left Ireland dissatisfied, discontented and a source of weakness and not a source of strength to the Empire,' he said to enthusiastic and loud cheers from the crowd.

Meanwhile, the much bigger party of those who had obeyed the call of the priests had also moved off. There were about 7,000 of them taking part in the march, over three times more than the number who had gone with the opposition. They marched through the Gorbals and Langside on the way, carriages carrying the priests, including Fr Tracey and Fr Munro. They too were accompanied by a considerable number of bands, likewise walking close to each other, each playing a different tune and creating a cacophony. As one newspaper put it, the overall effect was 'the reverse of pleasure'. They met on a field of a farm just by

Pollokshaws and from a platform which had been erected were treated to a variety of speeches from the priests. Fr Tracey appealed to them 'in the language of O'Connell' never to depart from their priests but to follow them wherever they went, a recommendation which was well received, judging by the cheers.

The priest then went on to comment on how during their march they had passed the site on a hill of the Battle of Langside, 'where Mary Queen of Scots, the last Catholic and patriotic monarch of Scotland [cheers from the crowd] had been defeated'. But on the other hill at Pollokshaws the Catholic church and schools had arisen from the ashes. They had in Pollokshaws the best churches, the largest congregations and the largest schools in the Parish of Eastwood, and he hoped the day was not too far distant when it would be the same in every parish of Scotland. That was received with even louder cheers.

It was the same old story. We know it today, they knew it then. They have their meetings, their commemorations, their big football matches, their marches, their Walks. As often as not these go to plan, uneventful and conventional. Then, after the long day, comes the evening and the night, and the celebrations, whatever they may be, assume a different atmosphere. The alcohol may start out as pleasant and much appreciated refreshment, but by night it can take on other more sinister guises, stoking those mysterious fires that they say burn deep in the Celtic psyche. That was what happened on that warm summer night in 1875.

The first sign of trouble was nowhere near where the marches or the rallies had been that day. In fact, it occurred in a completely different part of the city, in the burgh of Partick. There are a lot of public houses – hundreds of them – between Glasgow Green and Shettleston in the east, Pollokshaws in the south and Partick in the west side of the city. And the marchers had been in not a few of them on their long trek to and from the furthest parts of Glasgow. So too had the Orangemen – they hadn't been marching like the others, but it was a Saturday, after all. They had finished their week's work at lunchtime (it was a five-and-a-half-day, 55-hour week then) and with the pubs being closed on the Sunday, what better way to spend a part of the rest of the day than with some mates, with some drink? Many of them, of course, would have been in the city with their families that afternoon and would probably have seen and, more than likely, heard all those marching Irish bands. The disharmony of the music wouldn't have mattered to them, but their numbers would. And all that green! Of course, most of them acknowledged, just as the church ministers were saying, that Glasgow was losing its Scottish identity and becoming more and more an Irish city. If ever any of them had doubted it, that day in August 1875 convinced them. For there they were in their thousands, the marchers and their followers, flaunting their green, their sashes and banners, swagger-marching to the jaunty tunes of their flute bands, shouting their slogans and demonstrating their Irishness. And that day and its meaning was all they spoke about that night in the local pub!

The first indication of what might unfold later in the day had come when two factions of the O'Connell celebrants were congregating on Glasgow Green. The police, of course, had anticipated that there would be people at the gathering with thoughts other than of O'Connell or celebration. It wasn't long before one of them, an Orangeman, made the predictable move. All that green became too much for him and he made a lunge at one of the marchers, grabbing at his broad sash, furiously trying to rip it from him. But the sharp-eyed police instantly responded and he was promptly led away. There had been several other similar incidents throughout the events on the Green, but all were speedily dealt with by the large number of policemen on duty.

The remainder of the afternoon, including the city march and the gatherings at Pollokshaws and East Muir, passed without major incident, again due to the efficiency and alertness of the city police. It was a very different story that night, however. The first report of trouble was logged at nine o'clock, when the returning marchers were going west along Dumbarton Road. It had been a great day out for them, what with all the bands, all the other Irish voices around them and everything tinged with green, the green the poet said was 'that of their lovely green Ireland'. This had been one of the best Irish days they had enjoyed since leaving their beloved land. All of a sudden, however, there was another kind of reality to being Irish – Catholic Irish in Glasgow. It had been when they passed Partick Cross and were still marching west towards the suburbs where they lived, some to Whiteinch, others heading further to Yoker and Clydebank, that the first loud shouts were heard. There was the usual range of epithets which the opposing religious factions use to express their feelings about one another when the Guinness and whiskey, and the heavy and whisky, have been liberally flowing, as they had been that day.

Newspapermen who were there referred to the exchanges between the two groups in the temperate journalistic language of the day, describing the shouts as being 'party cries' mingled with 'uncomplimentary language'. As always, the yells and insults led to threats and challenges and counter-threats and counter-challenges – and then a stone came flying. The battle of Partick had commenced.

It was the Orangemen who started it, said the Irish representatives, predictably, when they were interviewed by the *Daily Mail*. They had invaded their ranks, knocking down some of the marchers and kicking them. The answer from the Orangemen was equally predictable, with denials and protests that it had been the Home Rulers who began it all and that they had been 'rather free' with the use of their pikes. Whatever the spark, whoever was the cause, it was Donnybrook right there on the main road through Partick, as well as a variety of surrounding streets. They went at each other with pokers, pikes and placards, stones and sticks with loaded heads, or as one reporter put it, 'a vigorous use was made by whatever weapon the mob had at their disposal'. Among the weapons that the police were later to collect was a large dagger with the word 'Faith' engraved on the blade.

After that initial confrontation, the battle of Partick continued and spread through the burgh, in scenes described as those of the 'wildest excitement'. More than 50 were arrested by the time matters had cooled later in the evening, but there was more to come. Word quickly spread to other suburbs of Glasgow about the events in Partick and the police were informed that a band of 30 Irishmen armed with stones and bludgeons were marching towards the burgh to do battle. Although every available policeman from the district had been called out, many of them were already pleading with the 50 or so rioters who had already been detained and there weren't sufficient numbers to stop the Irish reinforcements marching into the area. However, groups of concerned Partick citizens – not Orangemen – volunteered to join forces with the police. They stopped the rioters before they reached Byres Road and were even able to force them to retreat in the direction from where they had come, many of them running down the banks of the River Kelvin. While this was going on, however, matters began to deteriorate once more inside the burgh. Workmen had been laying asphalt on the pavements around Partick Cross that week and the

Irishmen stormed their store huts to collect every available tool they could – shovels, picks, hammers, everything they could get their hands on. Now they had even better weapons than their wooden pikes to take on the Orangemen.

Alarmed at this further deterioration in affairs, the superintendent in charge of the Partick police urgently sent for help to nearby Whiteinch. It's interesting to note that in those pre-mobile, pre-telephone days, the quickest method of requesting that help was to send a telegram! But then, the telegram boys of the day could really make their pedal bikes fly! Although most of them didn't need to be told, orders were sent to all local public houses that they should immediately close. So too did the remaining shops, which had been open late.

Equally alarmed at the threat of more violence, Provost Thomson of Partick summoned a horse and cab for a fast gallop to the police station at Hillhead to tell them about the alarming state of affairs in his district and some constables were immediately ordered to the scene. When the provost returned from Hillhead, he immediately went with a sheriff to Glasgow for a meeting with the chief constable.

Still the crowds continued to grow, each side attracting more followers, and when yet another mob of Irishmen, said to be about 1,000 strong, were reported to be on their way, the sheriff of Partick headed to the city, where he called at the military barracks at Gallowgate (they were just off Gallowgate in Barrack Street) and also at the ones at Maryhill (now the Wyndford housing estate). At both barracks he requested that detachments of soldiers be sent to Partick to help keep the peace, and he also considered it prudent to telegraph for these to be reinforced with more troops from the barracks at Hamilton should the situation require it. When the sheriff and the provost returned to Partick, there were still skirmishes erupting in various parts of the district, but these were not as bad as they had been earlier. Police reinforcements from the city and some suburbs had also arrived, which had helped considerably. They were to note that the hundreds of Orangemen who were present were now patrolling the streets in military-style platoons, six deep, with soldierly discipline, obeying all the drill orders being yelled at them by their leaders.

There was a further report of another big group of Home Rulers at nearby Yorkhill who were said to be waiting there till midnight before advancing into the burgh, while there was word that another hostile assembly had been halted and dispersed when a priest had intervened. Although there were continued outbreaks of fighting through much of the night, the army refrained from sending in the requested troops, their officers wisely concluding that if they turned their tough and experienced infantrymen amongst civilians it could only result in a bloody outcome. Nevertheless, they kept detachments at the ready just in case.

It wasn't until the Sunday morning that the first full assessment was made of the damage caused in the riot. Partick looked like it had been at war all right. There wasn't a single intact window in the Roman Catholic chapel and priests' house near the Cross. These had received such an onslaught of various missiles that even the window frames had all been completely destroyed. All the streets from the Cross to the River Clyde were strewn with bricks, tiles and stones. In one particular street, known at the time as Newton Street, there was hardly a complete window left and the pavements were littered with broken glass. Hundreds of shop windows and street lamps had been shattered. Bricks and stones littered the streets everywhere, together with the remnants of the weapons which had been in use, including hundreds of heavy branches wielded as clubs and sticks that had been wrenched from the trees on the banks of the Kelvin, as well as many of the tools looted from the watchman's hut of the asphalting squad.

It was a grim sight, but still the crowd lingered, seemingly anxious to continue battle. The authorities had had enough, however, and late on that Sunday morning, together with a bodyguard of senior police officers and two sheriffs, Provost Thomson marched briskly to the Cross, holding what appeared to be a document of some kind and followed by a huge and inquisitive crowd wondering what was about to take place. It had been decided by the authorities that the situation required the most stern of measures if it was to be prevented from recurring. The law provided for such eventualities, but to institute them required a declaration as ordained by Parliament. That was the reading of the Riot Act.

The usual flow of horse-drawn traffic which that busy intersection known as Partick Cross usually experienced was absent that morning, most of it veering clear because of the litter of debris and the prospect of more trouble. A police officer called for silence from the big crowd of onlookers and the provost read in as loud a voice as he could muster the words on the prepared document he had been carrying:

> Our Sovereign lady the Queen chargeth and commandeth all persons being assembled, immediately to disperse themselves and peaceably to depart to their habitations or to their lawful business upon the pain contained in the Act, made in the first year of King George the First, for preventing tumult and riotous assemblies as amended by an Act in the first year of Queen Victoria, Chapter 91.

The crowd had listened intently to his words and gave a rousing cheer when he concluded the official wording of the Act. When they had quietened again, he addressed the crowd once more, this time explaining that now that the Act had been read, if the crowd didn't disperse (and they would be given one hour in which to do so) the magistrates were empowered to take the most extreme measures. Those who did not go home would render themselves liable to severe penalties.

Police and court officials then toured the area, pasting up posters with the announcement that the Riot Act had been read. Despite that, there were still some who were bent on trouble, and there were to be a variety of skirmishes between the two protagonists for the remainder of the day. People from outside the burgh kept arriving, unaware that the Riot Act had been read out. They were told to disperse but were reluctant to do so. They were to be the first to realise that sightseeing after the Riot Act had been read would be far from pleasant. The police moved in on the thousands milling around and used their batons freely, resulting in many of the crowd receiving severe blows. Those who were injured could only blame themselves, said the *Herald*, as they should have headed indoors once the Act had been read out. Journalists noted that a large number of women were enthusiastically taking part in the trouble, rushing about and urging their boyfriends not to spare their foes, 'with wild whoops which would put Red Indians in the shade'.

By the afternoon, more crowds had gathered outside the police court and around the Cross, and the few shopkeepers who had opened up quickly drew their shutters down again, fearing violence. Three men passed by and were attacked by some of the crowd who recognised them as being of Irish descent. They were taken into police custody for their own safety, and requested to stay with the constables for a time.

Eventually they were taken out by the back door of the police station and led away.

Army Volunteers (the equivalent of Territorials), including men from the Artillery, began arriving at the police station to offer their services in order to restore peace. There were nearly 100 of them and they marched smartly through the streets breaking up the crowds. One group headed towards Kelvin Bridge and others went in a westerly direction, routing all those who appeared to be spoiling for trouble. Then sporadic fighting broke out afresh, the crowd seemingly getting out of control once more, agitators among them starting to stone the police yet again. By nine o'clock on the Sunday night the crowd had grown again and was moving around from one quarter to another. Then a cry went up that a man had a revolver at the west end of Dumbarton Road near the railway bridge. The Army volunteers dashed to apprehend him but he bolted down one of the side streets, went into a close and headed for the top-floor flat, where he was arrested in possession of a Colt six-shooter.

Despite the encouragement of the women and the continued presence of various groups of men obviously wanting more trouble, the remainder of the night was mainly confined to a variety of flare-ups, most of which died off as quickly as they erupted. Two men called at the Partick police station with a suggestion which they said would bring immediate peace. They asked the superintendent for a group of Orangemen to be sworn in as special constables. The police, most wisely, refused the request. As the night wore on things finally began to quieten down and the Army Volunteers were dismissed. There had also been trouble at nearby Cranstonhill and there was a demonstration in progress at Glasgow Green where, once more, Irishmen were wearing their green sashes and had their colours flying. But none of the other trouble spots in the city were anywhere near as bad as what had occurred in Partick.

The following morning, Monday, 9 August, most of the newspapers acknowledged that it was principally due to the wisdom of reading the Riot Act that the rioters had quietened down, although it was also suggested that exhaustion, not suppression, had helped. As a result of all the publicity about what had been the biggest civil disorder in the city for years, and despite the fact that the Riot Act had been read, huge crowds were to arrive in Partick on the Monday and the Tuesday. But they were neither Orangemen nor Irish, at least not professedly so – they were merely sightseers wanting to view for themselves all the grim damage they had read about in the newspapers, perhaps an understandable reaction in those pre-television days.

Monday was to be the initial day of reckoning for those rioters, about 70 of them, who had been arrested in the two days of battle. Partick Burgh Court was crowded with them, Orangemen and Irishmen, together with their relatives, when they made their first appearance before the magistrate. According to witnesses, it seemed that all of them had at least one black eye – many of them had two – while their faces were described as being 'serrated with cuts'. Wearing a varied assortment of blood-stained garments, they were, in the words of one reporter, 'a sickening if not ghastly spectacle'.

The least concerned about both the riot and their appearance in court seemed to be the actual offenders themselves. They appeared to be completely indifferent about their injuries, possibly consoling themselves, as one paper suggested, that they had been sustained in a good cause. The *Daily Mail* reporter said they displayed 'quite a hilarious mood, endeavouring to crack jokes with one another and even with their custodians'. Those who pleaded guilty were quickly disposed of, mostly being fined three guineas, today's equivalent of around £135, with the alternative option of two months' imprisonment. Those who pleaded not guilty were ordered to be remanded in custody and when being removed to the cells in batches of three and four, 'defiantly began singing songs, shouting to their neighbours and making as much noise as possible, rattling their metal drinking cups on the floors and cheering to the echo'. Journalists noted that they were supplied with tea, coffee and bread 'and possibly stronger liquors and were not having an unpleasant time of it', causing the *Glasgow Herald* to ask why so much indulgence had been shown towards them.

Who was to blame for the Partick riot? Was it the Irishmen who had consumed too much alcohol during their great day of celebration and were letting the world know all about it on their way home that night? Or was it the Orangemen, angered at the sight of all those Catholic Irishmen being perhaps over-enthusiastically Irish towards the end of their day of commemoration? From the observations made by journalists on the scene during and after the riot, who had obviously been careful in making their judgements, the Catholic Irish had been the least to blame. The Provost of Partick was also of that opinion. While it was difficult to know who to condemn for the trouble, the consensus was that the Orangemen had been the principal instigators of the actual riot. But that did not mean that their adversaries were not at fault; there might have been considerable instigation of a more subtle nature on their part. As in all events of that nature, there was so much more to the riot than the obvious. The *Glasgow Herald* was perhaps the most astute. After carefully considering everything that had gone on that eventful weekend in Partick, they concluded:

> We should have no objection to the efforts of Irishmen
> to honour O'Connell, not even if they built a church to
> him or put him in the book of saints. But what good
> have they done in Partick to the memory of the
> 'liberator'? They have done their best to disgrace the
> memory which they meant to glorify.

The *Herald* then examined the blame the priests had
apportioned on the Home Rulers for creating the initial
cleavage in the day's commemorating celebrations. Stressing
that they had not 'one pennyworth of interest' in the Home
Rulers, the *Herald* questioned aspects of the priests' role: 'The
action of the priests had probably a steadying effect upon the
temper of the O'Connell party [the Home Rulers], although the
general effect of their interference may be greatly doubted.'

It was noted by the *Herald* that a number of the Home
Rulers at Glasgow Green were Protestant and no doubt there
were some Orangemen among them. Was this the reason, they
asked, why the priests took such energetic action on the side of
the demonstrators who stood opposite the Home Rulers?

> Whatever be the truth of the matter, what but evil
> could be the effect of the unwise words of Rev. Fr
> Tracey where he described Mary Queen of Scots as
> the last patriot monarch of Scotland and where he
> boasted about having the best church, the largest
> schools and the largest congregations in the Parish of
> Eastwood and that it would not be long before they,
> the Catholics, would beat Protestants not only in
> Pollokshaws, but in every hamlet in Scotland.

The *Glasgow Herald* said they wished to point out to Fr Tracey that some of those who heard him that day may have belonged to Partick and it was not difficult to reach the conclusion that, in an ignorant mind, his phrase about 'beating the Protestants' in all the towns and hamlets throughout Scotland might produce the most disastrous results. 'His words may have been a bit of holiday humour, but to the ignorant mind words have all the significance of weapons.'

The *Herald* was also to note that it had been, perhaps, some consolation to know that the combatants on both sides were Irish, and while it had been the Orangemen who bore the greater weight of the blame, 'if one side was wicked enough to give the challenge, the other was as wickedly eager to accept it'.

In summing up that riotous weekend, the *Daily Mail* wrote:

> It is monstrous that law-abiding citizens should be subjected to the annoyance and disgrace of having their streets on a quiet Sunday evening converted into a common battleground for the rival factions which under the guise partly of religion, partly of political animosity, make it an article of their creed to fly at each other's throats.

While they also found it difficult to apportion blame, the *Mail* agreed that it had mostly been the Orangemen who had started the riot – as they put it, 'a few vehement Orangemen looking for a coat-tail to tread upon'. But their opponents were not excused: 'The extreme bigots of both factions who are so ready with their sticks and stones are rank cowards at heart. The peace of the community is of infinitely more value than the great and glorious memory of O'Connell or the pious and immortal memory of King William.'

In yet another editorial, the *Herald* again took a tough line, this time on the participants:

For a time it seemed the Irish mob from Glasgow would have borne down the authorities. Orange armies patrolled the streets. Irish armies faced the police and the special constables. The town might have been sacked or burnt, all because there was an O'Connell procession. Orangemen fretted and Home Rulers fumed. It is marvellous that Scotchmen – if any of them were Scotchmen! – should still be indifferent with those liable to be alarmed for their politics or religion. Whatever an Irish mob may be, Scotchmen ought to be above and beyond the reach of petty partisan feeling. There is one kind of contempt for their adversaries which they might exercise with good results and that is the contempt of indifference.

Provost Thomson of Partick said he regretted the events of the previous two nights and he deplored the fact that men could not pay tribute to the memory of an illustrious countryman without putting their lives and the property of their fellow subjects in jeopardy. He too blamed the Orangemen for starting the riot, but asked: 'Was it not because they had followed the Irishmen to pay them back for the insults they had been given during the day?'

Partick had been the riot so many predicted had to happen. It was one of the worst disorders of its kind that Glasgow has ever known. Yet, let's take a step back and have another look at what happened. After the battle, comparatively few weapons had been found. There was the dagger, of course, with its blade marked 'Faith', and police also recovered a poker, a sword-bayonet and a square-headed mallet – nothing really, considering that the numbers involved in the riot had been many hundreds. The man with the Colt six-shooter had merely been spotted with the gun and had made no attempt to use it. Tongue in cheek, the *Glasgow Herald* suggested that 'these bits of war material' be handed over to Kelvingrove Museum, 'there to be exhibited for all time coming as a consolation to wise men and a warning to fools'.

There was no report of any of the prisoners being found with concealed weapons. Black eyes and bloodied faces seemed to be the extent of their injuries. There were no deaths. No petrol bombs were thrown. No fires were lit. No barricades were erected. No policemen were seriously injured. No soldiers had to be despatched from the Maryhill Barracks, specially built, it should be noted, to cope with the likelihood of immigrant trouble. The riot had not spread to other areas of the city, where there was a far greater proportion of Irish settlers, areas such as Bridgeton, Calton, the Gorbals, Anderston and Townhead. Even at worst, the riot at Partick was nothing like the widespread disturbances they have known so many times over the years in Belfast or Londonderry. Nothing, either, like a much later age was to experience in places like Blackwater Farm, Toxteth, Oldham, Burnley, Bradford, Leeds and many others. All the dire forecasts about what would become of the city with all those immigrants pouring in were never fulfilled. Even in the days when Ireland was enduring the worst of its many decades of Troubles, Glasgow was not to experience anything like what that country went through. It certainly seemed that all the potential ingredients were there for racial conflagration of the most major kind, but some magic sanity seemed to prevail. I remind you of the comments of Lord Provost Bilsland about that great Irishman John Ferguson: 'The Town Council of Glasgow exercised a wholesome influence on him . . . It had improved him by toning him down . . .'

The Battle of Partick Cross

Did Glasgow also have that effect on all the Irishmen from both sides of the divide? Did the city 'improve' them too – tone them down? And did they, in turn, lend a special edge to the native complacency of the Glaswegian citizen? Is there really something about the Glasgow mix, some benign formula which benefits the native and ameliorates the incomer? Perhaps much of the answer lies in the story of that riot in Partick, which had the potential for disaster, yet ended so peaceably.

– CHAPTER 7 –

Who's Irish Anyway?

It was thanks to those sophisticated Roman occupiers who were in Scotland in the first century AD that the very first Irishman to come to Scotland was seen, and the details of his visit recorded for posterity. He would have been one of the ancient Celts, and it's not every Irish person that can say they are a true Celt. The present-day Irish are a melting pot of races, the descendants of peoples who went to Ireland for all sorts of reasons, from a host of countries. And the story of the Glasgow Irish would not be complete without a look at their origins.

Who are the true Irish anyway? Those with names like Kelly, Kane and Conroy, Hannigan, Flanigan and Lanigan? More than a few are of the opinion that this is indeed the case. Others believe the requirements are not only the name, but the religion also, and that only a good Roman Catholic with a real Irish name can really claim to be truly Irish . . .

If being Irish depended on any of these factors, then many of the most famous of the Irish would no longer have a claim to that nationality. Eamon de Valera instantly comes to mind. He is regarded as one of the greatest of Irishmen, a gallant freedom fighter and veteran of the Easter Uprising, their most outstanding statesman who served as both Prime Minister and President from 1959–73, a man seen by his nation as on a par with people like Lincoln, de Gaulle or Ataturk. Yet de Valera possessed neither an Irish name nor an Irish birth certificate. He was born in the heart of Manhattan, New York. His father was a Spaniard, hence the un-Irish surname, and he was christened Edward, changing that to the Irish equivalent, Eamon, when he entered public life.

The man to succeed him as President (1973–74) was Erskine Hamilton Childers, born in London, who didn't arrive in Ireland till he was in his late 20s. Then there's the first Taoiseach (Prime Minister) of the Republic of Ireland, the veteran politician John Costello – not exactly an Irish name. Among the nation's most celebrated freedom fighters, nationalists and Home Rule campaigners were Wolfe Tone, Robert Emmet and Charles Stewart Parnell; all were Protestants and descendants of immigrant stock. The antecedents of James Joyce, one of the famous Irish writers, arrived with the Welsh-Normans. Political party leader and Nobel Peace Prize winner John Hume, of Londonderry, one of the most devoted and popular politicians in the country, carries a Scottish name, and Sinn Fein's Gerry Adams has a surname which indicates his ancestors were from England.

On the other hand, the man who might be said to have been the most famous bearer of the name Lynch, that most Irish of names, is none other than the legendary South American freedom fighter Che Guevara. His father was a Lynch and he was named after him, Ernesto Guevara Lynch. Then there's St

Patrick himself. While the birthplace of the man who brought Christianity to Ireland has not been agreed on (it is thought to be in either Scotland or Wales), it's accepted that his parents were called Calpurnius and Conchessa. They were both Romans living in Britain with senior positions in the government, colonial administrators in fact. Other names often considered to be Irish, such as Fitzgerald, Butler, Burke and Beckett, originate from the Anglo-Normans who invaded Ireland in the 1170s. The Bonners originated in Germany and the Coggans arrived in Ireland with the first English invaders. Doyle, which is among the 20 most common names in Ireland, was a name they gave to dark Viking invaders. Walsh is the fourth commonest name in Ireland, but it too is from immigrant stock. And eight of the ten most common names in Scotland are among Ireland's 100 top names.

Having an Irish national identity is neither about name nor religion – it's about attitude. Even if you were born in New York and dad was from Spain, and you were given an English Christian name, you can still be the very best of Irish, just like Eamon de Valera or St Patrick. Being Irish too is not only about being descended from the Gael or the Celt, but being from the blend which had its origins in the assortment of invaders, incomers and interlopers whose main reasons for being there were to prey, plunder and purloin. Other immigrants trekked there from various parts of Europe seeking asylum from persecution in their own lands. Assorted speculators and carpetbaggers flowed in seeking fortunes in land transactions and sharp trading deals, and became settlers. So did those good souls, the missionaries, there to spread the word of God and the gospels. Today's Irish are descended from all of them.

So when did the flow of migrants from Ireland to Scotland begin? There's no real answer to that. The two countries are the closest of geographical neighbours. At its narrowest point, that is between Torr Head on the far north-east coast of Antrim and the most south-westerly point of the Mull of Kintyre, it's a mere 12 miles across the waters of the North Channel that separates the two countries. There's evidence from the archaeologists that voyagers were criss-crossing the channel in flimsy rafts and other small craft thousands of years BC, but it wasn't until the Roman occupation of Britain that the first record of a meeting with an Irishman who made the journey over the water to Scotland was made. That historic event would never have come about had it not been for the level of sophistication of the Roman invaders. They were the most magnificent army ever assembled: each recruit had to be at least 1.75m tall (about 5 ft 9 in.), endowed with the best of eyesight and hearing, and fit enough to complete a forced 36-kilometre route march, dressed in armour, bearing weapons as well as carrying equipment and rations, in five hours. There was another requirement of Roman Legionnaires that made them different from any other army of their day – each man had to be able to read and write. And it was because of this that the fascinating first record of an Irish man on Scottish soil was to be recorded for posterity. The incident was noted in his logbook by the commander of the Roman legions in Scotland at the time, the legendary commander Agricola, who had been sent by the Emperor Vespasian to complete the conquest of Britain and was in the final stages of doing just that when he was presented with the man from Ireland. It wasn't until nearly ten years later, after returning to Rome at the request of the Emperor, that Agricola was to cooperate with his son-in-law Tacitus on a biography of his life, with special reference to his career as the commander-in-chief of the Roman forces as well as his post as Governor of Britannia.

Tacitus had a special reputation of his own in the Roman

Empire, being regarded as one of their finest scholars, an accomplished historian and Latin prose stylist. In his book on the adventures of his illustrious father-in-law in conquering and colonising Britain, he included the story of his encounter with the Irishman. In the context of this book, it is worth retelling this encounter. I have taken a modicum of writer's licence in order to augment some of the detail which is all too briefly recounted by Tacitus.

The Roman commander the Irishman was to meet and converse with was one of the greatest soldiers that great empire had ever produced. In the year AD 77 Julius Agricola was appointed as commander-in-chief of all Roman forces in Britain, or Britannia, with the order to complete the occupation and subjugation of the entire country. A few years later he had moved north from the south of England, taking an easterly route in Scotland, where he recorded that he had met as much opposition from the weather as he had the native tribespeople. Despite that, he had marched on with his legendary Ninth Legion supported by two others, the Second and the Twentieth, to conquer the remaining parts of Britannia not already under Roman rule. It was Agricola who assembled a colossal army of over 30,000 for the last major battle with the wild and primitive northern tribes people called the Caledonii. They in turn had mustered a force of similar size, the two huge armies meeting in the famous battle of Mons Graupius, one of the greatest conflicts ever fought on Scottish soil. The site of the legendary battle is not precisely known, except that it was in the foothills of our biggest mountain range, the Grampians, which were to take their name from the historic encounter. Following the battle, Agricola returned to the south of Scotland in order to explore new routes for his armies to commute with their bases in the south of Britain.

They had set up camp one evening on the banks of the wide and bountiful waters they called the Clota, which we now know as the Clyde. As Tacitus doesn't pinpoint the spot, we must speculate on likely places for the campsite where they were to encounter a man from Ireland. Anywhere along the coast of what is now southern Ayrshire would be likely, perhaps in the vicinity of where the village of Ballantrae is now situated, as it looked directly over the coastline of the mountains of Antrim, the beautiful backdrop to the north-eastern shoreline of Northern Ireland, from where the Irishman and his party would in all probability have set out on their crossing to Scotland.

We can imagine the scene when the man from across the water and Agricola had their historic meeting. It's a late summer evening and Agricola with his legionnaires have set up camp on a high promontory overlooking the broad waters of the Clyde, taking in a splendid panorama of the huge rock of Ailsa Craig to the west, behind which lies the southern tip of Arran, and the Mull of Kintyre and coastline of Ireland.

Agricola had often spoken with his officers about that unconquered new territory across the water, the big island to which they had given the Latin name for winter, Hibernia, because it seemed that season predominated there. Scouts had already made expeditions there and they had heard stories of merchants who had also made landings and traded with its people. Should Hibernia be added to their still-growing empire? Agricola had debated this point with his senior commanders and they had agreed that it should be one of their next conquests, but first they should learn more about it and what they might expect if they were to send a full-scale army across the water in order to do battle. Would the tribes there be as wild, as fierce and as numerous as the Caledonii, against whom they had fought at Mons Graupius?

Who's Irish Anyway?

The first sign of strangers near their camp was when a cry went up from the sentries. There was a small group of them, one of the legionnaires told officers, but there was no danger as the alert pickets had quickly surrounded and captured the party. Their leader made it known to them that he wished to speak to their commander and when he was told this, Agricola ordered the man to be brought to him while the others were kept under guard. Two robust legionnaires stood on either side of him as he faced their general. Agricola studied him. He noted quickly that the man was not like the rough savages they had warred with in the north of the country. He had the appearance of someone used to better things, and after Agricola had summoned his interpreters they were to learn something of him and his party. To their surprise the Romans discovered the man was from that land out there over the water – Ulster.

He had fled his homeland, he said, because of problems with other chieftains and their followers, but would hopefully return. Enter the very first asylum seeker. In his long conversation with the man, Agricola gained what military information he could about the territory on the horizon, a place that he had already planned one day his brave legionnaires would invade and make their own. He wanted to know about their rulers and armies, and how well they were equipped. It was the philosophy of the Roman leaders in these expansionist times to consider the advantages, or otherwise, of acquiring each new territory. They did not conquer merely for conquering's sake. There had to be a purpose in every acquisition, and there was such a purpose in the covetous thoughts Agricola was entertaining about that island of Hibernia. In view of what they had experienced in these northerly regions of Britannia, it would be of great benefit to the Romans if Hibernia also belonged to his emperor. While he had subdued the main armies of the tribes in the land of the

Caledonii, he was still experiencing problems with the native people. After the battle at Mons Graupius he had anticipated that the tribes would come to him with an offer of surrender and then become peaceful and law-abiding citizens, even being accepted as subjects of his empire. Hadn't they done this in so many other lands in which he had fought and won and subdued? But not these stubborn and ferocious tribes in this land of North Britannia. It would be most prudent to follow the accepted policy of previous Roman generals that recalcitrant new subjects could be made more docile citizens if the state of freedom was removed from all their boundaries. Those boundaries included the land on the horizon. In his book on Agricola's time in Britain, Tacitus recorded these and other thoughts of his illustrious father-in-law immediately following that meeting with this first Irishman.

Beginning with his opinions on Hibernia, he wrote:

> Compared with Britain, it is of smaller proportions, but is larger than the islands of our own sea [the Mediterranean]. In regards to its soil, climate and the character and ways of its inhabitants, it is not markedly different from Britain. We are better informed, thanks to the trade of merchants, about the approaches to the island and its harbours. I have often heard my father-in-law say that with one legion and a fair contingent of irregulars, Hibernia could be overpowered and held and that the feat would pay us against Britain also, for so Roman troops would be everywhere and liberty would sink, so to speak, below the horizon.

Agricola had made his military assessment about conquering Ireland as a result of his conversations that summer evening with the newly arrived Irish chieftain. Following the interview with him he had ordered that the man be held, but not in the harsh fashion they would have detained the normal prisoner. He was to be something of a house guest or, as Tacitus put it, detained 'in the cloak of friendship'. Agricola kept the chieftain in reserve for some time as he considered he would be a useful man to accompany him and his legionnaires when they had a fleet available in Scotland to invade Hibernia. However, other circumstances were to intervene. Before he could translate his thoughts into action, there was word from Rome of more immediate problems nearer home. That news was quickly followed by a summons from the Emperor himself that his duties were urgently required there. When his successor took over as Governor of Britain, he was to become too embroiled with revolting tribes in the northern regions to contemplate an invasion of Ireland. In consequence, liberty was not to sink below the horizon.

With Agricola gone, the Irish chieftain would probably have been released. There was no record of his name (though it would be many centuries before surnames were in general use in Ireland and Scotland), nor was there any record of him thereafter. Maybe he did return to meet and make peace with his fellow countrymen who'd had him expelled. Then again, perhaps that very first recorded asylum seeker from Ireland stayed on in Scotland and settled somewhere. He may have wandered a few miles north to a part of the country which at the time was one of the most tranquil and sheltered areas in the land, where the wide river teemed with salmon and trout and the surrounding countryside was plentiful with wild game. It was truly a dear, green place. Who knows?

Indeed . . . who knows?

– CHAPTER 8 –

Oh, My Father Was . . .

They came as two tribes. The majority of them were Green. Most of the others Orange. Their colours are both there on the Irish tricolour, the flag which was designed to symbolise the reconciliation of the two communities: the green of the Irish Catholics and Republicans, and the orange of the Northern Irish Protestants, divided only by the band of white which represents peace (the desire and hope for it, that is) between them. Those of the Orange were arriving in Glasgow long before the gigantic tide which was to flow over during and after the Great Famine. Large numbers of them settled in the weaving communities of the part of Scotland nearest to Ulster, southern Ayrshire. They came in considerable volume as settlers to Calton, Glasgow's first industrial suburb, which was a booming centre of the handloom weaving trade. In the early years of migration around a third of

Calton residents were Irish, mostly Protestant Irish, although in later years it became more identified with Catholic Irish. It was those early Protestant Irish areas of Glasgow and Scotland which were to be the most attractive spawning grounds for the spread of that most symbolic of movements, the Orange Order. Scotland's biggest city was never quite the same after the arrival of those who were to become the Glasgow Irish. And those of the Orange Order played no small part in contributing to that.

It is old, it is beautiful, and its colours they are fine,
It was worn at Derry, Aughrim, Enniskillen and the Boyne,
My father wore it as a youth in bygone days of yore,
And on the Twelfth I love to wear . . . the sash my father wore.

You might know the first line of that famous Irish chorus; more likely you'll have heard of the last, especially those final five words. Some might even know all of it, and the verses as well. But every Glaswegian certainly knows the rousing tune that accompanies the words, and what it stands for. Orangemen are one of the most vital parts of the story of the Glasgow Irish, being yet another ingredient in the special cocktail that constitutes the great city's cultural and demographic mix.

Back to that sash – according to the song it was worn at all those legendary battlegrounds: Derry, Aughrim, Enniskillen and the Boyne. At the latter, the most famous of all the battles, soldiers are remembered as proudly wearing their sashes behind this man on the prancing white charger, his gleaming sword raised high as he led the charge – the darling King Billy himself on that glorious and memorable day of his, 12 July 1690, as he led his victorious army in routing the opposing Catholic forces.

Then we look at some of the facts – the king's white horse, for instance. No one is sure what colour it really was. Many of the older pictures show it as a black. Others have it a brown charger. Some historians swear it was a chestnut. So who knows? And the picture of him with his sword held high – that wasn't the case either. For the king had been wounded the night before while out reconnoitring the battlefield, a shot from a Jacobite six-pounder had ricocheted off his shoulder, putting his arm out of action and forcing him, on the day of the big battle, to be riding his black/brown/chestnut horse . . . wearing a sling!

The sashes they wore at Derry and the Boyne, etc. – the truth is that they didn't! When those legendary battles were fought, the Orange Order hadn't yet been formed. It didn't come into existence until a century afterwards. Then there's that all-important Orangeman's date, the 12th of July, when the big one, the Battle of the Boyne, is annually celebrated. Even that date isn't as it seems, for it appears the decisive battle didn't take place on the 12th but on the 11th! The irony is, the mix-up came about because of a Pope, Gregory. The confusion goes back to the sixteenth century, when his astronomers discovered their predecessors had got their sums wrong in calculating the precise length of one year. To compensate for the error they had the calendar revised. The Western world accepted the new changes, although we were not to institute them here in Britain until 1752. Therefore, we were still working with the old calendar in 1690 and the battle had taken place on that calendar's 1 July. This should have equated with the new calendar's 11 July. But in the process there was a leap year miscalculation and the battle which had really been fought on 11 July was recorded as having occurred on 12 July.

One more thing – the song, 'The Sash . . .', originates from a popular turn-of-the-century American tune, 'The Hat My Father Wore'. It turns out that this song was initially recorded in 1909 by the American singer Billy Murray, who goes down in pop music history as being hailed as the record industry's first-ever recording star. Murray, who had Irish parents, sang 'The Hat My Father Wore' accompanied by a barbershop group known as the Haydn Quartet. But if 'The Hat' really is the forerunner of 'The Sash', then there's yet another ironical twist to the story, for Orangemen would not be too enamoured of the original words that Murray sang with his pseudo Irish accent. They were:

> The hat me father wore on St Patrick's Day,
> As he marched, head erect, along Broadway!

There was no white horse, no sashes at the Boyne. Nothing really happened on the 12th, and 'The Sash' is derived from a song about taking part in the St Patrick's Day parade! Such stories are no small part of the myth and misconception surrounding Irish history, and it must have been one of these that influenced the decision to erect the statue of the great King William himself that we have in Glasgow. At one time it was the best-known, best-loved, and most-hated statue in the city, but then having such a statue in Glasgow is as controversial as having one of a Pope.

The King William statue was originally erected close to the Tolbooth in the Trongate, in the heart of the Glasgow Cross area. It was on the broad pavement of the north side of the road directly outside the premises of the Town Hall Working Men's Club, which was part of the old Tontine Hotel building. It takes no great stretch of the imagination to conceive what might happen if it was still there today. All the obvious things did happen way back in the nineteenth century when it was first erected – the daubings, the broken whisky bottles, the shouted insults, the climbing demonstrators, etc. It was an added insult that the statue was facing in an easterly direction, as though the King were looking in the direction of Bridgeton Cross, where so many of his supporters lived – or was it Calton he was looking over, the abode of so many of those who loathed him? The abuse got so out of hand that he was moved, just a little way at first, in a westerly direction along Argyle Street, away from Glasgow Cross. Still the statue copped it and eventually, in the words of the Glasgow Corporation spokesman of the day, it had to be moved as it was 'getting in the way of traffic'. The old Corporation were clearly no slouches when it came to spin doctoring. In fact, traffic had nothing to do with the removal of the statue. King Billy now stands mainly in peace and virtually unnoticed in leafy Cathedral Square, adjacent to the Royal Infirmary and the site of the original village which became the city of Glasgow.

Perhaps the main reason for it going unnoticed is that the statue, rather strangely, in no way resembles the customary pose of the king, the one on all those banners and photographs, with him atop a frisky white stallion, charging into battle with drawn sword. For reasons which were perhaps better known to the donor of the statue, the self-made millionaire James MacRae (one of the wealthiest men the city ever produced and at one time Governor of Madras), this King Billy is quite unique. He's on a much more docile horse and is dressed, most surprisingly, in a Roman toga, holding aloft an imperial baton and looking for all the world like one of that ancient empire's revered emperors. It is something of a twist, or perhaps it's just another part of Irish myth and misconception!

Incidentally, should it be a windy day when you are having a look at our unique Roman King Billy, don't think you're seeing things if the horse's tail starts swinging in the breeze. It really does move. Back in the days when the demonstrators used to vandalise it down in the Trongate and Argyle Street, the horse lost its tail. When it was repaired, the tail was reunited with the horse's hindquarters by means of a ball-and-socket fixture.

Orangeism came to Glasgow long before the main influx of Irish migrants during and following the Great Famine. It was introduced by soldiers returning from Ireland, men of the various fighting units known as the Fencibles, similar to the modern-day Territorial Army. Mercenaries from Scotland, of course, had been venturing over there since the thirteenth century, but the Fencibles had been sent to help suppress the 1798 rebellion against the British by the United Irishmen, led by the man who best demonstrates that nationalism was not confined to Catholics, that being the Protestant Wolfe Tone. Three years prior to this rebellion, the Orange Order – or to give it its full title, the Loyal Orange Institution of Ireland – had been founded there. It was the child of fear among the Protestant population. They were living in trying days. Their world, as they knew it, was in the midst of considerable turmoil. There was the threat of invasion from France, and the emergent American nation was also worrying them – their new navy had even captured a British ship in Belfast Lough.

Coupled with these anxieties, they were experiencing one of the worst-ever periods of sectarian violence at home. The most appalling atrocities were being committed, not least of them the Protestant schoolmaster who had his tongue and fingers severed and his wife tortured till she died. The government was in such dire financial straits, its armies so pressed, that it was unable to supply soldiers for protection and it was left to the citizens to defend their country. In 1795 sectarian violence had reached such a pitch that there was widespread and open conflict between the opposing sides. There were raids and counter-raids, more terrible atrocities, and equally terrible counter-atrocities.

The formation of the Orange movement can be traced to specific guerrilla activities between the two sides. The Protestant grouping was known as the Peep O' Day Boys. They had been making regular raids on Catholic homes, searching for acquired arms. To counteract these raids, the Catholics formed a militant secret society with Masonic-like oaths and rites, establishing a network of lodges throughout the north. They were to call themselves the Defenders, and operationally carried out much of the same terrorist tactics as had the Peep O' Day Boys. A militant Catholic society with similar secret oaths and rites to the future Orange Order – nothing is exclusive, and such secret societies were common at the time. Landless labourers and the land-poor cottiers whose plots were less than five acres, and who were partially dependent on working for others, often combined to force farmers to employ local men, to keep up wages or to ensure continuing access to cheap 'conacre' land. One such Catholic sect became known as Ribbon Societies, and they wore green sashes of their Ribbon lodges and swore in new members. There was only one obvious reaction by the Protestants – they would have to organise too in order to protect their rights. If the Catholics could have societies with secret oaths to do just that, why shouldn't they? There was no better time to do it than after one particularly fierce battle between the two, at a little crossroads hamlet called the Diamond. Nearby was the house of a man named Dan Winter. The little cottage is now a listed house, incidentally, where visitors are shown around and told that the lead shot from the battle still remains there in the thatched roof. The Defenders suffered the most casualties in the skirmish, at the conclusion of which the victors had headed to the nearby public house of James Sloan, proprietor of the Loughgall Inn, and declared their brotherhood in loyalty to the Crown, and committed themselves to forming their own exclusively Protestant defensive association.

An earlier defence formation had been known as the Orange Boys, the title, of course, referring to King William of Orange. His name originated in the town of Orange, in the south-east of France, from where some centuries before local princes had married into and become united with German nobility, inheriting extensive lands in the Netherlands. That name had been in complete accord with what the new association stood for, and they were therefore to call themselves the Orange Society, its members known as Orangemen. The right to form new lodges of the fledgling movement was authorised by a system of warrants, obtainable initially from James Sloan, the man in whose pub the Order was formed.

The Orange societies were an immediate and huge success among the Protestant population in Ireland. They offered members mutual protection against 'known and nameless enemies'. At the same time there was a tinge of the mysterious in the new organisation, with passwords, secrets and degrees offering escapism and status among members, and also creating male bonding between them. However, they professed not to be a secret society, more a society with secrets. Some of these would be incorporated in their initiation ceremonies, although these were not as sacred or rigid as those of the Freemasons and have been described as more silly than sinister. Each new member at these initiation ceremonies would take the Order's solemn oath, part of which required them to give no countenance to the 'unscriptural, superstitious and idolatrous worship of the Church of Rome' and to promise never to marry a Roman

Catholic, or stand sponsor for a child receiving baptism from a priest of Rome. These bigoted rules are stoutly defended by Orangemen, who point out that it is also part of the initiation oath that they always abstain from all unkind words and actions towards Catholics and use only their best efforts to 'deliver them from error and false doctrine'.

One of the movement's great highlights was to be their annual parades to church, when they could decorate themselves with their various sashes, collarettes and ribbons. One of these parades would bring the Orange Order to the widespread attention of the citizens of Glasgow. The soldiers who had returned after their time in Ireland keeping the peace after the United Irishmen rebellion had come home even more fiercely Protestant than when they had left. As it was put at the time, they returned to Scotland with 'Orangeism in their hearts and lodge warrants in their pouches'.

The south-west of Scotland was to see the first of these new Orange Order lodges, most of the Fencible soldiers coming from there. The first to be started up in Glasgow was the Brunswick Loyal Orange Lodge in 1813, founded by one of these returning soldiers, a John McWilliam, who had served with one of the Ayrshire Fencible regiments. The movement didn't exactly spread like wildfire: seven active lodges were formed in the city in the first few years, and that number remained for the next 17 years. It took them nine years after McWilliam's first lodge was formed before they got around to considering the first Glasgow Orange Walk.

There was little pre-publicity about that event, in Orange terms their 'historic and celebrated procession', which its members and followers had hoped would bring the Orange cause to the notice of the Glasgow public. They had wished, of course, that it would do so in a good light. As events unfolded, it was not exactly to work out in that way. The *Glasgow Chronicle* would not take too kindly to the events of that summer day of 12 July 1821. 'The harmony of the Glasgow Fair was interrupted by a procession of Orangemen,' it noted the following day, before giving details about the march. Three lodges of the Orange Order had met in the Lyceum Rooms, one of the most popular meeting places in the city, and debated which route they should take for their first-ever display of the Order. They had a band with them, plus the usual emblems, flags etc., with some of the men carrying symbolic swords. They moved off from the Lyceum Rooms, situated in what is now known as the Merchant City, then turned smartly into Ingram Street where, as the *Chronicle* put it, 'the first symptoms of disapprobation' were to be heard.

The reporter covering the story noted at that point that there was 'a boxing match taking place at the head of Miller Street which divided the attention of the spectators'. It is not clear whether the boxing match was the reporter's way of saying that there was a punch-up in progress, or whether a couple of bare-knuckle fighters were having an open-air contest. Whatever, the Orangemen's procession continued. They marched smartly along Ingram Street to the rat-a-tat-tat of a side-drum keeping them in step, and at Queen Street wheeled left to go down towards Argyle Street, where they turned left once more to head for Glasgow Cross.

The tap of the drum and the sight of the marching men drew crowds. After all, they had never seen an Orange Walk before. Not only were the crowds growing, however, but so was the hostility towards the marchers, decorated with sashes, collarettes, badges and other insignia (but no bowler hats, that new creation of the London hatter John Bowler not having caught on with the working classes as yet). By the time they reached Argyle Street the crowds had increased enormously and so too had the 'contempt', all sorts of epithets being hurled at the marchers.

The rat-a-tat-tat of the drumbeat seemed to quicken and the men's pace picked up. They feared the worst as they approached the Trongate. It was there, within sight of King Billy himself, that they came to a smart halt, meditated briefly, then dispersed as quickly as they could, heading in the direction and the safety of some nearby public houses.

It was then that the historic fracas erupted. Historic? Well, it was the first Glasgow Orange Walk after all. In the words of the *Glasgow Chronicle*, 'the crowd burst upon the parade'. What followed wasn't the kind of play-acting Donnybrook they had been staging in the show of that name down the road at the Scotia Theatre. This was the real thing. Orange sashes, banners, collarettes and bunnets were tossed in the air and kicked around, while the luckless owners were harangued by the exultant mob. One of the big flags that had been carried in the parade was snatched from its bearer's grasp and ripped to pieces by the besieging crowd of Irish Catholics. Fortunately, the battle was over quickly, the reporter noting that within five minutes there wasn't one Orangeman to be seen. They were, in fact, taking refuge in the pubs in King Street. Although it had been the briefest of skirmishes, its ferocity had so alarmed nearby shopkeepers that they immediately closed their premises and remained shut for some hours after. As the *Chronicle* put it, 'the procession appeared to excite dissatisfaction in every beholder'. A few Orangemen who had been detained by the police following the disturbance appeared in court the following day and entered into recognisance for their good behaviour. They were warned by the sheriff about their future conduct.

Despite that dismal outcome to the first showing of the

Orange movement in Glasgow, and the fact that no permission had been forthcoming for another one, the lodge members went ahead with their plans for the following year's march. This time it would be a much more impressive one which they hoped by its size would deter any troublemakers. All seven of the Glasgow lodges were to be represented, as well as one from Paisley and another from Pollokshaws, together with their followers, for this July 1822 Orange Walk. Their assembly point was on a piece of spare ground opposite the old infantry barracks just off Gallowgate, it now being known as Barrack Street, which links Gallowgate with Duke Street.

The *Glasgow Herald* was not in favour of the march taking place:

> We have been threatened for some time past with a Grand Orange Procession on this day, the throngest [the busiest and most crowded] in our Fair Week. The Magistrates very properly gave early intimation that none would be permitted. Notwithstanding that prohibition, the office-bearers of seven lodges assembled at nine o'clock in the morning opposite the barracks, from which they marched to the number of 127 in procession to Fraser's Hall in King Street.

Note the fastidious count the *Herald* man made of the marchers; he precisely recorded that there were 127 of them. At the command of one of their lodge officials, the men had marched off in procession towards Gallowgate, where they turned right along the thoroughfare past Glasgow Cross into Trongate to the statue of their great hero King William, raising their hats to give him a lusty cheer as they passed, and on to their destination, the Fraser's Hall in King Street. They met with what was described as 'little or no interruption' as they marched in procession, but perhaps this was because of the unexpected nature of the event and there being no pre-publicity about it taking place. However, it didn't take long for the word to get around, no surprise in that particular area, that particular era. Soon there was a sizeable and curious crowd of people gathered outside the hall, among them a number of what were described by journalists as 'zealous Catholics'. As most of them appeared ready to give battle they were obviously, to say the least, very zealous Catholics.

It should be observed at this point that it was still only a little after ten o'clock on a quiet Sunday morning, and already there was the prospect of a riot in the making. At that point, wrote the *Herald* man, one of the Orangemen casually wandered out of the hall where he and the rest of his colleagues had assembled and was immediately jostled and very 'ill-used upon', a quaint way of saying they set about him. His brothers inside the hall heard the commotion and a group of them rushed out in their comrade's defence, several of them ready to demonstrate that the swords they carried were something more than mere symbols, having drawn them ready for use. Fortunately, none were to be put to that use, and the morning's skirmish was sharply concluded with the smart arrival of a magistrate and a number of policemen.

It appears that most of the men they arrested had been the original assailants of the lone Orangeman, one of whom had arrived at the scene obviously ready for action, bringing with him a pitchfork which onlookers had seen him ceremoniously sharpen on the pavement outside the Fraser's Hall. The magistrate who had accompanied the police to the scene had been so concerned about its portent that he ordered the gathered Orangemen to be taken into custody at the Central Police Station for their own protection. There they were questioned by the sheriff about the nature of their meeting and in statements to him vehemently denied that they had met for a display of force or to excite any political irritation. In fact, the purpose of their meeting had been the exact opposite. Their true object, they claimed, was to bring to the public's attention the great need to collect money for the needy in Ireland. No procession had been intended.

Although the Great Famine was still some 20 years off, there had already been considerable suffering in Ireland due to poor harvests and deadly fever outbreaks, and there were regular public appeals to help the sick and poor. That very week there had been advertisements in the press placed by the Committee for the Relief of the Distressed Poor in South-west Ireland, informing readers that there would be church collections that Sunday on their behalf. The committee was also to intimate in their advertisement that money they had raised so far had enabled them to despatch the sailing sloop *Elizabeth* with 50 tons of meal for the poor of Clare and they had contracted to order another 50 tons. Near the advertisement was a news story that 146 had died of fever in the parish of Kilmore, Mayo, and that in Sligo there were 40,000 who had no means of subsistence; in some parts of the county the local committee could not afford to give more than 1 lb of meal a week to each individual.

The *Glasgow Chronicle* provided further details about what occurred after the men had been questioned by the sheriff. About 60 to 70 men from two Orange lodges had met in different pubs in the Gallowgate. After a while they had come out, assembled on the street and marched off, garnished with all their usual insignia and flags. 'On passing the statue of King William in Trongate they took off their hats and cheered. They cheered again at the head of King Street as the crowd gathered.'

They soon realised by the shouts and oaths now flying that the crowds weren't their kind and they hesitated, debating whether they should continue. Caution ruled, and they immediately headed for a pub in King Street where they took refuge.

While there was obviously a sceptical reaction to the Orangemen's claim that they were out marching on behalf of the needy, the *Glasgow Courier* reported that the Loyal Orange Lodge of Glasgow did, in fact, hand over a sizeable sum for precisely that cause. It totalled some £3 4s 11d. While it may seem a mere pittance, in today's terms that amount was the equivalent of £171.

As a result of these first two marches, the Glasgow Council decided enough was enough – they would only lead to further trouble. In July 1823 they announced that no further parades would be permitted. Perhaps it was just as well that they were banned in Glasgow after what was to happen at Girvan just thee years later. Some of the earliest of Scotland's Orange lodges had been in the south-west of the country and had resulted in numerous flare-ups between Orangemen, Catholic Irish immigrants and seasonal harvest workers, regular visitors for years, especially in that area. One of the worst of these had taken place during the Orange parade held in Girvan in 1831. The town's Orange Lodge officials had met with police prior to the march and there seemed to be no problems over the proposed route they should take for their walk as it was one which would avoid them parading through the centre of the town.

The police turned out in force along the agreed route and off the marchers went, 400 of them, for their celebratory walk. About half of the marchers, however, had come along obviously expecting much more than music, being armed with swords, pikes and bayonets, and as the local reporter was to record, 'quite a number of them were with pistols'. As they approached the bridge over the Water of Girvan, there was a line of policemen blocking the way ahead and reminding the marchers as they approached that the agreed route was not the one that went straight ahead and through the centre of the town. The Orangemen appeared to accept that at first before some discord erupted among them, the men at the rear beginning to push forward and urging that the march continue through the police lines. Their stewards bawled for them to behave – the march would follow the designated route. This appeared to make the dissidents even more determined to go straight ahead and head for the town. Anticipating this, groups of Irish Catholics had been waiting and when they saw the Orangemen attempting to advance, began throwing stones at them. That started it. One of the Orangemen fired his pistol in the direction of the police who had been blocking the way and a young constable named Alexander Ross fell, mortally wounded. The shot seemed to inspire the others who were toting guns and there were more shots aimed at the police. Not to be outdone, those with the pikes and swords then made a mass attack on the remaining police and anyone else who happened to be standing around, four people being critically wounded. It was mayhem from then on, bystanders and police running across fields in panic and jumping into the river in order to escape the maddened Orangemen who, it seemed, were out for the kill, even stoning one of the wounded policemen as he struggled through the fast-flowing river in a desperate bid to reach some kind of safety. It was like a mini-Battle of the Boyne as the cry went up from one of the Orangemen, 'The town is our own', at which they then charged up Montgomerie Street to the Green, or Dounepark, attacking anyone and everyone in sight.

Meanwhile, back in Glasgow, the resentment of the city's first two Orange Walks had grown and the city fathers were determined there would be no repeat of such behaviour. So they took the most effective course of action for that purpose and had all Orange Walks banned. Fifty years would pass before the council relented and gave permission for the Orangemen to march again. The 50-year ban constrained membership of the movement, which went into something of a decline, particularly after there was a House of Lords inquiry into Orangeism throughout the UK. Even the King (William IV) had become concerned about certain sinister aspects of its activities, mainly its growth among members of the army, a worrying number of warrants having been granted for the establishment of military lodges. Might it be that if the movement grew even bigger in the military they would have allegiances other than that to the king? There was even the suggestion of a plot involving the Orange Order in regard to the future of the monarchy and the King was to express his fears about the Duke of Cumberland, the Orange Lodge Grand Master in England, who, it was said, might be used by the plotters in furtherance of such seditious activities. The investigation carried out for the House of Lords, known as the Inquiry into the Origin, Nature, Extent and Tendency of Orange Institutions in Great Britain, exonerated the movement of any nefarious endeavours. But Parliament was not satisfied and some years later there was another Select Committee inquiry in which MPs were to speak of their alarm that the Orange Lodge movement in the military had now developed to the extent that it controlled the yeomanry (Cavalry Territorials) and was rife in the army. When the second parliamentary committee eventually made their report, they were to express not only their disapproval of the movement but recommend that the institution be suppressed. Following this there was considerable reorganisation of Orangeism, a government Anti-Processions Act even banning their demonstrations in the ensuing years.

Although they had already been forbidden from their July Walks through the streets of Glasgow, there was no restriction on Orangemen having orderly meetings, although it began to appear that the two didn't exactly go hand in hand. Six years after they had been banned from marching, there was another city riot, this time even worse than the one which brought about the parade prohibition. Catholics at the time had various restrictions placed on them, one of the most contentious being the fact that they were still banned from sitting as Members of Parliament unless they took an oath repudiating certain fundamental Catholic beliefs. In 1829 these unjust constraints were removed with the passing of the Catholic Emancipation Act, which also dispensed with the other remnants of legal discrimination against Catholics surviving from the penal laws. Civil rights for Catholics! Catholic Members of Parliament! The very prospect of that was to spark off a series of riots and protests in various parts of Scotland, a Catholic chapel in Inverness being attacked, a Presbyterian minister who spoke in favour of the Act was tossed out of his church and Glasgow University students petitioned Parliament against the concessions. As for the Orangemen of Glasgow, when they met that 12 July, it was just too much. There had been a considerable number of them on the streets fairly early on that day. Groups of them had been down at the statue of King Billy bringing with them spare bunting and ribbons with which they decorated their most beloved of kings. The newspapers hadn't liked that, one of them commenting:

> Some foolish people have dressed the statue as usual. When shall poor Ireland be relieved from party animosity? We perceive no tendency in the opposite party [the Catholics] to excite riot and we trust they

> have more sense than to notice this foolery each good
> and wise man must view with contempt.

The passing of the Act was to provoke the first open display of the Orangemen in the city since 1822 and it turned into yet another riot. It was 12 July 1829, and the Orangemen, still forbidden to march, were meeting in their favourite pub of the day, located in the Gallowgate, just by the Spoutmouth. They had brought their colourful sashes and collarettes with them and draped them around the windows of the pub, one of their banners proclaiming those victorious days of yore decorating the doorway, with everyone inside seemingly in a relaxed and jubilant mood, except when the subject of MPs being RCs came up.

Maybe it was their singing, maybe it was the sight of all those sashes and banners but, whatever, the word had got around about the Orangemen and a huge crowd descended on the pub. They were not there to join in the celebrations. The taunts and jeers from outside in the streets became too much for the 12 July celebrants and they poured out to confront their oldest enemies. The battles went on up and down the Gallowgate and into Hunter Street, then McFarlane Street, off the main thoroughfare. Again it was too much for the shopkeepers, who quickly locked up and fled the scene. The police station being nearby, they were able to rush men quickly to the scene, a Captain Graham, it being reported, together with some 100 constables, immediately breaking up the brawling.

They also toured all the local pubs, ordering the Orangemen to bring their celebrations to an end and leave the area before dispersing what crowds were still milling around the area. For the next few hours the police patrolled all the nearby streets, ensuring there would be no further outbreaks of violence.

The following morning in the Central Police Court, two

Irishmen, Bernard Carey and James Sweeney, said to be the principal ringleaders of the affray, pleaded guilty and were fined £3 3s (the equivalent of around £120) with the option of 60 days' imprisonment.

Although the second parliamentary inquiry threw the Order into considerable confusion for a long time, membership remained solid and was even to see a notable growth over the years, getting various branches together in the face of Irish support for the Irish Republican Brotherhood, or Fenian Brotherhood, forerunners of today's IRA, which had been established in Scotland and in 1867 had threatened to have their own parade in Glasgow, a move that was to be blocked by the Order's leadership, who warned of the consequences if such a march were to take place.

New branches of the Orange Institution continued to be formed in Glasgow in the years up to 1871. Now, almost 50 years after they had been barred from holding their parades, they felt strong enough to buck the authorities and conduct a small demonstration, but not a Walk as such. They held this small gathering, with a minor Walk of sorts, in a field at Busby, just outside the city. Despite the fact it was only a minor affair, the authorities were so concerned about what might happen that they called out the army to stand by, just in case. They were not required. Having had one peaceful display gave the Orangemen sufficient confidence to go ahead and plan their first one back in Glasgow, scheduling it for the following year, on the 50th anniversary of their original ban.

The 1872 procession was the full works, with banners flying, bands playing, sashes displayed and marching men singing the lustiest versions of the old Orange tunes, favourites at the time such as 'The Boyne Water' and 'The Protestant Boys', a verse of which went:

Oh, My Father Was ...

The Protestant Boys are loyal and true,
Though fashions are changed and the loyal are few,
The Protestant Boys are true to the last,
Though cowards belied them when danger has passed,
Aye, still we stand,
A loyal band ...

They had gathered in the morning in the very heart of the city, on historic Glasgow Green, the biggest-ever Orange gathering to date. Accompanied by their 80 bands, they had marched first of all right round the Green, the sounds of their stirring marches and the thump, thump, thump of their giant drums heard most audibly throughout the neighbouring suburb, the predominantly Catholic Calton. They heard it in the Gorbals too, as they came marching over the river and right through the heart of that other predominantly Irish-Catholic suburb as they headed for Cathcart Road to march all the way to Busby for their congregation point at a farm on the Eaglesham Road. Hundreds of bandsmen entertained the gathering for the rest of the day, repeated renditions of 'The Boyne Water' and 'The Protestant Boys' creating great enthusiasm; there were guest speakers and stirring speeches received with acclamation and, later, at the meeting in Busby, speakers attacked Gladstone for his 'popish proclivities'.

The boys were back in town.

– CHAPTER 9 –

They're an Alien Race

Religion has many virtues. It bestows on its adherents numerous blessings, but there are those with so much religion, it can make them hate much more than make them love. It was people such as this, who had made religion their profession, that were among those who were the most vociferous about the immigrant invasion of the Irish. Fearing the worst, the men of the cloth could only see the worst. They disliked them, they said, because they were of an inferior race. Presumably that was their interpretation of a race that was poorer than their own; a race that for generations had suffered all the indignities of poverty; a race whose misgoverned country couldn't even afford to feed its own children, which was why they had fled and were here. But more essentially, the Church ministers disapproved of them because of their religion. They were the children of the Church of Rome whose spiritual leader was the man they would preach was the anti-Christ. For that they were said to be the greatest menace to the Scottish race. However, in any rush to judge those Scottish clerics who were so outspoken about the multitude of Catholics that had descended on them, some consideration must be given to what reaction there may have been had the situation been in reverse. How would the bishops, monsignors and priests have responded had they, in turn, been so suddenly threatened with a horde of Protestants among them? Would they likewise have been so outspoken, or would they have chosen more subtle avenues to suppress or stem the invading multitude of those who were not only members of another Church but of a Church which was so against theirs? It requires only a modicum of imagination to picture that latter scenario at its worst.

One of the most disappointing, if not disturbing, aspects of religion is the intolerance which adherents display not only towards other religions, but to those of their own religion who do not worship their God in the same precise fashion as themselves. And when shipload after shipload of Christian immigrants descended on the city to make it their home, the storm warning cones were raised; with every arrival of them at the Broomielaw, they raised them even higher. For the majority of these Christian immigrants happened to be Roman Catholics, and they were coming to a very Protestant community.

It wasn't just in Glasgow that there were loud mutterings about all these Roman Catholics who it seemed were so suddenly arriving in their midst. Similar rumblings went on throughout the country, parish and town halls being regularly filled by local citizens with one very important and contentious subject to be discussed. 'Papal Aggression'. Motion after motion was moved, seconded, and unanimously passed that something had to be done on the subject. One Glasgow meeting was to platform 19 speakers vociferously condemning the state of affairs in the city. Petitions were initiated and circulated, and they flocked to sign them in their tens of thousands. The inspiration of a society which formed in Glasgow and had branches throughout the country was to oppose what it termed 'the aggression of popery', thousands flocking to their lectures on such provocative themes as 'The Persecuting Spirit of Popery' and 'Promoting the Religious Principles of the Reformation'. Even the new Lord Rector of Glasgow University, Sir Archibald Allison, the renowned historian, chose the controversial subject of the day to be the theme in his important inaugural address. He titled it 'The Intolerance of the Catholic Church through the Ages'.

Despite all the mutterings and rumblings, the motions, petitions and speeches, the immigrants still flooded in, nothing effectively having been done to stem the flow. None were to be more concerned or fly those storm warning cones higher than one of the most august groups of men in the country, men of great respect, men who were the very keepers of the nation's morals, the most professed group of Christians of their day. They called urgent meetings with one another over the subject. Every arrival on the quaysides of Broomielaw increased their fears and intensified their anxieties. Neighbour could confide to neighbour about their misgivings, their disquiet and dread, and committees convened to plan for a future they saw filled with apprehension and alarm.

After a year of such intensifying tension, it was now the general feeling among these men, each of whom was the most affirmed and dedicated of Christians, that something really had to be done. It had gone on long enough. They were now under the utmost of threats because of these new people from over the water who were now so proliferously among them. Their very way of life was threatened, their country could be inexorably changed. Their committeemen had gone into the subject in considerable detail and they were now armed with more facts and figures, opinions and attitudes, than ever before. All of them came to the same conclusion – something had to be done.

These concerned and worried men, who came from every part of Scotland, were the reverend ministers of the Church of Scotland. The time and place for them to make decisions and do something, as they felt they must, was at the General Assembly, the Church's annual general meeting. The new Christian arrivals flooding into Glasgow were causing much anxiety because the majority of them were not the same Christians as themselves – they were Roman Catholics. They felt they were being swamped by them, and were saying vehemently that something had to be done about them. Unless action were taken, they would be overwhelmed by the incomers. It would lead to catastrophe. Well, so they genuinely thought.

The year was 1922. There had been four years of peace since the awful First World War and the nation whose vast empire reached every corner of the globe was well on the road to recovery. Never mind that so many of those who had endured the hell of the trenches wondered if the bleak slums to which they had returned and were now confined were what they had been fighting for. Everything was relative, the politicians were telling them, and millions elsewhere in the world were living in much worse conditions, including the land from where those new immigrants had come.

With the terrible war in the past and the unknown horrors of the Depression still to come, 1922 was one of the better years. There was a mood of optimism and a feeling that if the good times weren't exactly rolling, they might be next year. There was plenty of work around and the professions and small business class were doing well. The mark of how well you had done in life was if you could claim to be a homeowner, a most rare and privileged class. Hundreds who had made it into that league were filling the newspaper classified columns with advertisements for that other status symbol of the era – domestic staff. Even those living in such places as the sandstone tenements around Byres Road, in the West End, deemed it a necessity to have their own servants of one kind or another. The current coffee table talk among the aspiring upwardly mobiles of the day was how difficult it was becoming to get suitable staff. It wasn't merely idle chat, designed to broadcast the fact that you were in a position to hire staff – it really was becoming difficult to find people to wait on your household table, so difficult in fact that the Ministry of Labour (in traditional government fashion) set up a committee of inquiry to look into the situation. There was a new attitude, the committee was told, among workers towards those who were domestic servants. They were becoming something of a music hall joke, and it was influencing young women away from such jobs. Mothers wanted something better than domestic service for their daughters. One witness was to tell the committee that young women who worked in shops or offices regarded themselves as a much higher class of people than servants. 'They look upon the uniform as a mark of servitude,' said the witness, adding that many were being lured away to jobs in hotels, where they could get tips as well as a wage.

Nevertheless, the middle class continued to fill the vacancies columns with adverts for household staff. Some wanted table maids or cleaners, others wanted nurses for elderly parents or nannies for the children, and in an age before takeaway fast food and coffee to go, most seemed to want the one member of household staff who could do all that, their very own cook. Not someone renowned for culinary skills, including those of the Provençale or Piedmontese. While their employers might enjoy thinking they were upper class, they were still really 'up a close' in their ways and most adverts for cooks would have the proviso that the essential prerequisite was for someone whose forte was 'just plain cooking'. The offered wage was always included in the advertisements, the current rate for cooks around £30, or even as much as £40, per annum 'for the right person'! That's right, £30 to £40 . . . per annum!

However, everything was indeed relative. To rent a sumptuous and spacious villa in, say, Pollokshields, cost only £5 a week and the latest model Rover saloon, capable of seating four or five and one of the prestige automobiles of the day, had just gone on sale. It cost only £550.

Football was going through a bad patch, with falling attendances worrying the administrators. Only 35,000 had turned out to see Rangers beat Queen's Park 4–0 in the Glasgow Charity Cup final at Ibrox Park, which then had a capacity of over 100,000. The total taking for the match, it might be noted, came to £2,056, which averages out at less than sixpence (2½p) per head at the turnstiles, yet it was the high admission charges which were causing the attendance slump. Shortly afterwards, Celtic and Hibernian FC did much better with their crowd for the final of the Scottish Cup, 75,000 seeing the Celts beat the Edinburgh side 1–0 to win the trophy for the 12th time, a record for the period unsurpassed by any other club and only equalled by Queen's Park.

None of that was of any concern to the hundreds of sombre-suited men meeting in Edinburgh for that year's Church of Scotland General Assembly. They were worried. The rioting in Belfast between the two communities was the worst it had been for years. There were regular gun battles with considerable deaths; matters had become so bad that hundreds of Catholic refugees from the latest Troubles were now pouring into Glasgow. Many of them were billeted at St Mary's Parochial Hall in the East End of the city, their presence seen by the churchmen as being not only yet another boost to the Catholic population but also a likely cause for similar riots breaking out in Glasgow itself.

All the signs were there, they were saying. Bigotry had never been so rife, nor the hysteria about it. One story that caused considerable talk around the time was when an investigation was called for over what was seen to be a blatant case of employment discrimination. It had arisen when two girls had applied for a job with a shirt manufacturer in the East End of the city. They had been asked that old Glasgow question, 'What school did you go to?' The girl who had attended a Catholic school didn't get the job! It seemed to be a classic case of the bigotry that existed in the city but, as it transpired, all was not as it first appeared. Following the story in the newspapers there were demands for an inquiry and reporters descended on the factory. There they were to discover that the biggest percentage of the workforce at the shirt manufacturers were, in fact, Catholic. The forewoman who had interviewed the girls was a Catholic herself. The girl who hadn't got the job had simply not been the best candidate.

Another source of anxiety which had considerably increased over the years, particularly since the end of the First World War, was the huge increase in intermarriage between Catholics and members of the Protestant faith. It was bad enough that these Catholic immigrants were here in the numbers that they were, but to have them intermarrying with increasing numbers of their flock was just too much, the specific objection being the strict rules of the Catholic faith which insisted that the offspring of such mixed marriages be raised in their faith, thus creating a 'second front' as it were, in the growth of Catholicism. It was also yet another sign of the breakdown in occupational, as well as sectarian, barriers to marriage. Because at the time those Irish Catholics were concentrated disproportionately in labouring and unskilled occupations, marriage with Protestants implied a marriage of people of different social standing. Factors such as these were giving the holy shepherds as much concern as the prospect of even more Irish people flooding over.

The hysterics about the girl who hadn't got the job at the shirt factory quickly died down, but the fear and foreboding that had been fermenting among Protestant ministers did not. The matter was eventually raised at the General Assembly in 1922, when it was decided that a full report be prepared on the subject and presented to the Assembly the following year, 1923. This remit from the General Assembly was interpreted as an instruction to consider and report on the problem of the Irish Roman Catholic population in Scotland. This had become of such concern to the Church that they had to make the perceived threat known to both Church and country.

It was with considerable trepidation, therefore, that they listened to Edinburgh minister, the Reverend William Mair, present the long-awaited and somewhat devastating report at the General Assembly in 1923. The disturbing conclusions it drew were made plain and clear from the title of the long study which had resulted: 'The Menace of the Irish Race to our Scottish Nationality'.

In his preamble before addressing the Assembly with the report's findings, the Reverend Mair said it had been the work of the Reverend Duncan Cameron of Kilsyth, and he had devoted considerable energy and devotion to its preparation. As a result of all their inquiries, said Rev. Mair, they had found that all the concern which had been aired the previous year, the facts and figures they hadn't been able to prove at the time, had been 'well grounded'. He stated that they had enough facts to justify asking the government to institute an inquiry into the matter (to loud applause).

The Rev. Mair then went on to deliver what was to be one of the most sensational reports of its kind ever heard by the General Assembly, a report which apparently they all wanted to hear, whether it be for its truths, its half-truths, its untruths, sweeping generalisation, overtones, undertones, innuendoes, insinuations and inferences. They were all included and it was a bombshell all the way. What follows is a summation of what the enraptured gathering of the reverends heard that day in Edinburgh:

> The overtures on which the General Assembly took action show that the alarm and anxiety which prompted them have been occasioned by the incursion into Scotland of a large Irish Roman Catholic population within recent years. The question of the Scottish Roman Catholic population has not arisen, nor is there any reason why it should arise. They have a right to call Scotland their country, in common with their fellow countrymen of the Protestant faith. Nor is there any complaint of the presence of an Orange population in Scotland. They are of the same race as ourselves and of the same faith and are readily

assimilated to the Scottish population. The Committee, therefore, interpret the remit from the General Assembly as being an instruction to consider and to report on the problem of the Irish Roman Catholic population in Scotland. They cannot be assimilated and absorbed into the Scottish race. They remain a people by themselves, segregated by reason of their race, their customs, their traditions and above all by their loyalty to their Church, and are gradually and inevitably dividing Scotland, racially, socially and ecclesiastically.

It is necessary to dispose of the possible objections that a considerable proportion of the Roman Catholic population in the industrial area of Western Scotland is of purely Scottish lineage. Statistics show that the only two counties in which a purely Scottish Roman Catholic population of any size exists are Inverness-shire and Dumfriesshire. In the first there were 1,800 Catholic children out of a total enrolment of 12,800, in the latter a mere 534 out of 12,712. In places like Banffshire and Aberdeenshire they were so few as to be almost negligible. The surplus of both populations of Scottish Roman Catholics in these two areas was not large and did not supply many recruits for the industrial areas of the country. The Highland Roman Catholics tended to cling to their home and native soil.

The problem, then, is almost exclusively an Irish problem and although they recognised that there were a number of Polish Catholics in coal-mining districts, the question did arise from the abnormal growth of the Irish race in Scotland.

In no other European country did the Reformation

have a more complete triumph than in Scotland. Sooner or later practically the whole body of the Scottish people adopted the principles of the Reformed Faith. Owing to the difficulty of providing preachers, certain isolated communities in remote parts of Inverness-shire adhered to the old faith, and the influence of powerful Roman Catholic families in Dumfriesshire succeeded in keeping sections of the peasantry within the fold of the Church of Rome.

It is true that the Reformed faith did not adopt the Presbyterian form of Church government to the exclusion of every other form. Among many of the nobility and the landed gentry, the Episcopal Church had devoted adherents, and in certain counties, notably Aberdeenshire and Forfarshire, a certain number of the humbler classes adhered to the Church of their territorial superiors. But generally speaking, the result of the Reformation was that the Roman Catholic Church was practically extinguished in Scotland, which thereby became homogeneous in faith and ideals.

It was not until large numbers of Irish Roman Catholics came over from Ireland that the Roman Catholic Church began to grow, to feel her power, and to assert her influence and this was the beginning of the destruction of the unity and homogeneity of the Scottish people. With the industrial development of Scotland in the nineteenth century, a demand for cheap labour arose. Industrial firms and great contractors advertised for labour in the Irish press and crowds of Irishmen and their families emigrated to Scotland to engage in building railways, to work in coal mines, in the great shipyards on the Clyde, and in the jute mills of Dundee and to labour in the construction of public works, such as the Loch Katrine water scheme. When they had settled down, they invited relations and friends to come across to Scotland, promising to find work and a home for them. All were welcomed by the employers of labour. The Irishman worked well, accepted almost any kind of habitation and was content with small wages. From the Clyde to the Tay, they spread themselves across the great plain of Scotland where the mineral wealth of Scotland lay, as did her great cities, and it was here they were to find their livelihood and make their homes. And, as they did so, the great exodus of the Scottish race was going on.

These were the people who wished for better conditions of life, higher wages and wider prospects. And because of the new economic pressure of the Irish race who had come to settle here, young Scots men and women – the flower of the nation – left their native land and sought their fortunes in America and the dominions. It was certainly to the advantage of the countries to which they went that the best of the Scottish nation migrated there. At the same time it was a grievous loss to the land of their fathers. Their places were instead taken by a people of a different race and a different faith, and Scotland was divided into two camps – Scottish and Irish.

There was no parallel to such movements in modern or in ancient times. In the great Glasgow conurbation there were now at least 450,000 Irish, almost every fourth person. In many areas it was every third person. The figures spoke for themselves. In 1881 there were some 327,000 of an Irish population in Scotland. In the year the report was being compiled, 1921, there were over 600,000. In one 20-year period the Irish population had increased by 32.5 per cent but the increase in the Scottish population had only been 18.5 per cent. In the 20 years before the compilation of the report, the Irish population had increased by 39 per cent, but the Scottish population had only gone up by 6 per cent. Thousands fewer Scottish children were now on the education rolls, but there were more Irish children.

The report revealed that the common allegation that the RC Irish produced more offspring than the native Catholic was not the case. 'It was just not true,' said the Rev. Mair. In fact, the previous year, in one popular mining parish where the Irish constituted about a fifth of the entire population, the Scottish birth rate had been higher than the Irish birth rate. When they had analysed the birth rates of what was termed the 'purely Scottish' city of Aberdeen in comparison to Dundee, where nearly a quarter of the population were Irish, it was the 'purely Scottish city' which had the highest birth rate.

In general, the fertility of both the Scottish and Irish working classes was much the same. The tendency to restrict the size of the family had not so far affected one any more than it had the other. Statistics did show, however, that the increase in the Irish population, and the relatively small increase in the Scottish population, had been due mainly to two causes – immigration of Irish into Scotland and emigration of Scots from Scotland. In one year alone, almost a quarter of a million Irish had come over and were living in Scotland. Other years had also produced six-figure numbers. In the same years there had been huge numbers of Scots leaving to settle abroad, mainly in Australia, Canada and America. In one three-month period an astonishing 34,000 had set sail for North America alone, boosting the year's figure of Scots emigrants to nearly 100,000.

A notable finding in their statistics research had been the discovery of the tendency for Scots to be up and off whenever the Irish population reached a certain proportion in their neighbourhood, whether that be village, small town or the district of one of the big cities. Because of this, many areas of the large cities, as well as certain villages and some small towns, were becoming exclusively Irish. Typical of this had been the Croy district of the parish of Cumbernauld, where the Scottish mining population had refused to stay after the influx of Irish. There was a disinclination of Scots to live and work alongside the Irish, just as there was a tendency for Irish foremen to employ Irishmen.

'This social phenomenon has a very sinister meaning for the future of our race,' intoned the report, which went on to warn that the time was rapidly approaching when whole communities would be predominantly Irish and that the great plain of Scotland, stretching from Glasgow to Dundee and Edinburgh, would soon be dominated by the Irish race.

There had been a suggestion that with the recent creation of the Irish Free State there might be a return to Ireland of at least some of the many thousands who had left to settle in Scotland. But the Assembly's report was to discount that with the view that Ireland could not provide for the maintenance of the natural increase in population, as it was a pastoral and agricultural country with few industries offering employment on a large scale.

One prominent Roman Catholic layman had said that the lure of 'reconditioning Scotland' – that is making it a Catholic country once more – had appealed strongly to their Church. If Scotland could be won for them, it could be a mighty lever for the control of the greatest prize of all, England. Glasgow had already become the largest Roman Catholic community in the country. If that could happen, some Catholics were prophesying, then even greater triumphs might be achieved. Within the next 40 years, that is by the mid-1960s, the Irish population in the industrial area of Scotland could rise to around 1,500,000 and the Scots would have lost control of the populous and wealth-producing parts of their country. 'And what will follow must be plain to any thinking mind – the rapid permeation of the whole of Scotland by an alien people.'

The report then reviewed some of the changes that had already taken place because of the big Irish presence in the country:

> Their gift of speech, their aptitude for public life, their restless ambition to rule, have given them a prominent place in political, county, municipal and parochial elections. They have also asserted themselves in cooperative and benefit societies. They have had an unfortunate influence in modifying the Scottish habit of thrift and independence. An Irishman never hesitates to seek relief from charity organisations and local authorities and Scotsmen do not see why they should not get help when Irishmen receive it.

Then there were the changes being brought about in Scottish customs because of the new immigrants. The strict observance of the Sabbath was already being eroded. It was now even becoming a day for 'political meetings and for concerts'. There were signs too of Roman Catholic propagandists at work, committed on behalf of their Church to converting the Scottish nation.

They already had their own schools (granted under the 1918 Education Act) and, in the minds of all those who cared about the Church of Scotland, that had been one of the most bitter blows, and not only in a spiritual sense. The advent of the Catholic school, said the report, had placed an 'unprecedented and intolerable' financial burden on the country. It had brought about a reduction in the salaries of teachers, and only absolutely necessary repairs could be done at schools because of the increase in the education expenditure. The 1918 Education Act had proved a great boon to the Roman Catholics and had made it, in proportion to its numbers, the most richly endowed Church in Scotland. Every year more than £500,000 was paid in salaries to Roman Catholic teachers in Glasgow. The expenditure in rates, taxes, fuel, light, cleaning, books and stationery came to more than £100,000, said the report, and it was incumbent on the Scottish people to consider before it was too late the grave situation in their native land and to devise means which, while they did no injustice to the Irish people, would:

> . . . preserve Scotland for the Scottish race and secure for future generations the traditions and ideals and faith of a great people, unspoiled and inviolate. Such an endowment of denominational schools in one city alone for the children of an alien race was surely unprecedented. The financial burden on the country is well-nigh intolerable and economy has to be practised, as some think, to the detriment of education.

Contemplating this, the report asked: 'What is to be the future of our land and of the Scottish people?' The investigators' view was that the incursion of the Irish race had been a misfortune both for them and for Scotland. It was a small country and small countries divided by creed and race never prove to be happy or harmonious countries:

> Ireland affords a striking illustration of the truth of this. Its racial and sectarian antipathies have embittered the soul of two peoples and impeded the high enterprises of civilisation. The Dutch and the Belgians, under diplomatic pressure entered into union in 1815, the one a Roman Catholic, the other a Protestant country. They failed to harmonise and in 15 years the union was dissolved. Fusion of the Scottish and Irish races in Scotland, just as it was in Ireland, will remain an impossibility. The Irish are the most obedient children of the Church of Rome; the Scots stubbornly adhere to the principles of the Reformed Faith. The Irish have separate schools for their children; they have their own clubs for recreation and for social intercourse; they tend to segregate in communities and even to monopolise certain departments of labour to the exclusion of the Scots.
>
> Already there is a bitter feeling among the Scottish working classes against the Irish intruders. As the latter increases, and the Scottish people realise the seriousness of the menace to their own racial supremacy in their native land, this bitterness will develop into a race antagonism which will have disastrous consequences for Scotland.

The report dissolved into an even gloomier mood, as it further contemplated the future. The Scottish race would be lost to civilisation through this invasion from over the water, and that loss would be 'immeasurable'. Scots would not continue to be Scots when they went to other lands, for, as they had already shown, when they migrated they became good citizens of those countries. While they might remember in song and legend the land of their forefathers, the generations who succeeded them would not know Scotland.

In its conclusions, the report was to ask if the Irish race or the Church of Rome would welcome the incursion of half a million Scotsmen into the counties around Dublin:

> Would the English people receive with open arms five million Poles into the industrial areas of Yorkshire, Staffordshire and Lancashire? God placed the people of this world in families and history, which is the narrative of His providence, tells us that when kingdoms are divided against themselves they cannot stand . . . It is incumbent on the Scottish people to consider, before it is too late, the grave situation in their native land and to devise means which, while they do no injustice to the Irish people whom they allowed to come into their country, shall preserve Scotland for the Scottish race and secure for future generations the traditions, ideals, and faith of a great people unspoiled and inviolate.

Rev. Mair resumed his seat to the thunderous applause of the nation's ministers, obviously shocked – and impressed – at the revelations in the vital report.

The Rev. Duncan Cameron of Kilsyth seconded the motion, agreeing that the Scots' nationality and civilisation was under threat. The Irish were moving in and Scots were moving out. He presented figures showing that in one year alone some 21,000 Scots had emigrated to countries of the New World from the Clyde. In that same period only 341 Irish residents in Scotland had likewise emigrated, and the previous year over 22,000 Scots had sailed off, but only 219 had left from the Scots-Irish communities.

Then there were those who were 'clocking on the dole'. There was no holding back the Rev. Cameron, who went on to claim that 60 to 70 per cent of such dole clockers were Irish, yet the population of Irish in Scotland was only 25 to 30 per cent. Furthermore, he thundered, charity organisations had been reporting that 70 per cent of those asking for relief were Irish.

Scottishness itself was being imperilled, and all because of the Irish. This great rally of the reverends was just getting warmed up. One of the great stalwarts of the Church of Scotland spoke next and while to the modern reader what he has to say might be all too predictable, the reverends sat up and listened intently. For the Rev. Dr John White of Shettleston, in the east side of Glasgow, was intently listened to when he spoke about the subject which was of the greatest concern to him, the Irish Catholics in Scotland, and the huge numbers of them who were here. A man who was some years later to be Moderator of the Church of Scotland, the Rev. White didn't mince his words when it came to that topic. He was a constant, virulent and tireless campaigner against Irish immigration to Scotland. He organised petitions around the countryside and got together deputations to call on senior government ministers urging them to do something about those hordes, as he put it, who were descending on Scotland.

The Scots were a superior race, he insisted, and the waves of people coming across the Irish Sea were supplanting them. Not only that, the Scots were being supplanted by people of an inferior race, corrupted by the inflow of them. They were a menace, he repeatedly uttered, and combating them had to be the main priority of the Church of Scotland.

The great Christian was unstoppable. His views beggared belief, yet they listened to him for he was the voice of many at the time. The question, he said, was not always that of the differences between Roman Catholics and Protestants. It was a question of how to safeguard the Scottish nationality:

> Our civilisation differs from that of these immigrants. The spirit of our institutions is widely different. The problem is how to regulate the incoming of these new forces from Ireland, Italy and Jewry so as to be a strength and not a menace. How to fuse these heterogeneous elements into one essential whole so that they should be Scottish and not foreign. The need is to have regulations of immigration as every other nation did.

And when he sat down, he was given the warmest of applause for his sentiments.

The Rev. William George Black, another Glasgow cleric and one of the final speakers, was to make some trenchant observations on the effects of migration into Glasgow. Black, who was chairman of the Glasgow Good Government League, said he knew that the west of Scotland was so 'permeated' by the increasing numbers of foreign nationalists that they could not say the Glasgow vote or the Scottish vote in the district really represented the opinion of the Scottish people.

'Glasgow has ceased to be a Scottish city. It is very largely an Irish city at the present time,' he said to rumblings of approbation. Not only had they been landed with all these Irish people, but it seemed to him that they had not got the best of them. However, there was one positive observation he had to make about them and that was 'the faithfulness of these people to the Roman Catholic Church . . . and that fact alone has to be a lesson to us'. Which brought an even louder round of 'hear, hear'. Mr Black concluded by telling the Assembly the matter was a serious problem and they were acting wisely in asking the government to make an inquiry into it.

In its summation of that day's somewhat sensational proceedings at the General Assembly, the Catholic newspaper, the *Glasgow Observer*, was to comment: 'The sum and substance of the report is that Catholics are overrunning Scotland at an enormous pace and that unless something can be done to stem the torrent they will very shortly possess the land.' Underlying the report were suggestions that Catholics be disenfranchised, excluded from public life, their schools cut out of the system and deprived of a share of the education rates. In short, the report was calling for the repeal of the Catholic Emancipation Act of 1829, said the *Observer*.

Never had the subject been so widely aired, so hotly discussed, so fiercely delivered. The Assembly had listened to the direst of warnings and a wide variety of fearful predictions that centred on fear of the destruction of the unity of the Scottish people. The incursion of the Irish race had been a misfortune both for them and for Scotland, said the minister. This social phenomenon had a very sinister meaning for the future of our race. Whole communities would be predominantly Irish and the great plain of Scotland would soon be dominated by them. There was a bitter feeling among the Scottish working classes against the Irish intruders. It was incumbent on the Scottish people to consider, before it was too late, the grave situation in their native land. Glasgow had ceased to be a Scottish city, and so on, and on, and on.

The General Assembly as a body was obviously extremely concerned about the influx of Irish Catholics, and did not hesitate to back up the lengthy report. The members had been impressed by the facts that were put before them and were to urge the government to appoint a commission to inquire into the situation, with a view to the 'preservation and protection of Scottish nationality and civilisation'.

Six years later, in a 'special investigation' on the same subject, the *Glasgow Herald* was to report in a series of articles on the situation 'which has often given rise to the cry that Scottish nationality is in danger of being submerged by the growing strength of the Irish community within our gates'. The *Herald* was to look at a variety of ways in which immigration from Ireland had affected Scotland, beginning with a review of the position as it stood at the time. By the early 1920s, it noted, the majority of the Irish community living in Glasgow and Scotland were second generation. In fact there were more English- and Welsh-born people living in Scotland, according to the census, than there were first-generation Irish. Nevertheless, the *Herald* found that there were still many widespread assumptions about the Irish community in Glasgow. The following were some of the more common:

> Who has not heard of the nepotism of the Irish foreman who keeps up the flow coming over the channel by reserving jobs for his kind from Connaught?
>
> Who has not been given to understand the lure of our dole to the idle, hard-up Free Stater who naively imagines he only has to find the fare to qualify for benefits not available in his own country?
>
> Who has not learned that the Irish hierarchy, with

the design of capturing Scotland for the Church of Rome, are ever urging their flock to migrate to Scotland in order that the Irish Roman Catholic race may eventually enter into full possession of the land?

The number of times such assertions were repeated, said the *Herald*, gave the impression that Irish migration persisted to a substantial degree. The paper planned to look at the facts behind such commonly held beliefs. On current immigration it was to report that migration figures were, in fact, considerably down. There were fewer shipping companies involved in the trade; in fact, there was now only one company running services between Scotland and Ireland, whereas in the past there had been several competitors.

In relation to poor relief, or benefit, once more the truth was found to be in complete contradiction to the theories. The *Herald* was to discover that in Glasgow at the time there were no Irish currently receiving outdoor relief – aid without the offer of shelter. And of the 58,000 cases who had required sheltered relief, only 90 had been natives of Ireland.

On the question of dole abuse, their inquiries were not to reveal any great exploitation of the dole system by the Irish. Dole money at the time, it was pointed out, could not be obtained by merely arriving in Scotland. Claimants had first of all to make 20 contributions before being eligible to apply for standard benefit. They also had to demonstrate that they were normally engaged in insurable employment and would continue to seek work only in such insurable employment.

There had been considerable changes over the years in population statistics. It was shown that births in the Catholic community in the previous six years represented nearly 19 per cent of births in the whole country. The number of Roman

Catholic school pupils had risen by just over 13 per cent throughout Scotland: in a six-year period in Glasgow and central Scotland, the number of Roman Catholic schoolchildren had gone up by over 6,000, whereas the number of Protestant pupils went down by over 12,000. In the 40 years from 1881 to 1921, the Roman Catholic population of Scotland, of which 90 per cent were Irish or of Irish extraction, had increased from 327,000 to 601,000. It was estimated there were around 650,000 Roman Catholics in Scotland, 450,000 of them living in Glasgow; about a quarter of the city's population. Two marriages in 15 were Roman Catholic; 40 years previously it had been two in 20.

What did the future hold for Scots and the Irish immigrants? The answer to that was very subjective. One unnamed writer quoted by the *Herald*, for instance, had only the gloomiest of prophecies for the future of the country. Writing at the time of the great influx of migrants, some 60 years previously, he said:

> The Scot is a man eclipsed. The Scots are a dying people. They are being replaced in their own country by a people alien in race, temperament and religion at a speed which is without parallel in history, outside the era of the barbarian invasions.

When the census of 1871 was published, around the same time another commentator had written:

> The invasion of the Irish is likely to produce far more serious effects on the population of Scotland than even the invasion of warlike hordes of Saxons, Danes or Norsemen. Already in many towns the population of Irish was up to 15 per cent. The emigration of so many labourers of the lowest class with scarcely any

education can't but have a most prejudicial effect on
the population.

It is painful to contemplate what may be the
ultimate effect of this Irish migration on the morals
and habits of the people and on the future prospect of
the country.

Such sentiments accorded with those of Rev. John White and
had perhaps even been studied by him.

In conclusion, the *Herald* made the point that it had been
suggested the Irish settlers would continue to be strangers in a
strange land, for mixed marriages could only take place on the
promise in writing that the children of the marriage would be
brought up in the Catholic faith. The Church of Scotland was
concerned about that and had little hesitation in making their
views on the matter known. In a letter to the Secretary of State
for Scotland, the Church spoke about the dangers of
unregulated migration, reaffirming the stance of their report
into immigration. If it was a case of a superior race coming in
and supplanting the Scots, it might not be so bad, they said,
because that would be for the good of Scotland.

But we are convinced that the very opposite is the case,
that a law-abiding, thrifty and industrious race is being
supplanted by migrants whose presence tends to lower
the social conditions and to undermine the spirit of
independence which has so long been characteristic of
the Scottish people.

This was a letter that may well have been penned by the ranting
Rev. John White himself.

The *Herald*'s inquiry concluded with the recommendation

that a revision of the Roman Catholic segregation policy in school and marriage should be replaced by a policy of cooperation. The *Herald* considered that a panacea for the whole situation could simply be, in the words of one of their letter-writers, that 'Scotsmen and Irishmen who have chosen Scotland as the land of their adoption, should pool their separate inheritances and develop these in cooperation for the good of Scotland that is to be'.

No revision, of course, was ever made by the Catholic Church on its policies in relation to marriages and schooling. Nor was there any public declaration on the merits of the letter-writer's panacea for Scotland's future. Nevertheless, a fair observation might be that public declaration or not, the good people of Scotland, and the Irish who had made it their adopted land, got on with their lives in a cooperative fashion which was indeed very much for the good of Scotland.

– CHAPTER 10 –

Sorry About That!

It was to take many decades before the Church of Scotland, after much debate and many reversals of views, was at last to own up to its unchristian stance during the days of the great immigration from Ireland. Various Church dignitaries in their own way were to offer their apologies for what had been said at the time. In June 2001, at the Catholic grotto in Carfin, Lanarkshire, a memorial was unveiled to the victims of the famine, and at the ceremony the Very Rev. Dr Andrew McLellan, a former and most highly respected Moderator of the Church of Scotland, offered his personal apologies for those deeds of the past. 'My forefathers did not welcome those who came across the sea from Ireland. I regret that and I am ashamed of it,' he said. Then, the following year, came a much-awaited apology from the Church itself, albeit in the briefest of terms.

It is Wednesday, 29 May 2002, at the General Assembly Hall, the mid-nineteenth-century building that is the headquarters of the Church of Scotland, its high spires dourly dominating the Mound in Edinburgh. Once again the annual Assembly, the supreme authority of the Kirk, is in session. It is exactly 78 years and 348 days since that other Assembly met in this same building and listened to the sensational and shameful resolution on 'The Menace of the Irish Race to our Scottish Nationality'. Now the Assembly is in session once again. There are some 800 commissioners in attendance for this annual and much-anticipated gathering, commissioners being the Church's term for the delegates who are made up of both ministers and elders, and who come from parishes and presbyteries throughout Scotland. They are all keenly aware that they are participating in another historic chapter of their Church. For the Church's supreme court has decided that it is now time to say sorry. After more than three-quarters of a century, the moment has at last arrived for opening up the cupboards and bringing out the biggest and most frightful skeleton of them all – that dreadful, almost spine-chilling attack on their fellow Christians from over the water. However, thankfully now it's different days, different ways, and the Church of Scotland is about to declare it has completely changed the views it had way back in those dark and less enlightened years of the 1920s and '30s. They've contemplated it for a long time and the decision has now been made – apologies are due.

The regrets come in a report to the 2002 General Assembly entitled 'Sectarianism'. The remorse of the Church for its past sentiments about the Irish is undoubtedly sincere and profound. It is in no way, however, profuse or fulsome, merely simple and to the point. The report to the Assembly, in which the apology is contained, mainly concentrates on the specific subject of sectarianism and how it should be tackled by the Church. Their contrition for those deeds of old emerges as the report unfolds.

Rather than rushing to conclusions on the matter in hand, the report makes it clear at the outset that 'we have instead approached the topic in a spirit of humility and with an attitude of listening'. There's the acknowledgement that sectarianism in Scotland is seen and heard 'in the small asides which say little and reveal much'. It is also most publicly evident in behaviour associated with football matches, 'although is by no means confined to such events'.

The Church makes the confession that their record on the issue in times past 'is far from blameless'. At that point, it delicately recalls the Church's views on the matter back in the 1920s: 'In the years around the Great Depression of last century, the Church and Nation Committee campaigned intemperately against Irish immigration into Scotland.' The infamous quotation is recalled from the letter written by the committee to the Secretary of State for Scotland on the subject of Irish immigration in which the Church declared that the 'law-abiding, thrifty and industrious race [the Scots] is being supplanted by migrants [Catholic Irish] whose presence tends to lower the social conditions and to undermine the spirit of independence which has so long been characteristic of the Scottish people'. This, the Church now accepts, was racism akin to the 'rivers of blood' speech of Enoch Powell in the 1960s:

> The Irish immigrants are shown in the worst possible light. No attempt is made at understanding the social and economic conditions both in Ireland and Scotland that produced the immigration and shaped the

character and lifestyle of the immigrants. Of course, the great majority of the immigrants were Roman Catholic and the sectarian implications are clear.

At that precise point comes the apology:

> From a current perspective, it is a matter of regret that the Committee and the Church could have taken such a position.

And that was it . . . a matter of regret!

Whatever observations may be made about its brevity, the Church's recognition of its murky attitudes all those decades ago towards fellow Christians is now at least conceded. They also recognise in the report that the 'demon in our society has been acknowledged and brought into the open' and that they are determined and committed to giving their full support to combating all forms of sectarianism. Perhaps sentiments such as these are worth more than belated apologies.

CHAPTER 11

Navvies: A Breed Apart

I've toiled at the end of creation, stripped to the
trousers and shirt,
I've hashed like the very damnation and squandered
my money like dirt,
And jobs that are nameless I wrought in, and deeds
that are shameless I've done,
And fights without number I've fought in, and paid like
the deuce for my fun.

The great Patrick MacGill, Donegal man, poet,
author and for many years a Glasgow Irishman,
wrote these words as the introduction to his
famous poem about the navvies, 'Down on the
Dead End'. MacGill himself had been one of
those legendary Irish navvies and worked in
Glasgow and various parts of Scotland
undertaking the most physically demanding
labour. Irish navvies had been a legend for
centuries. They first crossed the Atlantic as far

back as the middle of the seventeenth century when they went to Barbados to build the plantations for the British. In the centuries to follow they were building in America, Africa and Australia. Like MacGill, thousands of them came to Glasgow where, in his words, they stripped to the trousers and shirt, they toiled and hashed and contributed no end to the fabric of their adopted city.

They were a breed apart, the children of the dead end. They were born to a future which didn't exist in a country ravaged by a disastrous famine, a human tragedy on an unimaginable scale. Their God, however, had blessed them with the greatest of gifts, the will, the desire and the strength to become regarded as the world's renowned labouring-class workers. They were the navvies.

New technology and the universal use of all sorts of mechanisation, together with high-powered tools, means that navvies are not so prominent in today's world as they were in comparatively recent times. They're not even called navvies any more, the political euphemists of the census authorities blessing them in 1950 with the title of 'construction workers'. But for years the Irish navvy was one of the most prevalent sights in Scotland, men Patrick MacGill made legendary with names such as Blasting Mick, Carroty Dan, Moleskin Joe, Two-Shift Mulholland and Ben the Moocher. They were the core of the workforce, without which the universal transformation of Scotland through the Industrial Revolution could never have been achieved. The harbours, the railways, the roads, the quarries, the dams and, of course, the canals were all the result of the men with the big hands, big hearts and big appetite for work. From the middle of the nineteenth century, during and after those terrible days of the famine, they flooded into Glasgow to become the backbone of the Glasgow Irish community in the city. They had come to fulfil the demands of the big contractors who couldn't get enough of them and their skills for their huge work projects. All that was required of them to get the vital work for which they had come was a curriculum vitae of merely one word – Irish. As a navvy, that meant there were none better.

It was because they were from the poorest class, those who had been relegated to the bottom of the Irish pile, that they had to sever their roots and look for work in new lands in order to survive. As always, it was the poorest of the community who suffered most in Ireland's latest and greatest catastrophe, the famine. And it was they who were to pay the stiffest penalties when it was over. Ireland was to undergo sweeping agricultural reform, resulting in drastic changes to the rural working population. The principal landowners of the country had been absentee noblemen – the old Irish gentry – and businessmen, those who thought of themselves as professional gentlemen – lawyers, accountants and the like. Unlike the poor, they had been able to escape the worst ravages of the cataclysmic famine. But those who toiled on the land and had the good fortune to survive the devastating effects of the hungry years were to undergo changes to their lives from which there would be no escape. The great estates were being sold off in order to help the wealthy landowners through their financial difficulties, auctioned in lots to venture capitalists and wheeler-dealers of all kinds. These rapacious speculators were the mid-nineteenth century version of the unacceptable face of capitalism, financial hyenas who viewed the famine and its aftermath as a golden chance to snap up every acre they could for future investment and immediate return. That immediate return was, perhaps, their easiest bite – increased farm rentals. The new owners demanded cash or eviction. Out went the old custom of the small farmer being allowed to pay rent in alternative forms, such as supplying the landlord with labour or giving a share of his harvest. Now it was cash or nothing. Many of the small farmers weren't even given that choice.

Farm husbandry was changing, with bigger grazing tracts now being in demand, and if the small farmer's land had good grazing qualities, they would be evicted with no compensation so that their property could be included in the bigger tracts being created. The devastating result of that was clearances on a scale similar to those Scotland had witnessed in a previous century, when the biggest landowners had operated that very same practice, on that occasion the land being cleared of people and restocked with sheep. In Ireland it was cattle. The former tenants were rounded up and herded out to the poorest of land with the thinnest of soil, mainly in mountainous areas. Thousands of farmers were put off their farms, the cottiers were evicted from the tiny cottages which they had occupied in return for their labour, and the labourers, the hired hands who were also a vital part of what had been the rural system, were no longer required. The laws and the landlords had carved up the country in such a fashion that most of the vast rural population was reduced to serfdom equalling that of the poorest and most deprived of peasantry anywhere in the world.

These rural people, the small farmers, cottiers and labourers, were a collective species who for centuries had survived through their willingness to graft. They were a lean, muscular and brawny breed, as adaptable as they were resourceful. They were nature's basic engineers, the managers of situations which required their special skills, God's own labourers. When the country to which they belonged had no further need of them, they looked to the nearest place that did . . . Scotland.

They swarmed over in their thousands, offering what they knew best, the spit and sweat that was to earn them their reputation as the finest labourers in the world; not for them the traits of other nationalities that view toil with the greatest of temperance and prefer to philosophise about tomorrow, or be even less hasty and concentrate on the day after that. 'Resolute, dumb and uncomplaining,' is how the poet Robert Service described them, completing that description more kindly and appropriately with 'a man in a world of men'.

They were the muscle without which much of Scotland as we know it would never have been built: the magnificent Forth Bridge, on which around 60 navvies died, more than 100 received serious injuries and hundreds of others more minor injuries; the great harbours; the railway lines whose tracks were to criss-cross the nation, traversing vertiginous ravines and tunnelling through bluestone mountains as they reached out to the furthest and most remote parts of our country; the wonderful hydro-electric schemes; our canals, the very digging of which ('cutting the navigation' as they called it) was to bless them with that name, navvy. Although thousands of Highlanders and other Scots, as well as Englishmen and Welshmen, were also members of the great navvy army, it is the Irish who have the rightful claim to being the original navvies. They were the ones who pioneered the cutting of the very first canal in the British Isles, the Newry Canal in Northern Ireland, which links the Irish Sea to Lough Neagh.

So what if a poet had called them 'dumb', and others were to describe them as 'rude, rugged and uncultivated' – they were 'a class of community being in great numbers and possessed of great animal strength . . . a class of community by themselves, rough alike in morals and manners . . . they lived for the present and cared not for the past and were indifferent to the future'. Rude, rugged, rough, indifferent, so be it. They were the sinew and stamina upon which the Industrial Revolution would be founded, and without which the efficient and modern face of Scotland may never have fully emerged.

When the Irish left to migrate to Scotland, Glasgow was their principal destination, for it would be there they would be most likely to meet someone who had already arrived from their village or town and would help them gain the first toehold on their new lives as a navvies in Scotland, point them to the companies who were good to work for and the ones best avoided. For years they were a significant part of the human discharge from the little ships which docked at the Broomielaw throughout the first half of the twentieth century and the century before that. Unlike other nations' itinerant labourers with their big swags on their backs and their voluminous carpet bags, the brigades from the bogs travelled light. Invariably their entire worldly possessions would be the clothes in which they travelled and little else – usually nothing.

The big projects which were changing the face of Scotland as the Industrial Revolution gained momentum couldn't get enough of them. They were the bulldozers, the JCBs, the mechanical shovels, the excavators, the earth-movers, the ground-levellers of their day. They were the infantry of progress, hacking their way through mountains of rock, carving their way through quicksand and moss. They dug, they pick-axed, they shovelled, they lifted, they laid, they pushed and they pulled, they sweated and they bled – and suffered and died too – as they changed the face of Scotland from a rural agricultural society into one of the most advanced industrial nations of its day.

Navvies: A Breed Apart

Death and injury were horrifically commonplace in an age where employers knew little and cared less about safe working conditions. The navvies worked in the same clothes in which they slept and ate and enjoyed themselves in their free time. The hardest helmets they knew were their greasy brimmed hats; their only safety harness when they were sweating it out in precarious positions on high rock faces or tall new structures the grip of a pair of leathery, calloused hands that had spent years tightly grasping the end of a shovel. They neither knew about, or were offered, protection when they were down in the depths of some new underwater structure, laying bridge and harbour foundations. Such operations had to be carried out in caissons, huge chambers beneath the water level requiring the use of compressed air to prevent water seepage.

The navvies and tunnellers would go in and out of these deep chambers without the use of vital halfway-house air decompression, resulting in many of them suffering the horrors of the 'bends', the divers' disease caused by transferring from compressed to normal air pressure without a gradual process of decompression. Those who were afflicted with the 'bends' would experience the most excruciating pain from sore joints, so bad that many couldn't walk for weeks afterwards. Many went deaf, others vomited everything they ate. Some suffered paralysis – many became permanent cripples and unknown numbers died. Bizarrely, the only instant relief from their torment came when they were back inside the caissons and in the environment of the compressed air once more. Because of that, many men would spend much of their free time, even their weekends, inside the airtight compartments to delay the tortuous results of being returned to normal air pressure.

It was the same when they were tunnelling sections of the new Glasgow subway system, those underwater stretches where the trains rattle their way under the River Clyde between Bridge Street and St Enoch, Govan and Partick Cross. There was an oozing flow of mud above the navvies 60 feet thick as like moles they shovelled their way under the wide river, and in order to keep it from seeping into the big chambers in which they laboured, the air pressure had to be pumped up to over 30 lbs. They would work in the pressurised chamber for three and a half hours of their eight-hour shift, and dreaded the moment when, without any intervening decompression, they were transferred from their airtight chamber and thrust into the normal air conditions above the water level. The moment they surfaced, the first throbs would begin: the pains in their joints, the stiffness in any form of movement, the breathing difficulties. Some suffered so badly that they could walk only with the greatest of difficulty. No one wanted a navvy in that shape working for them.

The greatest and most hazardous project on which the Glasgow Irish navvies worked was the Forth Rail Bridge, one of the biggest construction projects ever carried out in Britain, the finished work being the country's longest cantilever bridge at 1,658 metres, or just over a mile. They flocked to the Forth from Glasgow for the thousands of jobs that were on offer; for the seven years that the bridge was under construction, it employed up to 4,100 men at a time. A big lure for the mammoth construction job was that the wages and conditions on offer were better than in most jobs. The simple fact that there were any 'conditions' on offer at all was somewhat rare, most workers generally being offered a basic wage with little or nothing else. As an illustration of just how rare the additional benefits were for workers, one of the extras on offer for the bridge workers was the fact that if they got injured at work, not only would there be an ambulance available, but there was also a works' hospital on site. And should the very worst happen, their funeral expenses would be paid (within certain limits, of course) and there were also accident and widows' allowances. All of which was a huge incentive to recruitment in those pre-National Health Service, pre-union-management agreement days. However, the benefits didn't come free: each worker had to contribute one hour's pay per week towards what was called the Sick and Accident Club. The maximum contribution, incidentally, for that one hour's pay was around 4p.

Despite the site hospital and the ambulance standing by, the bridge workers were to pay a heavy price for those good wages and conditions. The Irish navvies figured prominently in the horrific death and injury toll of the project. There were 57 recorded deaths, but because of poor record-keeping, the eventual fate of the 461 seriously injured, many of whom were to die later, was never actually known. A further 518 men were taken to hospital with various injuries.

There being none of today's safety procedures, many of the injuries came from the careless use of tools on the high beams. These would rain down from the towering girders onto the labourers and navvies working below. There is a recorded story of one rigger's spanner falling from his grasp 300 feet up on a high girder and ending up in the river below, after going clean through a four-inch plank of staging wood on its way. One of the luckiest men ever narrowly escaped death in a similar incident. He was left near naked, and undoubtedly near speechless, with shock at what had happened. A tool carelessly dropped from on high had plummeted with such speed that when it hit him in the top pocket of his jacket it rocketed straight through his clothing, exiting at his ankle with such force that it stripped most of his garments from his body in the process. Miraculously he was otherwise uninjured. Two rowing boats stationed at each of the cantilevers for the purpose of rescuing both men and materials were responsible for picking up eight workers and some 8,000 separate items which had fallen from the bridge during the construction process.

Scores of those who were taken to hospital doubtless died from their injuries, not least the unfortunate ones who contracted the painful decompression sickness through labouring in the underwater caissons which had been used to dig out the foundations of the main cantilever supports. It was the most demanding of navvy work, and hundreds of the Irish navvies who had come through from Glasgow found themselves labouring in this most hazardous of physical tasks with the likelihood of contracting the dreaded 'caissons disease', although it wasn't termed that then, little being known about the health hazards of such work.

Because of the prospect of water seepage, work in the caissons was carried on day and night, the only stoppage being from 6 p.m. on Saturdays till midnight on Sunday. But even then the air compressors had to be kept going all the time to maintain the air pressure, with watchmen constantly on duty in the chamber. At first, men worked eight-hour shifts with eight hours off, but as they increased the air pressure the shifts were reduced to six hours on, six off, and finally as the pressure went to its highest level, it was shifts of four hours working and eight hours off.

Despite the reduced shift hours, men continued to contract the dreadful 'bends' and, amazingly, such was the attitude of the times to the extreme danger of the navvies' work that when a manager made a study of the causes he apportioned part of the blame to the men themselves. This emerged in one of the first lengthy reports on the underwater labour which had been causing so many health problems. It was compiled by Wilhelm Westhofen, a German who had been appointed as assistant engineer on the bridge works, and was published in 1890, the seventh and last year of the bridge's construction. Westhofen was in charge of laying the foundations and building the piers on which many of the Irish navvies laboured in the caissons. His verdict on the men's health disorders was that much of the blame could be put down to their lifestyle, principally their drinking habits.

Westhofen's report claimed:

> Some of the most experienced hands suffered when they had been making too free with the whisky overnight, and a good deal of the disorders that ensued were traceable to the same source; though, on the other hand, wet feet or incautious and sudden change from a heated atmosphere into a cold and biting east wind, insufficiency of clothing and want of proper nourishment had their influence in causing illness among the workforce.

He went on to note that two men had died and one went insane and had to be sent back to his own country.

Westhofen observed that the main problem the men had to endure as a result of working below sea level 'appears to be that of severe pains in the joints and muscles of the arms and legs'. He was also to note that further diagnosis showed the disease to be the result of hard work and considerable sweating under high air pressure, probably causing small globules of air to make their way through the skin, where they remained. When the workmen returned to ordinary atmospheric pressure the air globules expanded, causing the most agonising of pains in their joints, elbows, shoulders, knee caps and other places. The only relief from the severe pain was when the men returned to work in the high-pressure chambers, which was why many of those affected spent the greater part of their time off back inside them, only coming out again when absolutely obliged to do so. Westhofen concluded that 'various researches were made by members of the medical staff in the endeavour to give relief or obtain a cure but so far not with any degree of success'.

Despite his observations about the Irish navvies' fondness for their drink, when he further commented on the workforce as a whole, Westhofen said that despite his comments about the Irishmen's lifestyle, they were mostly 'very hard workers and very conscientious and reliable men'.

Thousands of Irish navvies fanned out from Glasgow to provide labour for the major building projects taking place all over Scotland, one of them being the quayside at Broomielaw – unused but still solidly standing today – right in the heart of the city, where future generations of navvies would be able to disembark from their ships, saving them the hike in from peripheral harbours which reached out from the burgeoning city all the way down the river to Greenock. Not that the Broomielaw was the only harbour which required their muscle – thousands of other Irishmen had already worked on the ports and docksides at Ardrossan, Ayr, Arbroath, Aberdeen, Portpatrick, Leith and Stranraer.

The digging of the canals was one of the first of the major projects which required the tenacity and muscle power of the Irish, demanding the biggest workforce ever assembled in the country, made up of navvies from England and the Highlands as well as Ireland. They were to dig 140 miles of inland waterways so that ships could travel from Edinburgh to Glasgow, from Fort William to Inverness, and haul coal hewn by English brothers of the pick and shovel from the rich black seams in Lanarkshire. It was a truly gigantic project, involving considerably more than merely digging mile after mile of the biggest ditch (8 feet deep and 56 feet wide) ever excavated in Scotland. Quarries had to be opened up to obtain the mountains of stone required, kilns had to be built to make bricks, new railway lines developed to bring in building materials, the courses of streams and rivers were altered, and countless miles of new roads had to be laid for the construction traffic of the day, horse-drawn, steam-driven cranes and huge convoys of other horse-powered vehicles bringing in all sorts of supplies. For the Forth and Clyde Canal, for instance, eight reservoirs had to be excavated in order to control the flow of the new waterway. Ten big aqueducts had to be constructed, as well as numerous smaller ones, to take the new canal over rivers and roads. The most spectacular of these was the aqueduct spanning the River Kelvin, taking the man-made waterway 65 feet above the river by a 4-arch bridge crossing a 200-foot-wide valley. More than 30 bridges had to be built for road traffic to pass over the new canal.

With the only mechanical assistance being the few steam-operated appliances, the workforce required for such projects was on the scale of a huge army. One stretch of the new railway line going south from Glasgow required more than 2,700 men and 186 horses. As it advanced further south into Dumfriesshire it required more than 7,000 hands. A count made on one ten-mile stretch of new railway line showed that it required 168 stonemasons, 88 quarriers, 36 joiners, 24 blacksmiths, 44 carters, 31 odd-job men and 1,800 labourers.

Having such abundant legions of men in these rough camps, so often sited in the remotest parts of the country, was obviously not without its problems, such as maintaining some degree of discipline. Collectively the navvies – Scots, English and Irish – were the most basic of men. They worked hard, they lived hard, and when it was time to play, they did that hard too. Which was difficult when, so often, they were miles from the nearest pub, the nearest anything. That would lead to frustration and expose sentiments and feelings which might in more normal circumstances be suppressed. With no form of modern transport, the navvies had to be content with what life they could make for themselves on the sites on which they worked, invariably in remote areas that ruled out any form of commuting from lodgings in nearby communities.

Thousands of the navvies who had worked in Glasgow would go on from there to work on the new railway lines, where often they would meet up with Scots and English navvies – not always the best mix of men when times were hard. The contractors were aware of this, of course, and did their best to keep the nationalities apart by working them on different sections of the line, particularly the Scots and Irish navvies. But keeping the nationalities separate wasn't always possible and fights were commonplace, riots not unknown. At one time, the bush telegraph had it that there was about to be something of a war between the Scots and Irish navvies. Gangs of them had been working at Kinghorn, near Dunfermline, and feelings between the two camps had got so bad that the Scots gangers spread posters throughout the little town warning off the Irish. They were in gruff navvy-speak, under the threatening heading, 'Notice is given . . .', followed in smaller print by '. . . that all the Irish men on the line must be off the ground and out of the country by the 11th of this month or else we must by the strength of our armies and a good pickshaft put them off.' The contractors and subcontractors were also warned to get rid of their Irish workers, receiving letters from the Scots navvies to that effect. One read: 'You must warn all your Irish men to be off the ground on Monday the 11th of this month by 12 o'clock or else we must put them by force . . . for we are determined to do it.'

Matters looked so grim that the local sheriff had to be

summoned to give the Scots navvies a collective warning about their actions, and that seemed to cool matters, for a time at least. But problems flared up elsewhere. There had been more than 7,000 men working on the new Caledonian line, many of them camped out near Lockerbie. The villagers were up in arms at the behaviour of the navvies. They had plagued the district with their drinking, swearing and fighting, having been around for so long, said one of the village's justices, that some of the local youths had taken up some of the worst of their habits – 'drinking, swearing, fighting and smoking tobacco and all those sorts of things'.

It was the fighting part of it that was the worst, at least between the navvies, and it was the Scots and Irish who were at it again. It was so bad in fact that mobs of up to 400 a side were squaring up to each other with pitchforks and scythes, and the army had to be called up from Carlisle, 23 miles away.

The year following the scenes at Lockerbie, there was an even worse riot, this time at Gorebridge, ten miles from Edinburgh. Some 200 of the Irish navvies who had arrived in Glasgow had gone on to jobs there with the railway company, and found themselves being advanced on by more than 1,000 Scots, who had so convinced themselves that this was war that they had engaged a piper and bugler to lead them into action.

The navvies had been working on the Edinburgh–Hawick line under some of the worst conditions of any of the projects. Their accommodation was on the level of prison hulks, the food was atrocious, the predatory company stores they called 'tommy shops' (more about these later) consumed much of their wages, and the work was highly dangerous, involving a series of tunnels in which many of their mates had been killed. Every possible factor existed for the building up of frustration and resentment, and it had all come to a head one Friday afternoon in a

Gorebridge pub. That was where the contractors had chosen to hand out the men's wages and what with the drink and the fact that they weren't given the money they reckoned they had been due, the mood of the navvies took an ominous downturn.

That evening in the pub, a wandering salesman tried to sell watches to some of the Irish navvies. During the course of the salesman displaying the watches, some disappeared. The navvies merely laughed when he asked where they were, so he went to the police, who dragged off two of the Irishmen as suspects. In the early hours of the morning, some 200 navvies, ready for anything after their night in the pub, stormed the police station, releasing their fellow countrymen.

Worse was to come. As the navvies headed back to camp they were met by two other policemen who they beat up so badly that one later died. When word of this incident reached the camps, the Scots got an army of 1,000 together, complete with piper and bugler, and only the arrival of 60 dragoons, urgently called from Edinburgh, saved more lives from being lost – but not before the Scots got to the Irishmen's camp and burned their ramshackle huts.

Summoned to the site, the contractors sacked many of the Irishmen, but did agree to help the others rebuild their huts in order to start work again. The new huts, however, were the same pathetic collection of roughly erected lean-tos, the single men in crude bunk beds and up to 24 families housed in one communal building. When a *Herald* reporter visited them he condemned 'the degrading practice of having the huts of the labourers fitted up so as to accommodate the greatest number in the smallest possible space, without regard either to decency or the health and comfort of the parties occupying them'. The reporter went on to express how it was no great surprise that men reacted the way they did when treated in such a fashion as they were by the contractors. 'The immorality which such a system is calculated to produce must be obvious to all,' went on the *Herald* man, 'and it is not to be expected that people who are subjected to such a degrading condition and familiarised with all the indecent habits incident to it, will feel any great respect for the law enacted for the preservation of social order.' Incidentally, those responsible for the death of the policeman were never caught.

The worse-than-austere campsite at Gorebridge was typical of the conditions the Irish navvies and their families experienced. Employers made little provision for the men's welfare. They gave them a wage, and that was it, so the workers had to find or make their own quarters, these often being the most primitive of encampments composed of a series of crudely made 'humpies', often as not made up of sheaves of straw, better ones from whatever scraps of wood and canvas they could scrounge.

One newspaper reporter of the day, a man from the *Daily Mail* (known as the *North British Daily Mail* at the time), was sent to such a campsite to describe how the men lived during their hours away from work. He was shocked at the very appearance of these pathetic-looking bivouac settlements, describing them as 'miserable hut villages' that might be equated with the dwelling of a primitive African tribe. The reporter had clearly been taken aback at the navvies' crude living quarters, going on to describe the very sight of some of the rudimentary shelters as leaving him 'with no little astonishment'. As he continued with his tour to various work sites, it struck him that each settlement he came across appeared to be more wretched than the last:

> They present a picture of squalid poverty which is new
> to the people on this side of the channel [that is,

mainland Britain]. One of them is made of a few sticks and some rotten straw; its dimensions would not be enough for a pigsty. Smoke escaping through their doors gave them the appearance of a hayrick on fire. A Hottentot's kraal would in comparison be a palace.

Rather than leave their wives and children alone in the city, some navvies had their families accompany them to live in such rudimentary settlements, which surprised the *Daily Mail* man somewhat, though he described the children he came across as appearing 'healthy and frolicsome and the women contented and happy'.

When it came to accommodation, however, it could be said that the navvies on such locations had a better deal than the ones who relied on city lodgings, in the dosshouses. The lowest of these basic premises are often referred to in Glasgow as 'models'. In fact, the real 'models', taken from their title 'model lodging houses', were the very best of them! When a count was made of ordinary lodging houses – as opposed to 'models' – in the centre of the city in the 1840s, it was found that more than 500 of them were used by the navvies and other itinerants. They were home to more than 10,000, who slept in them every night.

With no health, sanitary, housing or any form of environmental standards being enforced, anyone with any kind of premises – an old shop, a disused house, the corner of a hayloft, disused stabling – could set themselves up in the lodging-house business. Anything was suitable for the dossers. They would be charged varying tariffs for their night's stay, anything from two to five pence in old money (one to two and a half new pence) per night. Many of them opted for the one-penny tariff, and no accommodation was more basic in these wretched hovels than that penny stay. Lodgers would be allocated compartments measuring around 12 feet by 10 feet, the size of a small bedroom. In the tiny boxroom there would be an average of three beds, the blankets of which were old hessian sacks. But you didn't get a bed to yourself. It had to be shared with others, usually two or three to a bed, making nine people crammed into one tiny compartment. If you had the cash, however, for one and a half pence you could get a bed all to yourself. This would merely be a narrow, straw-stuffed and stained mattress tossed on the floor. If you were really flush and could spend as much as five pence for your night's stay – which few of the navvies could afford, for that was almost a day's wages at the time – you got the best deal available, a curtained bed with sheets and blankets and even a small square of carpet on the floor.

The density of the population in and around the main area that housed these ramshackle lodging houses, the streets surrounding the Glasgow Cross–Briggait area, had no equal anywhere in Europe. In an area of just two square miles, there were some 300,000 people living in the most appalling conditions. It was the most densely populated city in all of Europe, bearing in mind that the city itself only stretched from Anderston in the west to Calton in the east, Cumbernauld Road in the north to Main Street, the Gorbals in the south, each point bordering on open countryside or by small rural villages. In that congested part of the Glasgow Cross–Briggait area there was an incredibly compressed spread of around 5,000 people per acre. Just imagine 5,000 people standing on the pitch at Ibrox, Parkhead or Hampden, with every surrounding acre being likewise crowded. It was like that in every street of the entire city-centre area, each of them teeming with thousands. Many of the occupants were there to escape the confines of their dismal accommodation, all of them mingling with street sellers and hawkers of every description, some with handcarts, others with donkey carts, some merely lumping their wares in sacks and boxes.

When the handloom weavers held an inquiry into the conditions in which people were being forced to live in areas such as this, a government commissioner informed them that having seen the most degraded of living standards in England and various countries overseas: 'I can advisedly say that I had not believed until I visited the wynds of Glasgow that so large an amount of filth, crime and misery and disease existed in one spot in any civilised country.' Little wonder, then, that when a policeman had been called to one of the lodging houses around that time, and made to go into the house, the smell from its interior hit him with such impact that he promptly fainted and had to be revived.

There were good people in the city who cared and became concerned enough to try to help. One unnamed Glasgow philanthropist with some friends had become so disturbed about the reports of the atrocious living conditions that they formed what became known as the Model Lodging House Association, in an effort to raise the standards of the basic accommodation available, being widely used by the growing influx of immigrants from Ireland. From then on the 'model', despite many people's memories of them, became the best of the lodging premises. They had bunk beds and dormitories, and for around three new pence you could get their best accommodation: your own bed in a small cubicle, separated from the others by a thin wooden partition which was topped with wire netting to keep out intruders. In other words, your very own bedroom, even if it measured only seven feet by four feet. In comparison to other places which were not 'models', it was a veritable boudoir and must have seemed almost an earthly paradise for the navvies and others who used them.

The models became hugely popular with the labourers and itinerant workers and soon there were more than 80 of them offering 13,000 beds in the city, four times more than there were in the next biggest city to introduce the model, Edinburgh. With a good model to stay in, and perhaps enough money left over for a good Saturday night out, there must have been times in this vastly changed city that a tired and weary navvy almost felt he was back home in Cork or Killarney.

There were lots of Irish pubs, and it seemed that every second man you bumped into when you asked for a Guinness was either from your part of the country or the neighbouring one. And wasn't there more Irish entertainment available than anywhere outside of Dublin! All the regular favourites came over on tour, shows with names that left little doubt about which side of the water they originated from, such as The Girl of Balliemoyle, The Bleak Hills of Ireland, Kathleen Mavourneen, The Lily of Leinster and the Son of Hibernia. Goodness, even the circus featured Irish acts like O'Donaghie and the Fairy White Horse. If you wandered down to the Scotia Variety Theatre in Stockwell Street they had the show everyone loved, The Donnybrook Fair, in which there was a cast of 'at least 100', with the performance ending every night with an act which had the audience howling, a rumbustious, riotous re-enactment of the actual Donnybrook pandemonium punch-up. What a finale that was! At that same theatre, incidentally, around the turn of the century the stage manager was a tall, dignified gentleman named Arthur Jefferson, whose young showbiz-mad son Stanley was to become the legendary slimmer half of the incomparable Laurel and Hardy.

Whether he was Moleskin Joe, Hellfire Jakey or Blasting Mick, the occasional night out at such a show for a hard-working navvy could make him feel like he was in seventh heaven. If it was only a few pints of the black stuff he could afford, there was no shortage of pubs, the city at the time averaging one for every 30 families, and when they were in full swing on a Saturday night there was theatre galore out on those hustling, bustling streets, in which, as one writer of the day was to put it, there was 'amusement with your ale, bliss with your beer, comfort with your cigar, poetry with your port, songs with your sherry, wit with your whisky, civility with all, and admission free'.

On the bigger projects on which the navvies worked, such as the canals and railway lines, they were enslaved to their masters by the imposition of an iniquitous practice known as the truck system, together with yet another equally infamous scheme, the company store (the accursed tommy shops). The truck system had been in operation for centuries. It was a brilliant innovation by the labour operators which not only boosted their profits by reducing the costs of their workforce, but also gave them the most rigid control over the navvies, a control which had all the hallmarks of slave trading. The truck system basically meant that the labourers could be paid in any fashion they chose. That rarely meant handing over actual cash – instead the employee would be rewarded for his labours with the basic goods he required to sustain his humble life: meal, potatoes, tobacco, beer, moleskin trousers, hobnailed boots. Wages were usually paid fortnightly or monthly, but in order to survive that long, workers would be given on request regular advances, or subs as they were known. But the sub, usually in the form of a ticket or a voucher, could only be spent in the store owned by the company, on the site of the project where they were working.

The company store sold everything the men and their families required – everything, it is said, except coffins. If you were on good terms with the man who ran the store, he might return you some of your advance in hard cash, but only after he had taken his cut. He would be far from generous, usually demanding around 20 pence for every 50 pence he handed over. There were infamous stores on various projects around Glasgow as late as the mid-nineteenth century, workers being compelled to use them whether or not they were on the wages truck system. One at a coal mine in Garthamlock, now part of the city's eastern housing schemes, was notorious for its prices. In the village store, paraffin sold for eight pence a gallon, but miners were forced to buy it at the company store, where a gallon cost twelve pence. A 4 lb loaf of bread which cost two and a half pence in the village sold for three pence at the company store. The company store's butter was usually rancid and the meat was described as only being fit for the crows.

At Blochairn the company store operated as a franchise. The owner paid the ironworks an annual sum – some hundreds of pounds – for the privilege of running the store. At one of the big Clyde shipyards, where wages were paid fortnightly, subs on the men's wages were doled out in the form of coloured tickets, or vouchers, which denoted the amount being granted. But these could only be used for purchases at a specific local grocer, that grocer being the brother-in-law of the shipyard owner. Everyone, it seemed, was in on the act.

The vouchers could only be obtained from the company timekeepers when the workers arrived for their shifts in the morning, the timekeepers being paid a percentage of the total of tickets they handed out. Not content with that, they would only permit the hungry worker to have some of his advances in hard cash on the condition they got a further cut.

As the famous folksong goes, they went 50 years and what did they get . . . 50 years older and deeper in debt. The navvies really did owe their very souls, it seemed, to the company stores. Nor did it stop at that. The long chain of graspers wanting or demanding some share of the men's miserable wages seemed endless. Men with children had money deducted for the upkeep of the school, and young pupils had to provide a penny or tuppence a week for their fees. Then the man who sharpened or repaired their vital working tools had to be paid, usually around three pence a week. The vicious truck system and the company store were to linger well into the nineteenth century and it was not until the dying years of that century that the last traces of it were to be eventually outlawed by Parliament.

The *Daily Mail* ran an admirable campaign against the system that exploited these poorest of workers. In an example of pioneering journalism, they had reporter William Cameron seek work as a navvy in order to reveal the real inside story of the conditions these men had to endure not only at work but also as a result of the practices of their employers. Cameron was to discover that the navvies' masters were charging them a shilling per pound for the vital wage advances on which they relied so much, their wages only coming every fortnight or even longer. He concluded that if a man got an advance on his pay it would cost him an extortionate 180 per cent per annum by the time he had paid it back.

The men who are the working descendants of Glasgow's Irish navvies now wear hard hats and donkey jackets with their company name printed on the back and are known as construction workers. But they are still out there in all sorts of weather, in the major construction works, engaged in the ever-changing face of the nation, working for such giant companies as McAlpine, where they were originally known as McAlpine's Fusiliers, Tarmac and Wimpey. So many of them are associated with the latter that it is said the firm's name – WIMPEY – is an acronym for 'We Import More Paddies Every Year'.

Of course, for those who didn't like the itinerant life of the ordinary navvy, there was always other steady work available. There was plenty of employment for coalminers, those children of another dead end: a deep, dark and dangerous dead end. Although this had not been a traditional form of work for natives of Ireland, the demands made of the miner were as harsh as those on the navvy, and immigrants to Scotland very quickly adapted to the requirements of occupation in that industry. With the same big bands, big hearts and big appetite for work, they could get themselves work down any one of the hundreds of coalmines in and around Glasgow at the time of the great migration. Many who navvied on first arriving in Glasgow moved on in pursuit of better money and a less itinerant way of life to the coalfields of Lanarkshire, the Lothians, Ayrshire and Fife. In Lanarkshire and in Glasgow itself, it is estimated that around a quarter of the mining workforce were Irish.

Being a miner appealed to the family men, for the job didn't require them to be on the move as much as the navvies. They didn't have to live in navvy camps or travel so far to their work site, and if they wanted to work in and around Glasgow, there were mines galore always requiring men. Because of high transport costs, many mines were concentrated in the vicinity of the city, scores of collieries being opened up to mine the rich seven-foot seam between Glasgow and Hamilton. In the 1870s there were more than 200 working collieries in Glasgow and Lanarkshire, making it the sixth-largest coalfield in Great Britain.

Although they could graft with the best, being a coalface miner was more difficult for the Irish immigrants than it was for the young lads born and bred in mining districts. The Irishman was usually bigger and more angular than the wiry, bony and sparer-framed colliers, who would have been working underground since leaving school as immature 12-year-olds. If a coalface hewer at that time were to be asked what it was like where he worked, a likely response might be for him to point to a kitchen table and tell you to get under it and imagine yourself swinging a pick or scraping with a shovel in that space for up to ten hours a day, the eight-hour day not being introduced in the pits till after 1879. You can get your body into positions like that when you've been doing it since youth, but for the fully developed man this form of labour, hunched foetally in a tiny space, can be agonisingly difficult. They would kneel, lie, twist, trying always to claw forward into the coal, then shovelling back what they had just won from the seam. Kneeling forward, throwing back, kneeling forward, throwing back, hour after hour, the human moles grafted through their long shifts. Irishmen did become miners, but because of the physical difficulties they were more likely to be found at work in the many other tasks underground, such as hauling bogies and hutches, clearing tunnels and managing the forest of pit props the miners required, rather than moling their way through a three-foot-wide coal seam.

In many of the mines in which the new immigrants found work, there was the same iniquitous truck system many of their navvy brothers suffered, that is being forced to use the company store, or the tommy shop as they knew it in many districts. The only face-saving aspect of the system as it operated in the Glasgow and Lanarkshire coalfields was that it wasn't as drastic as it was at the lead mines up in the high villages of Leadhills and Wanlockhead, where the wages were paid annually – in arrears, and minus the deductions from whatever had been spent at the company store during those previous 12 months. This meant that for many, when they had tallied their year's wages, there would be precious little hard cash remaining to show for 12 months of hard work. Nevertheless, it was bad enough in the mines in and around Glasgow at the time. In 1860 half the miners in Scotland were subject to the abominations of the villainous truck. To get their hands on hard cash, men were sometimes forced into buying goods from the store and then reselling them, often for as low as half price, all for the feel of some copper and silver coin of their own.

Like the navvies who had laboured in the caissons – the underwater work stations of tunnel and bridge projects – those working in the deep coal mines were toiling in the most hazardous and hellish of occupations. They worked in the most horrendous of conditions, invariably with water everywhere, either dripping on them through the roof or seeping up through the floor. Photographs and old film depict some of the grim and forbidding aspects of the underground work, but nothing conveys the stench down there in those fearful and unpredictable tunnels where life is a world apart, a dangerous, dim, dusty and unsanitary world. There was no smell anywhere like there was down in those depths, the pervading odour of manuring pit ponies and sweating humans. There was no place for the men to sit and eat their packed lunches, nor was there any provision of proper toilets. So, just like they had to find somewhere out of the way to eat their lunch, they would have to find somewhere to urinate or defecate. Their waste, like that of the pit ponies, would subsequently get into the water, and the bacteria would transfer into the open sores from which the miners perpetually suffered through the constant chaffing when they crawled, scraped and squeezed their bodies through jagged cavities of stone and coal.

The era of the questioning working man had not yet arrived, and the miners accepted the diseases with the same meek heroism they did the dangers. There were gassy tunnels that gave them searing headaches and robbed them of their appetite, perpetual damp that got into their joints, causing inflammation and giving them all sorts of sores, agonising boils and the perpetual irritant of dermatitis. At least such things didn't kill, but there were plenty of other illnesses that did: lung diseases like miners' asthma, the crippling breathlessness known as pneumonoconiosis, miners' phthisis, which they called the black spit, and bronchitis. Almost all underground workers were showing symptoms of at least one of these diseases by the time they were 40. The best known of all the miners' occupational diseases was miners' nystagmus, a rotatory oscillation of the eyeballs which prevented them from accurately focusing their vision, together with side-effects such as headaches, giddiness, night blindness and photophobia, the dread of the light. Miners were almost certain to die of one or other of these diseases.

The Irish miners of Glasgow didn't have to travel far to find a coal pit. There were seven in the Shettleston area alone, fifteen of them in and around Baillieston, two at Kelvinside and others at Jordanhill, Polmadie, Toryglen, Possil, Robroyston, Govan, Maryhill, Tollcross, Mount Vernon, Millerston and Bishopbriggs. If there were no jobs available at any of these pits, there were plenty of others just over the Glasgow boundary. Thousands of men who had come to Glasgow had found underground jobs in nearby Rutherglen and Blantyre, some of the big pits at the latter belonging to William Dixon and Company, owners of the Govan Iron Works, much better known as the famous Dixon Blazes at the head of Crown Street in the Gorbals, a 24-hour-a-day nightmare inferno of iron making and one of the most awful establishments in the entire city for its noise and noisome stench, situated right in the heart of Glasgow's most densely populated residential district. But then, the concept of 'environmental health' was largely unheard of in those days.

Navvies: A Breed Apart

The Dixon mines at High Blantyre (there were five of them) had a big immigrant workforce. About half of those who worked at the No. 2 and No. 3 pits were Irish. The No. 2 and No. 3 pits were to become infamous names in British industry that cold, wet autumn of 1877, the talk of every working man in the country and the source of more grief than any single workplace that Scotland has ever known.

It was just before nine o'clock on a Monday morning in October 1877 when it happened. Some 233 men had left their homes as usual, long before dawn, for their early shift, which began at 5.30. Because they didn't have a change of clothing, some of their grimy work clothes had still not properly dried from the previous day's darg in the wet and muck of the deep mine. They walked in silent, cheerless groups, as always in Indian file, some on one side of the road, some on the other, heads down into the blustering wind that was threatening a gale, the first spit of rain from the ominous weather front that was moving in from the Atlantic spattering their faces as they trudged to the pitheads. If this morning was a foretaste of the oncoming winter, then they were in for a hard one. It was almost a relief when they reached the pithead, albeit one of the most bizarre kind. At least they were out of that chill morning wind, crushing themselves into the crowded hoists, their gates clanging shut, ready for a headlong plunge into the bowels of Lanarkshire.

They were deep pits, No. 2 and No. 3 at Blantyre, 150 fathoms deep (900 feet), and they would have taken a copious gulp, as they always did, of the last few precious moments of fresh air before the cage hurtled at breakneck speed into the depths, so fast it made their innards heave and had them wondering, as always, if this might be one of the journeys where the brakes failed. Even if any of them survived a disaster like that, they would be a bag of broken bones for the rest of their lives. The fear of that worried some so much that they would stagger thankfully out of the cage, then retch up that morning's breakfast and what was left of their previous night's supper.

They had been down at the coalface for more than three hours when it happened, and the noise could be heard in every house in the village and nearby villages too. Anxious faces peered from windows, staring at the huge column of smoke coming from the direction they all knew was that of the No. 2 and No. 3 pits. The houses quickly emptied, their occupants running to the pithead, the wives first and the men who had been asleep after their nightshift following. There is no mistaking a coalmine explosion. The one that morning had come with a terrifying rumble that shook the very earth beneath them with the most fearful of bangs, the like of which even the men who had been to war said no gun or exploding shell could ever match. The fireball of the explosion, flashing through all the tunnels of the mine, looking for an escape route to blow itself out, sought freedom by roaring up the lift shafts, shattering the housing over the hoist platforms and badly injuring a group of young mechanics who had been there preparing one of the cages.

Somehow word that something terrible had happened quickly spread throughout the city. Before there was any official news, a rumour swept round the stocks and shares dealers and other financial men at the Royal Exchange in Glasgow that morning. It was 'whispered with bated breath that no fewer than 400 men were imprisoned and it was feared nearly all had perished'. There were no further details, apart from the fact that the men had been involved in a mine disaster somewhere nearby, until the rumour reached the offices of the Glasgow newspapers. The *North British Daily Mail* checked with William Dixon's, the biggest of the mine owners, to ascertain if anything of that nature had occurred at one of their pits. The rumour was true, admitted Dixon's, although the numbers were not. They gave the details as far as they knew them: 233 men were involved. They had all been at work down in the heart of the mines, and were trapped. They were sending for help.

By that time, men on horseback were galloping as fast as they could from Blantyre to nearby mining centres for rescue squads, while one was heading to the Royal Infirmary in Glasgow with the news that a five-carriage train filled with wounded men would be on its way to them as soon as possible, and they should stand by to receive it.

Three surfacemen at the Blantyre No. 2 and No. 3 pits had already made their way underground following the explosion to make the first assessment of what had happened. They knew by the nature of the blast, the flame and the extent of the devastation that it must have been the most feared of mine disasters, a firedamp explosion. These fears were confirmed as soon as they reached the bottom and came across the first pile of bodies not far from the pit cages. The indications were that few, if any, of the 233 men who started work that morning would be coming out of the mine alive. These first rescuers quickly collected what bodies they could, stretchering them to the pithead and taking them straight to the joiners' shop there, going through the age-old colliers' procedure of washing each man's face so that a wife or mother or someone could recognise him. But even when all the coal dust had been wiped away their faces were still black, scorched by the furnace heat of the explosion. More and more bodies were brought up, many of them naked, their clothes having been blasted from their bodies.

Those first rescuers came across the most harrowing of

sights. There was a young boy (at that time lads as young as 11 and 12 worked underground) who when they reached him said, 'What kept you from coming?' and at that very moment fell dead. Not far away was a miner sitting peaceful and still, as though patiently waiting for them, his eyes wide open. But he too was dead. Another had his tobacco pipe in his mouth, his heavy pick in his hand, as though he was still at work, but again he was dead. The rescuers couldn't stay long underground because of what they called 'chokedamp', a mixture of oxygen-deficient gases which cause suffocation instantly, if bad enough, and are usually present following a firedamp explosion. Because of the chokedamp, the first rescue team could only work for half-hour periods at a time before racing back to the surface for air and rest.

Every woman from the village was there at the pithead, and many of the children too. They had come running from their houses, humble terraced-cottage dwellings called miners' rows, which from a distance looked like lines of redbrick cloches. Some of the women stood in silent, traumatised groups, just staring ahead as though they had experienced it all before. 'She's got her man and three sons down there,' said one pointing to another. A young miner who was there said that every one of his dozen relatives had been down the pit that morning: brothers, uncles, father. Other groups of women were not so silent, the *Glasgow Herald* reporting, as it was later described with 'unintentional superiority', that the Irishwomen were 'tearing at their hearts and rushing about in a half-crazed state, strong men having to interfere to prevent them throwing themselves on the corpses'. Others rushed to uncover the faces of the bodies to see if they could be identified. Some of them were studying the boots on the feet of the worst-scorched victims, boots they knew all too well from cleaning them, greasing them, taking them to the cobblers and helping their menfolk take them off their feet when they came home, exhausted from their labours. A Catholic priest was there, too, a reporter noting that 'such had been the nature of the catastrophe he had found the task of consolation altogether beyond him'.

The storm that had threatened that morning broke by early evening and torrents of rain lashed fiercely down, soaking the huge crowd that waited in vain for a father, a son, a brother. *How Green Was My Valley* had never been as hellish as this. By nightfall only a few remains had been recovered, together with four badly injured men, writhing with the excruciating pain of their burns. There were still 197 men left down there, but there was no longer any need for the doctors and nurses at the Royal Infirmary in Glasgow to stand by, for the special train ordered for the injured had been cancelled. Considering the gas content of the lingering foul air at the pit bottom, it would certainly be only bodies the rescuers would bring up when they eventually managed to make their way through the dark and polluted tunnels down there.

In the ensuing days, when the air had cleared, the bodies of many of the 197 missing men were recovered, but it was to take up to a month before all of them were located. The final death toll was some 207 men and boys, the worst-ever mine disaster in Scotland. The last one had been 26 years previously at Nitshill, just over the Glasgow boundary, when 63 men had died, again many of them Irish miners. Only 26 of the 233 men who had gone to work that morning at Blantyre No. 2 and No. 3 had survived, most of them badly injured. The 207 who were killed left 92 widows, 33 of them being those of Irish miners, and 250 fatherless children. Eleven of the victims were lads under 14 years of age. The explosion had completely devastated the mine workings, which was why it had taken so long to recover all the victims. Such was the extent of the injuries of some of the men in the horrendous blast that many of the coffins had plates screwed to them bearing the words 'Not to be opened'.

They never knew precisely what sparked off the explosion that had been caused by a build-up of firedamp, a highly combustible mixture of gases mainly composed of volatile methane, and formed by the decomposition of coal in the workings. The Blantyre mines had been known among the miners as 'gassy', and just weeks before the disaster there had been another firedamp explosion, which was confined to one small section and killed only one miner. Yet despite it being a 'gassy' mine, the Davy safety lamp wasn't in general use, the men still using the older open-flame 'tally' lamps on their leather hats. The fact that one of the dead miners was found with his pipe still in his mouth showed how lax working practices had been.

About a third of the men and boys who died at Blantyre were from the local Roman Catholic community, sharing such names as Brannan, Kelly, Murphy, Docherty, Tonner, O'Neil, Dolan, Boyne, O'Byrne, Connelly, O'Bryce, Larkin and Conlan. Some had only recently arrived in the district, one of them having been there for just a few days. Like so many of their navvy brothers who had worked on the canals, tunnels and bridges, whether on perilous heights of soaring new structures or in the deadly underwater depths of the caissons, they had gone bravely to their workplace frontline. And they had paid the ultimate penalty for that bravery.

It was the country's biggest contractor of the age, the wealthy MP Sir Morton Peto, who was to tell Parliament of the real worth of these hard-working men, the Irish navvies, so many of whom had come to Glasgow. No one knew them better, for Sir

Morton's huge contracting company was rated at the time as the employer of the world's biggest workforce, with building projects throughout Britain, Russia, Denmark, Canada and the Argentine. Sir Morton was seconding the Address to the Crown at the opening of Parliament. He chose to speak of these men who had been so much in the news, and not always for the best reasons. This is what he told Parliament:

> I know from personal experience that if you pay him well and show you care for him he is the most faithful and hard-working creature in existence; but if you find him working for fourpence a day and that paid in potatoes and meal, can we wonder that the results are as we find them? [This was a specific reference to the wretchedness of some of the Irish navvies working on the railways.] But give him legitimate occupation and remuneration for his services, show him you appreciate those services, and you will be sure you put an end to all agitation. He will be your faithful servant.

– CHAPTER 12 –

The Amazing Adventures of Hannah

Hannah was all the talk of the Glasgow Catholic Irish in the early years of the last century. She was the central character in a long-running serialisation which was featured weekly in the main newspaper of the Glasgow Irish at the time, the *Glasgow Catholic Observer* now known as the *Scottish Catholic Observer*. Hannah was a young girl from Ireland who came to Scotland on her own, one of the countless destitute and unfortunate victims left in the wake of the Great Famine, and her adventures in the big city were faithfully followed by thousands of readers of the *Glasgow Catholic Observer*. When Glasgow Irish met other Glasgow Irish, Hannah was sure to come into the conversation. She was as important to them as a soap star might be today. Maybe even more so, for although Hannah was a fictional character, she was real to the readers and her experiences, her fortunes and misfortunes, her reactions, her aspirations and her observations about life in the new country, the new big city, were theirs too. Which is why they so enthusiastically anticipated every episode of the long-running serialisation of the story of Hannah. She was living and seeing it all just as they had. She saw and reflected on the city with the eyes of the newcomer. She loved the great things it had to offer. She endured the not-so-great, varied and unanticipated hazards of the innocent abroad.

Reading it now, nearly 90 years later, is like lifting a curtain on the attitudes and reflections of Glasgow and Glaswegians, Scots and Scotland, of another era. The story itself is hardly even penny-thriller material, yet it reveals so much about interactions of the day. It contains scathing racial references which, irrespective of the politically correct, would just not be tolerated today. Yet they are expressed without reservation or reluctance in this otherwise seemingly innocent tale of the young girl from Ireland which literally breathes with attitude of a bygone age. The story of Hannah was a rare and revealing episode for me during my research into the great migration of the Irish to Scotland, contributing much to the understanding of Glasgow, Glaswegians and the Glasgow Irish in those transient times. And in this considerably shortened version of Hannah's life and times in Glasgow, I have endeavoured as much as possible to adhere to the essence of the original script.

The story of Hannah, the young exile who had come to Glasgow on her own, begins back in rural Ireland. Hannah's parents had died, presumably victims in the wake of the Great Famine, and the surviving children couldn't earn enough to keep all of them. It's the simplest of tales, full of all sorts of unanswered questions and written in a style that would make the most basic Mills and Boon seem worthy of being a Booker contender. But the story of Hannah reveals much about Glasgow as it was nearly 100 years ago.

The weekly serial was highly popular among the Irish in Glasgow at the time because, simple as it is, it was the story of themselves, a story with which they empathised more than any other of the day. Hannah could have been one of them, from their very own family. Her experiences were their experiences. Her background was their background. The trauma of the departure from home and hearth was theirs. The great adventure of moving from one life to another was theirs. So too were the advantages and benefits which it brought. So too were the downsides, the sadness, the misfortunes and the heartache of the exile.

And all that shared feeling of highs and lows was for a girl who never really existed. Hannah was created by Patrick Dougan, a budding author of his day, just after the turn of the last century. His great new work had been called 'An Exile of Erin' and was to be serialised by the *Catholic Observer*, their weekly newspaper in Glasgow, over a period of many weeks beginning in October of 1915. They billed it as their 'Grand New Serial', a story which every reader would love. And love it they did as they avidly followed the story of Hannah and all her adventures in her new city, her new country.

The story of Hannah as it unfolded week after week in their newspaper was to become the talk of the community wherever they met, from street corner to steamie to saloon. And they could hardly wait till the following week's edition of the *Observer* to read how Hannah, the new immigrant, was now faring and what else might be happening to her.

The story of Hannah is worth retelling in as much detail as possible, despite the flaws and imperfections in the story itself, for it reveals as much about the attitudes and feelings of the immigrant and the native communities as any academic study might. But first, and to appreciate the full story of Hannah, some understanding is needed of just what the Glasgow of 1915 was truly like when the young exile from Erin arrived there to begin her new life.

In many aspects, the physical appearance of Glasgow 90 years ago would be broadly similar to the city we know today. The basic street plan of the city centre has altered little. Neither have many of the buildings, though they were not nearly as clean as they are today, having at the time already taken on the grim black blight of the smoke-staining from the thousands of tenement coal fires – the only source of household heating – as well as that of the putrid clouds belching from the forests of tall chimney stacks of the factories and works in nearby suburbs like Anderston, Gorbals, Townhead and Bridgeton. It's near the end of 1915 when the story of Hannah begins in the *Observer* and therefore I have concentrated the following aspects of Glasgow from the closing months of that year.

The First World War is little more than a year old but already countless thousands have been and still are being slaughtered on the horrendous battlefields of France and in Flanders. Despite all that, many aspects of life in Glasgow continued just as they had been in those early years of that century. Going into November they were already anticipating whatever small pleasures there might be in the coming festive season, although there would be no lengthy work breaks and celebrations would be mainly confined to Hogmanay and New Year's Day. The poultry and game shops were stocking up with turkeys and geese, ducks and fowls priced from ten old pence to one shilling (that is 5p to 6p) per pound. Sounds amazingly cheap, but then that sum was the equivalent of today's £1.90 to £2 per pound.

War stories dominated the newspapers and, as relief, any non-war stories were read with more than customary relish. One story which made the news late that year was the court case involving a Glasgow workman called James Garvie. James had lost his arm at his work in a paper mill at Linwood and had successfully sued his employers, who admitted liability. He was awarded £380. Even translated into what would be the equivalent sum today, £14,440, it was paltry recompense for such an injury.

Many advertisers were using various aspects of the war to promote their products. In their latest advertisement, the makers of Waverley, the popular cigarette, were proclaiming their cigarettes were 'always in the firing line!' They were selling at three old pence, or today's 1½p, for a packet of ten.

It was with some obvious reluctance that newspaper readers turned from page one of their paper, filled entirely with display and classified advertisements of all descriptions. For the advertisements were about the only regular good news in the press that season. Once they turned to the news pages inside the paper, there seemed little else but grim reading.

New names in far-off locations had become part of everyday language. Places which were headline news day after day, map locations such as Flanders and Loos, Bessarabia and Salonika, Dardanelles and Dwinsk, Suvla Bay and Gallipoli. And all of them meant battles – and deaths and casualties, especially those latter two placenames in far-off Turkey. The Allied forces had landed at Gallipoli that April in 1915 and the battle plan was that the Turkish troops would be routed and it would be all over in 72 hours. Now it was near the end of the year and those who survived of the 500,000 men that had landed on that remote

Turkish beachhead on the Gallipoli Peninsula were still there – more than 300,000 of them having become casualties.

There was little cheer in any of the news from those faraway battlefronts. The newspapers were filled with death announcements, page after page of them, many of them accompanied by small head pictures of yet another father, another son, with the news that they had either been slain at the front or that they were 'missing in action', the most compassionate way of putting it that a soldier relative had either been blown to smithereens or else drowned in the sea of mud surrounding their trenches.

But despite all the heroism and sacrifice of the Glasgow men who had gone off to fight – the city was to provide an incredible 200,000 volunteers and conscripts – sadly there were still those whose only view of the carnage in the killing fields was that it could be a means of making money. Perhaps the most miserable of these schemers were the ones who, after reading that day's death notices, would call at the houses of the newly bereaved professing to be a representative of the newspaper which carried the story of their relative in the services. And, for a fee, they would glibly announce, with mock sincerity, that they would be able to supply a 'fine reproduction photograph' of the one appearing in the paper. Of course, it was a stipulation that the bereaved relative would first of all have to hand over the fee. The rest of that pathetic story is too sad, too predictable.

In many ways life was to continue just as normal for this second year of the Great War and indeed for the subsequent years. Families went on with their lives as best they could. They planned their holidays and the steamship companies were offering day sails down the Clyde from Broomielaw to Dunoon at 5p return, accommodation was available at places such as Ayr for 40p a week, and if Rothesay was your preference, there was full board available for £1 a week. On the jobs front, bricklayers were in demand at 5½p per hour and there was plenty of work for labourers and navvies for the big project at the Rosyth naval base, the terms being the going rate of 4p an hour, but note! – 'excellent accommodation' available in the 'hut village'. Office boys were wanted by city firms with a starting wage of 25p a week, and they were so short of carriers for delivering the hundredweight sacks of household coal that women had been recruited for the arduous task, although it was pointed out in some newspapers that even though they had to resort to such a practice, 'women in employment would not become a general thing'!

There was still plenty of entertainment to be had at the number of theatres and venues with live shows throughout the city, which was just as well with the news from Gallipoli deteriorating by the day, and likewise in other areas. A weekend visit uptown and you could find a show to suit the most varied of tastes. The King's Theatre was featuring a gripping drama entitled *On Trial*, and the forever popular thriller *Raffles* was on at the Theatre Royal. The biggest crowd-pleaser, of course, was variety and there seemed no end to your choice. At the Empire in Sauchiehall Street the current show was simply billed by a title which said everything – *All Scotch*. Its big attraction, according to the posters, was that it featured 'the finest bunch of beauties – all kilted'!

Round the corner at the Pavilion there was an all-star show called *Just in Time*, while down the road at the Alhambra there was the legendary Harry Lauder starring in his own show and over the river at the Princess's in the Gorbals the tartan was still flying high, their big show being *Rob Roy*. The production at the Olympia, Bridgeton Cross, was a touch more exotic, the star being Phaoros, hailed as the 'great Egyptian illusionist'. While he confounded them Lady Pot astounded them at the Trongate Waxworks, this lady being billed as the 'world-famed midget'. Admission prices began at 1½p and you could get the very best seat in any of the theatres for 25p.

The latest writing gadget was in vogue, supplies of typewriters just having arrived from America, Royals selling for £10.80 and Underwoods at £12.80, or almost the equivalent in today's terms of what you would pay for a computer. And as if to demonstrate very little in life is really new, the rave toy for Christmas that year was the little two-wheel contraption they called SKA-cycle – in fact, an exact replica (with the exception of the use of modern materials) of the mini-wheeled scooter which was one of the rage presents of Christmas 2000. Hoey's at St George's Cross was selling them from 13p to 33p.

If you wanted to get away from it all there were fares available by sea to Australia for just £18, or if cash wasn't the problem £45 for a first-class cabin and service. You could travel much cheaper, of course, that is if you were fit and destined for a life in the Outback, the state of Queensland luring migrants with agricultural experience with subsidised fares of just £7, or £10 if you had a wife to bring along, plus £1.50 for each child.

And so it was to the Glasgow of the 1½p theatre seat, the 5p return sail to Rothesay and the 13p scooter into which the teenage Irish girl called Hannah Purcell arrived. The serialised story of the exile from Erin starts with a description of the young migrant's background.

It tells how she has already been living in Glasgow for some 13 months, having migrated from her native county of Cavan. There she had lived with her family in Belturbet, a small village in the beautiful heartland of West Ireland near where the River Finn meets with Upper Lough Erne. But the beauty and serenity of rural tranquillity are scant compensation for empty stomachs. The Purcells had lived in what the story describes as a cabin near the river. In the jargon of later years, the use of the word cabin as one's homestead sounds somewhat appealing, with even an idyllic undertone. But a cabin in rural Ireland of those times was in reality something completely different. Thousands who lived in the Irish countryside dwelt in similar cabins to the Purcells, and there was little of the idyll about them, for they were the most basic of abodes. Crude wooden shelters, little more than dilapidated huts, usually sited on the worst aspect of the landowner's property for whom they worked. The tenure of a cabin would usually represent part of their wages. It was also an excellent hold over the tenants who, if they ever dared become demanding, faced the prospect of not only losing their work, but their only home, their cabin.

When Hannah's parents had died, her sister and two brothers continued living in the family cabin, but without the support of their father's wage, there wasn't sufficient income to maintain all four of them. It was the old Irish story. To live meant to leave and in order for the others to survive on what income there was, Hannah said she would go across the water, like so many others had done from Belturbet and its outlying villages whose litany of names sound as though they're the work of some fanciful lyricist: from Ballyconnell to Ballyhaise, Derrylin to Tullyvin, Derrylaney and Drumasladdy as well as Killashandra, Magheraveely and Carrigallen. The human haemorrhage had flowed from them and hundreds of others for decade after decade.

Hannah Purcell had now been in Glasgow for just over a year and the promised land had so far lived up to her expectations. Within days of her arrival she had found herself a good job with comfortable accommodation, working in domestic service for the family of a prominent King's Counsel called Amplefold, who lived in the West End. Her employers are kind to her and she is happy working for them. To their surprise, however, Hannah tells Mrs Amplefold she plans to leave her job. She lives with the family in the West End and this means that there was no nearby Catholic church for her to attend. Being the devout Catholic she was, this has caused her some concern. She has only managed to take part in two masses in the past month and has missed Benediction. It has made her increasingly upset. When informed of her plans, Mrs Amplefold tells her how difficult it will be for the family to get someone as good, honest and hard-working as she has been but as she is also a Catholic, she sympathises with her and understands her problem.

One of Hannah's new friends in Glasgow is a Protestant girl called Nelly Morrison, who tells her about a job in the city warehouse, Central Stores, where she works. If she writes to them she will probably get work there. She does; there is a tearful farewell from the Amplefolds' children, who have grown to love her, and she speaks of her anxiety about the new job and what kind of people she might be meeting there. But her friend Nelly assures her the staff in the warehouse are friendly, even the boys. But Hannah is not interested.

Because she wrote such a neat letter of application she gets a job in the stores department of the warehouse. They call it the 'G' department. The manager is a Mr Forbes, who Nelly says is a proper gentleman, but there is also a Mr Pendleton, a cashier, who is not so nice. Hannah takes lodgings in Castle Street, Townhead, with the parents of Nelly Morrison, sharing a bedroom with her friend. How strange she feels that first Sunday living there, getting up early in the morning for mass while her friend lies on in bed, getting up at a more leisurely hour to go to her church! And how strange, too, to be living in a bedroom without a crucifix or an altar at which she could pray, like she had at home in Cavan. The tears fill her eyes at the thought of it all.

One night in August the two young working girls go walking in the West End. As they pass nearby the university, the big clock there is striking 7.30. They have gone to that part of the city with the intention of listening to the organ recital being held in the Art Galleries, the author commenting on how the galleries 'looked somewhat dreary with its dark red stone frontage having a neglected appearance and giving the impression that such a building including the so-called art treasures contained within was scarcely worth the enormous sum of money expended on it by a sound, practical, level-headed Corporation'.

The girls discuss the evening's entertainment, debating the high tone of what is on offer at the Art Galleries and the low tone of what is on at the new picture shows. Hannah has been warned by her local priest, Fr Joyce, a Tipperary man, about the sort of films they are showing in the picture houses. She should be very careful of what ones she should go to, he told her, and she should discuss with him which ones to see. Probably he had in mind such films as were being screened that week in the Bijou in Cowcaddens, the main one being *The Fisher Girls' Folly*, supported by *The Black Diamond*.

The girls, having debated the high and low tones of how they should spend their evening, take the course of moral rectitude and avoid the cinemas showing these doubtful films. They walk home, all the way from the West End via Anderston Cross, taking in the sights as they go. At Anderston Cross there's a big crowd round a black man who says he is a doctor. He is selling something: 'Pure herbs,' he shouts to the crowd. 'Pure herbs are nature's remedy for all the diseases that trouble humanity.' The girls stand at the back of the crowd as the man continues with his spiel. 'Look at the people who live in the country,' he goes on, 'and then look at those who live in the towns. The country people are nearer to nature and believe more in herbs and vegetables. Town people go for drugs and chemicals.' Then he says that he has been over in Ireland: 'Ireland is the place where people love the natural and healthy life. They scarcely believe in doctors for they hardly ever need them.' And one of the main reasons why all those Irish folk are so damn healthy, he says, is because they regularly take the same ingredients which he has specially made up in his bottled mixtures. 'And if you want to be like them in Ireland, free from indigestion and bad health then you couldn't do anything better than buy one of these bottles.'

The two girls decide on the pictures after all, but instead of the Bijou they go to the St Enoch Picture House, where the main film on the programme is a travelogue featuring scenes of the Irish countryside. On the way Hannah reflects on the colourful life that is the Glasgow street scene of the day, so much more lively and vibrant than life as she knew it back in Belturbet. At nearly every intersection they pass all the way along Argyle Street there's an almost endless variety of street-corner musicians, singers, sleight-of-hand artists, jugglers, performers of all kinds and gospel preachers, as well as men who say they are doctors and claim that their pills, lotions and mixtures will alleviate every known ailment or affliction and cure any disease or disorder. There is never a dull moment, it seems, in this big and bustling city which has become her new home.

Hannah's work at Central Stores is much more demanding than her routines at the Amplefolds' household. Her job in the 'G' department is to check all the goods that come in and then methodically place them on the tall shelving of the department, which means spending considerable time climbing up and down high ladders to the uppermost shelves. She is exhausted when she returned to her lodgings in Castle Street after a hard day's work.

Hannah is discovering how different life in a big city can be from her rural Ireland. She has never known snobbishness before – she does now. It is rife at work. Each position in the store is finely graded, and those doing the coarser work, or that which requires more muscle power, are looked down on by others doing what they consider to be less coarse work. Those in each of the various grades keep strictly to themselves, separating the workers into cliques, each division displaying great jealousy towards the others. Then the cliques are further segregated, this time by religion, creating even greater divides between staff. Hannah reflects on her colleagues' attitudes towards what work they do, what wages they receive and what religion they are. Each creates their own problems, but none more than the religious one.

One day while walking home from work she is surprised when one of the other girls walking with her says, 'So do you think most people at Central Stores have scented your religion?' Hannah replies by saying that she had been only three days in the job when another girl asked her outright which church she went to. Her response had been that she went to the oldest one in Glasgow. She teased the girl by saying that whenever in a strange place she always looked out the oldest church because that was the true one. Not satisfied at that, the girl had then asked who the minister was and eventually was given the answer that it was a priest in charge. The other girl had been surprised at that. 'Are you really a Roman Catholic?'

'Why?' Hannah wanted to know.

'Because you look so respectable that I thought you would be a Protestant,' the girl had instantly retorted with not a trace of shame. Hannah by this time had become acquainted with another Irish family, the Reillys, who lived in Monteith Row. They had been living in Glasgow for some years and she had struck up a friendship with Maurice, the Reillys' son. Offended at the attitude towards Catholics at the warehouse, she tells the story of the incident to Maurice, who explains: 'That is just the way, Hannah. To be a Catholic in Glasgow is to be all that is vile and disreputable.'

The story moves on to Hannah and new friend Maurice having a night out at a Cavan reunion being held in the National Halls in the Gorbals. As they pass the Princess's theatre in Main Street they have to walk round a big crowd milling outside the theatre, waiting to go into the panto. A car stops beside them and a man gets out. Hannah recognises him as Mr Pendleton who, she tells Maurice, is a 'big boss' at work. Recognising Hannah, he raises his hat to her and walks on. Maurice is surprised at being told the man's name. 'That's not his name,' he says. 'I know him. He is George Rankine, a convicted embezzler and forger,' he insists. It's all reminiscent of a scene from one of the old black-and-white silent films with subtitles and dramatic piano music, as Maurice, the good guy, reveals to the heroine, Hannah, the real story of the shady character who has entered the plot, in this case, Rankine, aka Pendleton.

Going into the National Halls for their great Irish night, the author describes the life-sized portraits of prominent Scots on the walls of the big hall. They include those of John Knox, George Wishart, the Protestant martyr, and Robert Burns, plus another described as 'someone called James Watt (we Irish are far back in engineering!)'. George Wishart is labelled 'a religious fanatic' and 'as for John Knox, how curious, how funny that a gathering of Irish men and women should contentedly sit in the presence of such intolerable blasphemy. A Catholic bishop in the chair, a Catholic audience, all presumably from County Cavan. A coincidence peculiar to Glasgow life, no doubt!' Only Robert Burns receives a kind word, being described as 'Scotland's only great man'.

The Bishop makes a speech; because of the big crowd and being away at the back of the hall, Hannah cannot hear it all but the occasional sentence catches her ears.

'Our Catholic forefathers . . . fighting for liberty . . . very near its accomplishment . . .' At that she looks at the portrait of John Knox. She catches some more of the Bishop's speech, but just snippets: 'Ireland has kept the faith through it all . . . we will persevere . . . letting no obstacle hinder our progress . . .'

There's a huge roar of response when the speech is over. It's now the interval and Hannah looks around her. There are long tables covered with white cloths on which there are plates of doubtful-looking pastry. Tea of a kind is to be had from urns on the tables. Her eyes roam round the people at the function. It's her first time at such an occasion and she is surprised at the sort of people who are there. A flood of thoughts go through her mind as she compares those at the reunion with the people she knew in Cavan. Is this a gathering of Irish people, much less natives of Cavan, she asks herself? Strange there is not one there she recognises.

She notes how the men wear fashionably cut suits and how well dressed the women and girls are. Had these people really come from Cavan, with its thatched houses and windswept hillsides and rugged, battered land? If they had, they would be talking as they would at home about their crops and their recent mission in the chapel, the coming county council elections and other subjects of interest to them in their district. In this hall, so unlike any other anywhere in Cavan, they talked about business, about books and plays and politics and, of course, the Bishop's speech. Alas, what changes life in the city of the stranger brings!

And the concert itself. For goodness' sake, it isn't all that Irish. Even the songs are not all Irish. One lady even sings the 'Bandelerrio'. An Irish ballad? She reflects on the last night she had spent at a reunion in Ennisfarne and how different that had been. No fancy concert pitch-piano. No platform. No long tables with fancy vases displaying fruit and flowers. Instead there had been a big turf fire and everyone sat about on buckets and upturned creels and piles of turf sods specially selected for the purpose. No fancy pastries, but instead wholesome home-baked scones, potatoes and boiled eggs and a barrel of stout in a corner. And the singing! It had been real Irish songs by real Irish people.

Then there was the dancing. At this reunion in the Gorbals it is waltzes, polkas and Circassian circles. What insufferable bosh! Let us have a good old-fashioned barn dance. At that thought, she gets up on the floor with Maurice to dance in a quadrille and then asks to be taken home. She has had enough of the Irish reunions as they understand them in Glasgow. The whole thing had seemed a mockery, a sham, in fact an insult to a really Irish gathering where, unlike here, everyone acted naturally and thoroughly enjoyed to the full the homely pleasures of Irish friendship.

The next day at the Central Stores there is more talk among the staff about Roman Catholics. A man called Andrew Petrie offers to let her read his book of the day, *The Awful Disclosures of Maria Monk.*

'You won't be a Catholic if you read all of this,' he tells her as he proffers the book. He says it would also do her good if she and her Catholic friends went to see Sarah McGrath, the 'escaped nun', who was giving a talk at the City Halls. 'Look at this,' he says as he shows her a bill for the City Halls meeting. It reads: 'Popery exposed. Sarah McGrath, who was for five years in a convent in Ireland, will tell you how she was treated there and how she escaped. General Marshall of the Salvation Army in the chair. Admission two shillings, one shilling, and sixpence. God

Save Us From Popery.' 'You don't need to tell the priest about it,' Petrie tells her.

After all the talk on the subject at work, Hannah feels she has to pay a visit to her priest. She goes to see Fr Joyce and tells him about the conversation at work. He warns her not to engage in serious discussion with Protestants about the tenets of their faith. Still curious about what Andrew Petrie had told her about the City Halls meeting, she asks the priest if he would forbid her from going to see the 'escaped nun'. He replies by saying that while he would not forbid her outright from going, his advice would be for her not to do so. She says how different that advice would have been had she asked her priest back in Ireland. She says if she had asked him that he would have hunted her from his door. Fr Joyce explains that the clergy in Ireland have no half measures whereas a certain laxity is allowed them in 'heretical countries' where Catholics are obliged to do many things which are never expected of them in Ireland. He then asks her to make a promise that she will not go to the City Halls meeting. However, as Hannah is curious about the event, she replies that she cannot make such a promise.

After the meeting with the priest, she in fact decides to go to the City Halls evening and arranges to meet one of her friends, a Mrs O'Neill, by the bank at the corner of Candleriggs and Argyle Street. She knows her Glasgow fairly well by now and makes sure that on her way down to that part of town from Castle Street she avoids the terrors of nearby Ingram Street and the houses by the Ram's Horn Church, where her safety would be doubtful because of a gang of garrotters who are terrorising that part of the city. Despite the fact it is a mere 400 yards from the main traffic, it is a quiet and dangerous place and nowhere for a girl on her own to be.

Outside the City Halls there is the usual gathering of street performers, to whom the police seemingly take a very liberal attitude and give much scope. One was known as the Green Orator, famous for his speeches on Glasgow Green. He is haranguing the crowd about the nun. He says she has never been in a convent in her life, except as a charwoman.

Hannah pays her one shilling entrance money and immediately reflects on how much better the money could have been used for good, as a donation, for instance, to St Vincent de Paul or for St Anthony's Bread, a Franciscan charitable trust. Inside the hall, General Marshall of the Salvation Army and a woman in nun's clothing are seated at a table on the platform, two jugs of water in front of them. The General speaks first, after a round of applause. He says they are all anxious to hear what the sister has to say about her experiences in the Church of Rome.

'We can all sympathise with her cause,' he says, at which a voice from the hall shouts, 'A question!' The General ignores the remark and continues to speak. He says that Miss McGrath has suffered many indignities at the hands of that institution infamous in history. 'What history?' comes the voice from the hall once more.

The General then comments on how some people are there to cause trouble and no doubt are members of 'that Church'. 'I think it is high time we exposed some of Rome's wickedness,' he says, again being met with the voice from the hall. 'Time's up,' comes the shout.

Eventually the nun gets up to throw back the veil covering her head and Hannah is surprised to see a young woman of about 25. She begins to speak about the miserable life and experiences she had in the convent.

'Which convent?' a voice demands, the woman replying that she would only say that it was in a remote part of Ireland before continuing with her talk. 'Whilst in the convent there . . .'

Now there is more than one voice coming from the hall, so many in fact that she has to stop speaking. 'Fraud! . . . Swindle! . . . Humbug!' come the shouts one after another. General Marshall immediately leaps to his feet calling for order.

At that, another member of the audience, who Hannah recognises as John Boyle, the commissionaire at Central Stores, stands up and demands to know where the convent was. The General shouts back that he will have him removed from the hall.

That brings about a further eruption: 'Romish intolerance!', 'Papish hooligans!' The disturbance gets worse, with cries both for and against the Catholic Church. It gets so bad that proceedings can not go on. Alarmed at the agitated state of the audience, the Salvation Army general hurriedly escorts the nun from the hall. 'Rush them . . . rush them!' came one loud shout.

Fighting breaks out. Everyone, it seems, is engaged in what is now a full-scale riot, the wooden seats in the hall being broken up and used as batons by people to club each other.

Police whistles sound as uniformed men rush into the hall amidst what is now absolute pandemonium. Alarmed at what had been likely to happen, Hannah and her friend Mrs O'Neill had made to flee from the hall but are now caught up in the tremendous crush. It is too much for Hannah and she faints as they go through the exit door.

Hannah doesn't know where she is when she eventually comes round some two hours later. The room in which she is lying is strange to her and the first thing she notices is the wallpaper, immediately thinking how lovely it looks. It is an attractive blue colour with gold stars and white stripes. Then she looks upwards to see a porcelain crucifix with a holy water font below. She had one just like it, but smaller, in her little cabin back in Ireland. Above the crucifix there is a picture of the Sacred Heart. She tries to get up but almost screams with the pain coming from her injured ankle and elbow before falling back on the bed again.

Hannah then hears the comforting voice of a woman asking, 'Are you all right, dearie?' She asks where she is and the woman reassures her she is in safe hands and that she is Mrs Boyle, the wife of the Central Stores commissionaire who was also at the City Halls meeting that night. She tells Hannah that her husband suffered a head injury in the riot but managed to bring her home to their house in the Gorbals. Their son Terence has gone to tell the Morrisons at Castle Street, with whom Hannah lives, what has happened.

Mary Ann, the Boyles' daughter, who works at Templeton's Carpet Mills, comes in. Hannah says she didn't realise how many friends she has in Glasgow, at which Mrs Boyle replies, 'Ach now, God and His Holy Mother watch over the Irish. And what better would we want?'

When Terence Boyle tells the Morrisons about Hannah, Mrs Morrison comments to her husband about how considerate these Irish people are. She goes on to say that Nelly, her own daughter, would not have bothered going to tell anyone so quickly. Her husband agrees. 'You are quite right. The more I know about Irish people, the more I understand the great injustice that has been done to their character by those who had a purpose in belittling them.'

The doctor called to see Hannah diagnoses a severely bruised ankle and advises that she should be off work for about ten days. Just after he leaves, Maurice her friend comes to see her. His mother had also been injured in the City Halls mêlée and had suffered a bruised shin. She tells him a messenger came to the house from Central Stores with a note from Mr Pendleton saying how sorry he was to hear the news and that he hopes she will be well soon. After telling him about it, Hannah asks Maurice if he is sure that Pendleton is the rogue he thinks he is, the question making him comment on how anxious she seems to defend the man.

'Then why did Central Stores engage him if he is what you say he is?' she counters. Maurice gives a most surprising explanation to Hannah. It is because Central Stores, although staffed by Gentiles, is owned by Jews and Pendleton was one. 'They stick by each other at all costs. They don't care because Pendleton's offences were not against Jews. They were against Gentiles. And because of that it didn't matter. They accept him as one of them and can therefore be trusted.'

There's a knock at the door and Rupert Pendleton arrives at the house, comes into the room but doesn't look at Maurice. Maurice goes over to the Jew and stares him in the face saying, 'Do you remember me, George Rankine?' Pendleton says he does not and says his name is not Rankine. Maurice stares at him then says, 'There's a mistake somewhere,' then leaves the room. Hannah asks Pendleton if he knows Maurice; he says he has never seen him before.

The Boyles' house in the Gorbals is just a few hundred yards from St Francis's Chapel. Hannah enjoys her short stay there, for there's lots of other Irish people about. The house is over a shop and on a Saturday night they have a sing-song and a dance and an old Irishman comes in with a fiddle, but they behave themselves and set an example to the Protestant families living across the road. The Boyles ask if she would like to stay on at the house when she is better, but she says it would not be fair to the Morrisons and, anyway, Nelly, the Morrisons' daughter, has been going to benediction with her and she could even become a Catholic.

That's good news to Mrs Boyle who tells Hannah, 'So you are thinking of bringing in one of the lost sheep? Well, good luck to you. We could be doing with one or two more to make up for Sarah McGrath.'

Terence Boyle walks Nelly Morrison home because she stayed late visiting Hannah and it is too dark and dangerous to walk home alone. On the way they pass the old Duke Street jail and they get into a discussion about offenders, Terence saying they were not hanging so many people now in Scotland as they wanted to show the world that it had a clean record. 'Hardly anyone is sentenced to death now, unless they are Irish,' he says. Nelly goes silent at that and he has forgotten for a moment that she is a Scotch girl.

The story switches back to Pendleton. He is on foot in the west part of the city centre and on his way to a house in an exclusive part of St Vincent Street, just off North Street. At the time it is one of the most exclusive parts of the city, its house owners being the top professional people and, as the story goes, 'even royalty frequent the area'. Pendleton goes into one of the best houses, one of the most magnificent-looking in the street and even more so inside. He is met at the door by a footman in full livery costume, that including a spectacular red coat and yellow breeches. In the hall there's a beautiful chandelier and expensive oil paintings and a stair carpet made from the most highly priced Brussels, that being the best quality of heavy pile worsted carpet, firmly gripped to the broad staircase by elaborately fashioned stair rods shimmering like polished gold. It's all in stark contrast to Pendleton's own humble accommodation, two rooms which he rents at the YMCA building in Bothwell Street.

The footman leads him from the head of the stairs to a drawing-room in which wealth, luxury and affluence are all highly evident. Pendleton doesn't act like a guest or a visitor. On the contrary, he acts as though he belongs there. A man and a woman sit at the huge table in the room. Nathan Halterberg and his wife Rachel are typically Jewish in appearance and speech.

The man's short stubble and dark whiskers don't improve his dark complexion and aquiline nose. His expression is hard to describe; not exactly cunning but shifty. Mrs Halterberg is a splendid type of woman, physically so at any rate, with good features and large black eyes that are spoiled by thin, cruel-looking lips and an abandoned expression. Jewels sparkle on her arms and fingers and are even set in her hair. They greet Pendleton.

'Benny, my boy. You are late. Vat keeps you so much?' Their speech is dotted with such 'vats'. They then ask him, 'Vat success now?'

He says they will have to wait. 'The fish are a little shy and need careful angling,' he tells them. A woman called Sarah, his cousin, is smoking and appears to have been drinking, but needs more, telling them that she wants some champagne. Pendleton has other things on his mind and speaks to her about a ploy he has. He tells her about the Irish girl Hannah and her boyfriend Maurice and that he needs her help in order to put the girl off the boy. She could do this by infiltrating Maurice's family, spreading bad news about the girl. The woman Sarah says the plan seems a bit elaborate.

'I don't think so,' says Pendleton. 'I have a strong desire to show I can pull off a really difficult job and also gain a victory over the so-called virtue which the Catholic Church boasts as distinguishing her adherents from other Christians.' He is determined, he says, to show them that 'vice can overcome virtue'.

Hannah returns to work and Andrew Petrie tells her he heard

about her accident but didn't come to see her in the Gorbals as it is too Irish where she was staying and as he is an Orangeman it would have been too dangerous. She laughs at that, for, despite all his remarks about popery, he is quite friendly.

Life at Central Stores improves for Hannah. She is given a much better job and although it carries more responsibility it means she is less physically exhausted when she goes home at night.

At this point in the adventures of Hannah in Glasgow, the long serial moves into no less than supercharged overdrive, events tumbling out of the *Observer*'s pages at a breathtaking pace. And if you once again imagine it as that silent movie, the piano music would be rattling it out to keep up with the action.

Hannah's new post is in the clerical department at Central Stores and the crafty and, by this time, obviously evil Pendleton is quick off the mark, telling her that some accounts need urgent checking before the auditors arrive and because this needs to be done immediately she would need to come to his home and help him with the work! Hannah, and who would blame the innocent Irish lass, blushes at the suggestion, but nevertheless complies with what she accepts as a bona fide work order. Pendleton arranges for her to be taken by chauffeur-driven car to the house, not his own quarters in Bothwell Street, but instead to the sumptuous mansion he regularly visits in St Vincent Street. She is overwhelmed by its opulence. The two women, Aunt Rachel and Cousin Sarah, are there but leave them alone and to Hannah's great shock, as soon as the two leave the room, Pendleton, whose gall as well as his guile apparently knows no bounds, proposes marriage to Hannah with the confession that her beauty had completely fascinated him. Without hesitation she turns him down. Undeterred at her rejection, Pendleton, with a cruel grin, says that if that's the case, then he will force her to marry him.

In the meantime, Cousin Sarah has agreed to help with Pendleton's scheme and moves in with the Reilly family. She goes to a church fair where she meets Catherine, a sister of Maurice, and tells her that Hannah is not the girl for her brother. She was not being faithful to him and had been visiting a certain house in St Vincent Street and if she didn't believe her she would even take her along one night to see for herself.

Believing the woman, Catherine confronts Hannah with the story but is told by her that it is none of her business. Pendleton, becoming more evil by the minute, steps up the pressure in his attempts to blackmail the Irish girl into marrying him. He calls her to his office, where he tells her the auditors have discovered discrepancies in the books and that she could have made the responsible entries.

It's a very serious matter, he goes on, and the prospects are that she will be charged with misappropriating company funds amounting to £100. He further terrifies Hannah by outlining the consequences. As it can only be Hannah who did the deed, there will be charges and an appearance in court. Hannah is horrified at what she hears from him and gullibly asks if he thinks she is guilty. At that, Pendleton, the hardened sycophant and double-dealer, quails before her innocent gaze. But he still thinks his ruse will work and culminate with his bedding the young Irish girl. It's a most delicate situation, he says, and if he took her part it would appear as though he had condoned it. She asks again if he thinks she is guilty and he prevaricates. Hannah is now reduced to having to ask Pendleton for his help and he invites her to the house once more, where he now tells her the situation is even worse than was at first thought.

Hannah tells Mrs Boyle of her predicament and about Maurice breaking off their friendship after being told by his sister about Hannah's visits to the big house in St Vincent Street.

After leaving Mrs Boyle and worried sick about what might happen to her, she then returns to the mansion looking for some assurance about her future. The footman, as usual, shows her through to the huge lounge where Pendleton is on his own. Once more she asks if he thinks she will be convicted. He says nothing is surer. She then asks if he can prevent a prosecution. His reply to that is that she should make herself independent of Maurice and anyone else. How on earth can she do that, she asks. By marrying him, he says. Hannah tells him she thinks it is an outrage not only what he has done but what he has suggested. Pendleton storms from the room, leaving Hannah on her own. After waiting for a time, she then makes to leave the house but goes through the wrong door and finds herself in a storeroom in which there are lots of cases of jewellery and precious stones. One bag instantly comes to her attention, as she recognises its contents to be jewellery which she used to look after in her first job in Glasgow, at the Amplefold house in the West End. It dawns on her that the house is being used for handling stolen goods, so she grabs the box with Mrs Amplefold's jewels and quickly flees from the mansion.

When Pendleton discovers there's a missing bag he leaves a note at Hannah's house saying it must be returned or he will have her charged with burglary. Pendleton goes to see a disbarred Jewish lawyer called Myers at his scruffy office off the Gallowgate. Myers, struck off the lawyers' rolls because of his addiction to drink, then contacts Hannah and tells her that unless she hands back the jewellery within 24 hours Pendleton will tell the police she stole the gems from the Amplefolds in the first place. Hannah then goes to see Fr Joyce and tells him the whole story, saying that she would like to return to Ireland. 'Yes, go to Ireland by all means,' says the priest. 'For there the spirit of faith is to be found which, alas, seems to have entirely departed from this land once belonging to the family of Saint Peter.'

Hannah returns the stolen jewellery to the house in the West End and tells Mr Amplefold, the King's Counsel, how she came by them and also how she is now being threatened by Pendleton. Mr Amplefold says she will need to have an answer for the charges Pendleton is making. He tells her the date of the burglary at his house and it so happens Hannah says she has plenty of witnesses to prove where she was that night, for it was the evening of the City Halls event with the former nun Sarah McGrath. Mr Amplefold then says there will be no further problems and that he will personally deal with the man Pendleton.

The story ends there. Hannah's friend Nelly Morrison and her mother are both converted to Catholicism and after Hannah takes a short trip home to Cavan, where there is a reunion in the old-fashioned Irish way, the exile from Erin returns to Glasgow where Fr Joyce conducts a double wedding for her and her boyfriend Maurice and Nelly and her friend Terence. And there the story concludes, not precisely in the following terms but leaving little doubt that dear Hannah and her close friends live happily ever after.

Despite the flim-flam naïveté of the story of Hannah, the Exile from Erin, it was no fairy tale. The lengthy serialisation over many weeks in the Catholic paper did reflect attitudes of the day, one of the reasons it was so popular with readers. And those attitudes in the otherwise simple little tale reeked of intolerance, racism and bigotry. Just reflect on some of the breathtaking comments in the story.

The workmate who thought Hannah was too respectable-looking to be a Catholic; Maurice, the boyfriend, telling her that to be a Catholic in Glasgow was to be all that is vile and disreputable; Robert Burns being Scotland's only 'great man'; the Salvation Army general thinking it was high time they exposed 'some of Rome's wickedness'; the wealthy Jews with their cunning and shifty looks, cruel-looking lips and faltering English; the struck-off alcoholic lawyer with the Jewish name; and Pendleton's desire to gain a victory over what he calls 'the so-called virtue which the Catholic Church boasts as distinguishing her adherents from other Christians'.

Despite the fact that there are still some people around who hold some of those views, Glasgow is a much more tolerant city than it was in the days of Hannah Purcell and Rupert Pendleton. And we should all be thankful for that.

– CHAPTER 13 –

Spirited Companions

When we drink, we get drunk,
When we get drunk, we fall asleep;
When we fall asleep, we commit no sin,
When we commit no sin, we go to heaven.
So let's all get drunk and go to heaven!
                    – Old Irish Drinking Song

Of all the places in the world to which the Irish would be scattered, in nowhere else but Scotland could the natives match them in that favourite pursuit of theirs – drinking. For the first time ever, they were to find themselves in a community where the locals consumed more whisky than they did themselves. And that wasn't just the way it appeared, it really was a fact.

Whisky was the universal drink of Glasgow and Scotland, particularly since the early part of the nineteenth century, when the government had actually reduced the excise duty – no, it wasn't a magnificent gesture of benevolence, merely an endeavour to cut down on illicit whisky making! When the exodus from Ireland was at its height, the Sheriff of Lanarkshire made the observation that the people of Glasgow drank two or three times as much whisky as any other equivalent population in the world. In the years of the Great Famine, Scots on average were consuming over ten pints of whisky per annum, per head, more than the Irish. This was not so much due to a lack of desire on the part of the Irish, perhaps, but more a mark of the prosperity gulf between the two countries at the time. With the humblest of acknowledgements to Burns, freedom and whisky, and Scots and Irish, certainly went together.

As they were to discover, their new home town of Glasgow could be the liveliest of cities. Only those who knew what to expect from big city life, having perhaps been to Dublin or Belfast (and they were in the minority), would have experienced some of what was regularly witnessed in Scotland's fastest-growing community. The new arrivals from over the water might have been strangers on our shores, but they were to see that there was at least one bond they had in common with the natives – drink! There's a tendency in the twenty-first century to consider that the drink culture, which obviously abounds in Glasgow and throughout Scotland, has never been more prevalent. At times there's good reason to identify with that viewpoint, but there were also some wild and rip-roaring days around the years of the mid-nineteenth century when the Irish immigrants were flooding into Glasgow. All sorts of things, of course, can be read into statistics, which are a science of interpretation and appreciation as much as they are one of assimilation and compilation. But however they are viewed, the facts are that in those years of the immigrant rush more than 450 people were arrested every week in Glasgow for being drunk and disorderly and of the 570 who were jailed every week for various crimes, 480 of them were there for being in an unfit state through drink – and that was when the city had around a third of the population it has today.

The amount of spirits, mainly whisky of course, being knocked back was, in the mildest of terms, prodigious. Exceptional or extraordinary is probably closer to the mark once you get acquainted with the quantities consumed. The average intake of spirits throughout Britain per head at that time was around eight pints a year, or, to be accurate, eight pints less a couple of 'halfs'. Remember, that average was calculated from the whole population, drinkers and non-drinkers. In Ireland, on the other hand, it was 13 pints. Here in Scotland it was 23 pints. Taken as an average among imbibers alone, that would represent several pints of whisky per drinker, per week. Little wonder the city needed 2,200 spirit dealers – that's one for every 18 families – to cater for such a thirst.

None of the statistics, of course, include the substitute spirits to which many resorted, such as ether and laudanum. That's right, they actually drank the stuff for pleasure, if that's the right term. Ether was more popular in Ulster at the time, in fact it was regarded as something of an Ulster phenomenon, particularly in and around the towns of Pettigo, Strabane, Dungiven, Toomebridge, Portadown, Cookstown and Draperstown, where they reckoned around 50,000 (that was one in eight of the population in the area around these towns) were hooked on this bizarre concoction, more associated with a hospital haze than happy days. Local historians say 'the aythur' craze all began when a Dr Kelly from Draperstown, a man who loved his drink, was swept up by the active temperance movement of the time and rashly took the pledge. There would be no more alcohol for him, he swore. Within days he was desperately missing his kicks, although he was still determined to keep the pledge. He knew that ether taken in a specific fashion could bring that certain smile to your face, and he began experimenting. Taking a snifter of ether is not exactly like downing one of whisky. The problem is that the ether tends to quickly turn to gas on contact with the mouth, but the bold doctor soon found a way round that by taking a little at a time, about an eggcupful, and quickly following it up with a chaser of ordinary water. The kicks came immediately, putting a whole new meaning on the expression high spirits! The downside was that being the kind of highly volatile stuff ether is, you had to make sure you didn't light up a smoke for a while, or belch too deeply near any flames, or else you would be doing the kind of act normally associated with the circus! Despite such dangers, it became so popular that some local shebeens in the area sold nothing else, the London *Times* even reporting in 1871 that 'market days in some of these Ulster towns no longer smelt of pigs, tobacco smoke or unwashed human beings, but of ether'.

So, why ether? Blame the government, said its drinkers. A new tax had been imposed on legitimate spirits, resulting in a clampdown by police on home-distilled whisky. London was interfering in Irish ways again. Vile as it was, ether became an acceptable and popular alternative.

Laudanum was its equivalent in Glasgow. It was an equally weird – and just as foul – substitute for the pleasures that the real stuff supplied. Although popular among a certain set in Glasgow, it was more widely used throughout Britain than ether. The laudanum drink was made from a mixture of opium derivatives and alcohol. Like ether, it was officially used for medicinal purposes, mainly in the relief of pain, and used to feature as one of the essentials of the family medicine chest, alongside iodine, methylated spirits and castor-oil. Basic drinkers appreciated laudanum because it was cheaper than whisky unless, that is, you were one of the writers and poets who took to it (it was an 'in' drink with many of them) and would mix the opium with some fine brandy. Like ether too, it had its dangers, although you could burp and smoke without becoming a human flame-thrower. When over-indulging, laudanum had some terrible side-effects, such as dizziness, an unusually flushed face, severe stomach pains, constipation and depression. And all for the sake of a drink!

The use and consumption of whisky in Scotland at the time was as endemic as it was prolific. You came across it, so it seemed, at every turn of life. If someone did a job for you, he would expect a 'half' as a tip. When you told a barmaid to have one herself, she didn't just put the money in the jar, she had her 'half' there and then. Roundsmen delivering bread, coal and meat could always anticipate a nip if their supplies were generously measured; the more generous, the bigger the nip. It was whisky galore, and no one was trying to hide it.

Glasgow City Council was having so many problems with females being apprehended for inebriation that it was to purchase a large home in Ayrshire for conversion to a reformatory specially for what they termed 'degraded, drunken women'. Later, it was even to consider plans to send males also fitting that description to a remote Hebridean island – a sort of alcoholics' Alcatraz. A former inspector general of the Royal Irish Constabulary on a visit to Glasgow at the time was bowled over by the amount of people that he noted were having some difficulty walking in a straight line. He commented: 'In no city in Europe, the US or Canada I have visited did I see such a number of drunk persons.' He had obviously been witnessing some of the 10,000 who the Sheriff of Glasgow and Lanarkshire had estimated were drunk on a Saturday, who remained that way all Sunday and were still half-cut when they turned up for work on a Monday morning. Glasgow was definitely one of the liveliest of cities in those days!

A writer at the time who used the pen-name of 'Shadow' regularly wandered the city streets on those nights, recording for his booklets some of the images of the day. The number of public houses somewhat staggered him. In some streets, he wrote, it appeared that almost every shop, one after another the whole length of the street, was a public house. 'It's as if the authorities had licensed them all out of a gigantic pepper-box, sending them all broadcast over the city, in accordance with the popular adage, 'the more the merrier'. 'If every pub had been given a spire,' he went on, 'Glasgow would be the most beautiful city in the world.'

The pubs didn't have spires, but they did have large clienteles and they did much to show the face of Glasgow in that age. It wasn't the prettiest of sights, although it would be nice to think otherwise. Let's face it, when an average of 65 people were being taken in every day by the police for being drunk in the rather small city centre of the time, and when a senior law official reckoned weekends saw 10,000 drunks on the streets, just imagine what the general tenor of behaviour was back in those days in Glasgow!

Drunkenness was rife, and drunks lying in the gutters a common sight. Robbers would relieve them of whatever was left of their possessions. Drunken quarrels between acquaintances and among families were a regular sight, as was children being publicly thrashed or otherwise mistreated by parents or other adults. The crudest behaviour prevailed on the streets. If there was a public flogging, or hanging, the general public would gleefully flock to see it in their thousands, as bevvied as they would be celebrating the Fair.

The *Glasgow Herald* sent one of its reporters at the time for a walk along Saltmarket and the Briggait to take in the scene. Again, 'lively' seems to be how he found things. The streets were thronging, as he put it, with evening strollers, described as 'shoving, pushing and boring people'. They were also packed with horse cabs, fish barrows and donkey carts, with all sorts of hucksters selling all sorts of things: fish, oranges, cheese, handkerchiefs and 'Brummagen' razors.

> There's a man bellowing out on the Irish pipes and an old blind fiddler scraping away at a tune which sounds a bit like 'Rory O'More'. Oyster shops, their gaslights blazing and the low eating houses they call tripe shops with their 'indescribable and overpowering smells'. The public houses are doing a roaring trade and there's much shouting and angry roaring. When the hour of 11 arrives [pub closing time] men and women are rowing, swearing, screaming and laughing and every now and then one collapses into the gutter. Boys and girls are screaming out songs they have just learned in the public houses.

The reporter appears to have been horrified at everything he observed, commenting on how little regard there appeared to be for what he termed 'decency and decorum from the sickening saturnalia'.

The *Herald* man goes on:

> With the bustle of everyday life at its throngest, when all classes are pushing along intent only on their own business, the good and the bad, the respectable and the rough, shouldering each other for a share on the

footpath, can you form any conception of what they are like when the wheat has been separated from the chaff? A graphic sketch of the conditions around the High Street, Saltmarket, Bridgegate and Trongate, between the hours of midnight on Saturday and six o'clock on Sunday morning would astonish many of our featherbed philanthropists who devote so much thought into bettering the conditions of Australian savages.

So there! Those rough and ready hordes he came across that night had obviously made a lasting impression on the *Herald* man. He wasn't the only journalist to come up against the edgier side of Glasgow. One of them, a *Daily Mail* writer, concentrated specifically on what he termed 'the rough'. We call them louts, yobs, hooligans and other things today. Then it was merely 'the Glasgow rough'. On his wanderings one weekend night in the city centre in the 1860s he carefully noted the groups of them congregating in the city centre near Glasgow Cross. He knew it was them before he saw them, their loud, raucous and vulgar cries filled the street before they came into sight.

The young men were easy to spot, the journalist wrote, being distinguished in general by:

> . . . a close-cropped head over which a cap, drawn pretty well back, giving him a slouching aspect to his whole person, his face, white and flabby in appearance and indelibly coarse in expression, is closely shaven, and a dirty white woollen scarf envelops his neck which boasts of no such ornament as a collar; a frieze coat generally unbuttoned with the collar drawn up around his ears, a pair of corduroys

and thick-set, ill-shapen Bluchers [old-style shoes, their laces tied over large tongues] complete his costume. You generally find him lounging with his hands in his pockets about the mouths of the low closes. At midnight, however, these ones wake up and become lively, they congregate in knots in the middle and corner of the streets, generally accompanied by their female companions. From these knots of men and women you will hear laughter, loud and coarse, obscene jests, oaths and curses. They only move when a policeman comes on the scene or a drunk passes, upon which they will pounce and either rob him or a girl will lead him off to one of the local dens. The streets are like rabbit warrens and the garrotters, burglars, pickpockets, prostitutes and other criminals have no problem in escaping in them.

At that point the man from the *Mail* was accosted by prostitutes, one telling him she had 24 previous convictions. The roving reporter had had enough of the 'rough', and without even making an excuse he left the scene and concluded his report.

There were, of course, certain times of the year when describing the city as being lively would be putting it in the mildest of terms. The Glasgow Fair was one of them. Everybody celebrated the great summer occasion, which was virtually the only decent holiday break of the year. For some it meant an entire week off work, although for the majority it was merely a long weekend to enjoy what there was of the social scene, perhaps one of the theatre shows that were on at the time, or the carnival on Glasgow Green. 'Come and see Batty's Royal Menagerie' proclaimed the big colourful posters pasted around the city. 'The baby elephant is the only one ever exhibited in

Europe and as seen by Her Majesty the Queen and the Royal Family at the Royal Zoological Gardens!' Others would crowd aboard one of the dozens of steamers plying the ever-popular day and weekend excursions to any destination that had a pier and, for the occasion, those places seemed as far off and inviting as the Costa Exoticas of much later times.

The Clyde had rarely been as busy as it was during the Glasgow Fair of 1861. It was at the height of the immigrant inflow and as hundreds of little steamers struggled up the Clyde with their incredible loads of those who would become the city's new residents, they were passed in the opposite direction by other little steamers heading out on 'doon-the-watter' cruises, also packed with people, although nothing like the standing-room-only of those arriving from Ireland. It's not just a cliché to associate the Glasgow Fair with the worst of the summer weather – the two really do coincide quite a lot. They did that summer of 1861 when intrepid newspaper reporters were once more out writing about how the 'rough', and the not-so-rough, were enjoying their much-anticipated mid-July break. They were undeterred by the grimmest of wet weather – well, you have to be if you really want to enjoy life in the west of Scotland – and the crowds had been there at the Broomielaw from early morning, determined to enjoy what they could of their holiday despite the downpour. And what a downpour it was. The *Glasgow Herald* man described that Fair Friday's weather as 'bleak, churlish and sunless'. The rain was continuous, falling in torrents and putting a right damper on the 200,000 who were out to relish their annual holiday.

After the amount of rain that had fallen on the Friday, they had anticipated better things for the Saturday, but as it was to turn out, it was another day of the same. Thirty-eight steamers had sailed out from the Broomielaw to all the usual Clyde estuary points, although because of the weather they were not so packed as they usually were at such a time. Nevertheless, cheered by the accompaniment of the little ships' orchestras – a melodeon, fiddle and drums trio – merrily beating out their favourite Scottish foot-tappers, those hardy and optimistic trippers ventured on their holiday cruises hoping for the best. What they got, it appears, was the worst . . . the very, very worst. The *Herald*'s man was there to count them all out, and again to count them all back in, and it was the latter stage he vividly described.

> It was most lamentable to see the plight of the number of people on returning to harbour after enduring the tribulations of a day in the wind and rain. The finery of the females, poor things, was utterly demolished; frills and lappets [small pieces of decorative lace] which were once neat and tidy were plastered to their necks and bosoms like wet dishcloth; their hats acted like sponges, perpetually distilling rainwater onto their dishevelled hair. The male part of the holiday folk were in a similar mess; they were steeped in dirty rainwater from their noses to their feet. As for parents, say with half a dozen little responsibilities, they looked miserable to the extreme. Not a few of them had taken refuge in drink and wore the wild expression and countenance of those who deem themselves both injured and insulted and are determined on satisfaction.

Few have described the Glasgow inebriate in more appropriate terms than that. His report continued:

Towards the evening the whisky began to operate and the aspect of the street became more Irish and less nice! Groups of excited men were fighting here and there; scores were zig-zagging along in tipsy exaltation and no small number of human forms lay in the gutter in a state of sweet beatitude, unconscious of whether they were reclining on the pavement or on a bed of down. Policemen and porters were literally worked beyond endurance in trundling these disgusting brutes off the streets; and perhaps the police officer never had before such a mass of drinking incapables. Relatives came seeking their belated friends during the night, but identification was almost impossible until the fuddled visage was placed under a [water] pump for it was so encrusted with mud that the mother had no small difficulty in recognising her own son. In fact, scores of them lay in 'glaury' state . . . so completely transmogrified in external appearance that they looked much more like men crusted in mud than enclosed in ordinary clothes. Altogether Saturday night was the roughest night experienced in Glasgow for a long time. Those who were visibly drunk or required help amounted to a few hundreds. Surprisingly, there were no assaults which required the help of the surgeon!

So this was the kind of Glasgow into which the immigrant flood poured. If it was thought of as lively before, it certainly became even livelier with the presence of these new arrivals. For, despite those statistics showing the Scot to consume much more spirits than his Irish counterpart, it certainly didn't seem that way when the newcomers set about their jars. At one time in Dublin there had been a public house for every five dwelling houses in the city.

The Irish and their drink were as synonymous as the Scots with theirs.

Mark Twain once said: 'Give an Irishman lager for a month and he's a dead man. An Irishman is lined with copper, and the beer corrodes it. But whisky polishes the copper and is the saving of him.'

There was a lot of that copper polishing to be done when they settled in their new land.

– CHAPTER 14 –

Jar Jars and Jaw Jaws

Only solitary men know the full joys of friendship.
Others have their family; but to a solitary and an exile
his friends are everything.
From *Shadows on the Rock*, Willa Sibert Cather
1873–1947

When a hard day's darg is over, what better way to spend a night than with your fellow countrymen, jar jarring and jaw jawing? We are back in the days when a pub didn't have to smother itself in green, deck itself in harps and shamrocks, adorn the front window with bales of straw, a scythe and an old paraffin lamp, and give itself a name including 'Paddy' or 'Jinty', or something unpronounceable in Erse, for it to be clear that it was an Irish pub. Back in the days of migration, Irish pubs in Glasgow really *were* Irish pubs. They looked like pubs did in Donegal, Skibbereen and Sligo. They sounded like them, smelt like them, and their customers jarred and jawed and jostled in them just like they had in the villages they'd left behind.

Many of these pubs did have Irish names, of course – real Irish names, which belonged to their owners, who were real Irish people. In the Gorbals, for instance, where most of these pubs were located, there was Molloy's, McNulty's, McKenna's, McCondach's and Beacom's, Doyle's, Finnigan's Roper's, Sweeney's, Quinn's and Rosie's, as well as others with names that left little doubt over their nationality: The Emerald Isle, The Bhoreen, The Kildonan, The Mally Arms, The Turf and the Pig 'n' Whistle, to name but a few.

Their clientele's conversation would invariably turn to those places they had left behind and the poverty and privation, hunger and hardship they had known there. Yet there was no place on earth for which they held greater affection, for it was home, and despite the harsh reality of life in Ireland, it was still the dearest place in their hearts. As the black stuff flowed, the dearer it became. The night would wear on, and when they had rid themselves of their troubles – their work shifts, gaffers, wages, digs and aches and pains – the conversation would inevitably drift to the ould place, the ould customs and the ould times – and they were always the *great* ould times. There was no stopping them once their minds were back in the old days, in those fondly remembered places.

Let us eavesdrop on a group of Irish workers on a typical Friday pay night back in the early 1950s in Molloy's, at the corner of Oxford and Coburg Streets, in the Gorbals, crowded to the doors, as it would have been every week. The subject of their conversation mainly centres on happier times back home, times associated with communal events such as weddings and dances . . . and funerals. Wakes were counted as being among the best of the good old times.

They're a mixed bunch, mainly from Mayo and Donegal. One of the men is from a wee place called Doochary, which nestles beneath the Derryveagh Mountains in Donegal. He talks about some of the great weddings he attended there:

'Sure, at our village weddings what we did was we would dance and drink and drink and dance, and when you couldn't do any more of either you would go home and get yourself a sleep, and when you had done that, you got right back to the wedding celebrations again and got on with the drinking and the dancing. As long as there was still some poteen or stout in the barrel, you just kept going. It would be like that for two or three days, at least.'

There is no stopping them once they've started the fond ramble down those happy Memory Lanes. The Doochary local has gone on to describe some of the tricks he and the other lads got up to at weddings:

'If it was a wedding in the summertime there would be some larking, I'm telling you. We would be out there looking for those wee ants that you would get all over the place on the warm days. Little red things that used to give you the most awful bite. The idea was to see if you could fill a whole jar with them, then let them loose during the celebrations and watch the havoc they created! There was one time, and mind, it wasn't me that did it, that one of the fellas got a jar full of them and did he not sneak his way into the newly-weds' bedroom and put them between the sheets, then go round telling everyone what he'd done. That night they all gathered round their wee cottage for their first night together. You know, I can still hear the screams of the pair as those wee red devils started their biting.'

A fellow from Rosturk in Mayo chips in to say that he used to be a strawboy on wedding days. None of the others have heard of such a thing, so he explains that it's a special custom in his part of the country. 'Went right back to the real ould days,' he says, 'so far back they said it was in the dark ages that it started.

We would just turn up at weddings, as uninvited guests, like. There would be nine of us and we would all get decked out in these queer costumes, women's petticoats or ones made of straw and men's long johns and things like that. We would be disguised with masks and wearing these big straw hats, cone-shaped things that came down over the head and face and rested on the shoulders. They said we were like the mummers they have in other countries that did the same thing at weddings there. Anyway, we used to take a big long pole with us and after doing a dance outside the wedding, we would poke it through the door with a note pinned to the end of it, just four words: "Send out a drink." They always did. Usually a couple of ould characters, a village biddy and her ould man, would tag along wi' us. They would dress up as well and get up to all sorts of antics outside the wedding house, play tricks and the like. Like us, they would never say no to sharing in the wedding drink . . .'

Another man from Mayo joins in. He too remembers the strawboys at weddings. 'And another thing,' he says, 'You never got married on a Friday in Mayo. You always went for a Wednesday if you could, for that was the luckiest day. There's a poem about it: "Monday for health, Tuesday for wealth, Wednesday the best day of all; Thursday for losses, Friday for crosses and Saturday no day at all."

'Did any of you go to the matchmaker for a wife?' he asks suddenly.

Before anyone has the chance to answer him his brother adds: 'We had a matchmaker in our village. There was another one up the road as well. Och, they were all over the place back then, old boys that had never made it to the altar themselves. They made it their business to know who was who in your area. If you were after a woman and were out of your element at meeting them, like a lot of our fellahs were, the matchmaker was your man.

Sometimes he could fix you up in a couple of weeks. It depended on whether you had a good bit of land, well stocked and that, and it was easier still if you didn't have an old mother or father that had to be lived with. If you did, then he'd probably have to go round a few women before he got one who would agree to that. There could be complications too, if the women's parents wanted their say, for they would be wanting to talk about a dowry.'

The man sitting next to him, yet another of the Mayo party, is celebrated for his collection of pithy Irish sayings. Although he listens intently to their conversations, his only contribution is to pull one of these out of the hat at appropriate times. That's why they call him Proverbial Pat, whatever the subject, Pat has a proverb for it. And he has been waiting for the chance to say something after all the talk about weddings and marriages. 'Aye, and you know what the man said when his wife died after a lifetime of marriage,' he says now. '"Never make a toil of pleasure," he said, as he dug the grave only three feet deep.'

They are still roaring with laughter at that when another round of the black stuff arrives and the conversation takes a change of course, from weddings to funerals. There are nods of agreement when a Donegal man says that he enjoyed them, or at least the wakes, even better than weddings at home. But before the wake came the centuries-old ritual of the 'keena', when the mourners entered the house of the deceased, approached the coffin and bent over it, praising the departed. The eulogies would often be accompanied by a complimentary anecdote or two, simple little tales like the time they had been a great help fixing up a house, or had taken the mourner's side in a scrap. The others, standing around listening, would clap their hands at the stories. When they were all finished, the whiskey, snuff and tobacco would be taken out and everyone would enjoy a glass.

The older ones, including the women, would pass round a clay pipe, filled with walnut plug by a member of the household. Afterwards there would be strong sweet tea and sandwiches, interspersed with roll-up cigarettes, passed around on plates. It was recognised that that was what some of them were there for: a good snifter, a smoke and their fill of tea and bread.

'Three bad habits,' breaks in Proverbial Pat, 'drinking the glass, smoking the pipe and scattering the dew late at night.' At that he takes another big draught of his Guinness, looking straight ahead as he waits for the next turn of conversation.

'You talk about your matchmakers!' someone starts. 'Why, there was no better place to meet the girls than at a good wake. There would be the ould fellah lying there in his coffin with his rosary between his fingers and all us young ones smoking like chimneys, the girls all sitting on the boys' knees and flirting away.'

One of the Mayo men claims that the wakes they had back home were better than the ones in Donegal, which tended to be a bit sombre. 'We had more games than youse at our wakes. There was no end to them: Hart-a-brog, Priest of the Parish, Sitting Brogue, Frimsy Framsy, Silly Ould Man, Webs and Forfeits – and that was just some of them.'

Some of his companions haven't heard of those games before, so he explains how some of them were played back home. 'Well, what you did in Sitting Brogue was sit on the ground in a circle holding your knees up and you would get an old shoe and pass it to one another beneath their knees. Somebody is picked to be in the middle of the circle and has to try and catch it as the shoe gets passed around from one player to another. The one they manage to catch it from takes their place.

'You got the best laugh, though, in Forfeits, especially if one of the lassies loses and for her forfeit had to kiss some ould slobbering Jake in his 80s that struggles to keep his clay pipe in his mouth!

'The priests were always complaining about our games, but as soon as they went away we'd start up the really good ones, like Frimsy Framsy. Now there was a game! We would all chant to the person that was nominated for the chair, "Frimsy Framsy, who is your fancy?" Whoever the person in the chair chose had to go up and give them a kiss. Then that person took the chair and somebody else got nominated and kissed. I'm telling you, you can forget all about your matchmakers after a night of playing Frimsy Framsy! It got that bad in our parish that the priests went around banning all the games at wakes, but if you stayed around long enough someone was bound to start them up again once the churchmen were all home in bed.'

Pat can't let the subject of the wakes go past without one of his sayings, and when there is at last a gap in the tales about the wakes, he has his little piece ready. 'To be sure, it's no time to be going for the doctor when the patient is dead.' The group of men looks puzzled as they contemplate that one, but only for a few seconds. Soon they are off again, this time on the subject of those priests and their watchful eyes. It reminds a man from Limerick about the dances in his little village.

'We never had a hall or anything like that for our dances and had them instead in whoever's house was big enough to let a couple of dozen of us in for a night's birling. They would be organised by a couple of touring musicians, a fiddler and an accordionist, well that would be all there would be room for, and away we went for a great old night, with the older ones having a game of cards at the interval and a raffle at the end of the night. You always got a laugh at the raffle when they announced the prize. Somebody's old donkey would keep turning up time after time, the previous winners not having bothered to collect it. The priest used to come and warn us about the dances where you held your partner too close. The "intimacy of the embrace", as he put it, was sinful. We would all dance right prim and proper while he was there. Then when he left we would all have his "intimacy of the embrace"! We used to have a whole chain of these house dances, a different one every night for a fortnight with the same musicians doing them all, collecting their fees at the end of the fortnight, shouting out each person's name as they went up to hand over their money. It was only a few pennies from each of us, but it was enough to keep them happy. But oh, the nights I remember loitering about after the dance, hoping there would be a girl waiting to be walked home ... And wasn't it always the night when you did meet a girl that the priest would be on his patrol looking for courting couples and chasing them away! Ach, but bless him, he was a fine man.'

Priests! What better subject for a proverb from Pat; he has a whole collection of them on the men in black, even one on the very topic of how watchful they can be: 'Three with the best sight,' he says, pausing to make sure he has everyone's attention before going on. 'The eye of a blacksmith on a nail. The eye of a young girl at a contest. And the eye of a priest on his parish.'

That isn't the end of the conversation. Another of the men from Mayo, this time from a village just outside Claremorris at the far end of the Plains of Mayo, begins to talk about the difficulty he had in learning his catechism. 'Our priest was a right fierce old bugger,' he says. 'You know what? He tried to make me learn that book wi' the catechism backwards because it had taken me more than a month to learn it the right way. He warned me that if I couldn't answer all the Bishop's questions on it, I would be put out of the chapel in disgrace. That's when he said to me, "There's only one thing for it, boy, and that's to learn the book backwards." I ended up I didn't know if I was coming or going wi' the thing. I think that's what put me off reading for life, so it was. D'ye know, I've never read a thing since. Except the racing pages.'

'We had one just as bad,' says the man from Rosturk. 'Used to make a point of reading out loud in chapel how much money people were putting in at the Easter and Christmas collections and the less ye put in, the louder he would say yer name. By the time he got to the ones who had only put in a copper or two, he'd be bawling their names out. He was the manager at our school as well and see if ye really got in his bad books, like I did a few times, he'd threaten to send ye to Artane, Letterfrack and the like, ye know . . . the industrial schools.'

One of the men has never heard of the industrial schools. 'You spent too much time up in the MacGillycuddy's Reeks,' he is told before the schools are described to him by a man from Gweedore in Donegal, who speaks now for the first time all night. 'They were like reform schools, for the bad boys. Well, that was what they were supposed to be, but a' the time they were full of poor orphans. Bloody shame for them, so it was.'

The man from Doochary in Donegal, the one who described the wedding in his village, tells the rest that his brother Seamus had been in an industrial school for stealing potatoes. 'It was just half a bag of thumpers to help out mother when she hadnae a thing to put in the dinner pot. But the potatoes were for the priest's house and they caught him red-handed, and because there had been that many of them lifted, Seamus got the blame. So they had him sent away . . . My God, the stories our Seamus told us about that place. It was run by the Christian Brothers and when they got a leathering, they would make the boys stick their head out of a window before pulling it down on their necks to hold them in place. And do ye know what they did wi' the boys that wet their beds? They called them "sailors" and made them parade wi' their wet sheets in front of the whole school in the morning before taking them to the laundry. If they did it again, they would make them run around wi' the wet sheets o'er their heads in front of everybody till they dried out.'

'Talkin' about wettin' yersel,' says a big lean man called Declan, who comes from the townland of Carnamoyle, six miles outside Derry and within sight of Lough Foyle. 'That reminds me of an ould uncle of mine. Cathal Lynch was his name. He lived up by Glentocher in Inishowen. D'ye know, he would save his pee and put it in a sheep's bag, then hing it up the chimney above the turf [peat] fire. He would keep it there till all the pee had dried out, then he'd cut the bag down and grind it all up till it was like a paste. Then he put it in ould jam jars and went round selling it for curing the baldness. He'd sell it to men that had good heads of hair too, telling them it would stop them losing what they had. He swore that because of his magic paste, as he called it, there wasn't a bald man in the area. Sure enough, I never remember seeing one there!'

Pat has to come in here. He looks around the group as if he's about to make some kind of pronouncement. 'What butter or whisky will not cure, there's no cure for.' That gives the boys their longest moment of contemplation yet.

The mention of the turf fire in the house of Cathal Lynch has the man sitting next to Declan, like him from Donegal, reminiscing about the days up the hill above his wee cottage cutting the turf. 'We'd dae a week really hard at it cutting the turf, a gang of us like, and we could bring back enough to keep three wee houses going for the rest of the year. But it's the smell o' it I miss. Yon really oily turf that would burn that slow, one big piece would dae ye for the night. And the heat it gave off as well! We used to bring back bog timber wi' the turf. You'll no' know about that stuff unless you've been cutting the turf. It's the oldest wood in the world, they say. Been in the bogs since the time of the Ark. D'ye know, it's that hard you couldn't knock a nail into it. We used it for making furniture and for the roof of the house. But by gees, it wouldn't half make you sweat when you were sawing it up.'

The mention of old Uncle Cathal's weird cure for baldness gets them onto talking about the great storytellers their villages had, ancient folklore medicines and cures being one of their favourite subjects. And they are hardly into the subject when Pat is telling them, 'Time itself is a good storyteller.' They let that one pass.

The village storytellers of whom they are talking were invariably the oldest members of a village, who had made a habit of listening to, noting and remembering the tales of those older than themselves.

They would retain every little scrap of all the tales they had heard, mentally filing each story, every little crumb of information. The stories of each generation would be added to the one before that, and the one before that, and before that again, each of them becoming part of a living library of the history of Ireland. There were many of them who had never in their lives read a newspaper or book, yet could enthral a cottage audience for an entire evening with their stories of past times. Some could take their collective tales back to the most distant history. There were those whose wonderful stories went back even to the days of the Vikings, days of the *'fad fado'* as they called it, something similar to the Aboriginal's Dreamtime.

But there was nothing they enjoyed more than having a jaw jaw about their aches and pains, and the remedies for them. Doctors were for the rich, but the traditional medicines were for everyone, and over the ages in villages and townlands the old ones had fostered and harboured them as sacredly as they would the family Bible – and few things were more precious than that.

A man from Limerick belches loudly and announces that he is plagued with indigestion and will be for the rest of the night. He is having terrible problems with 'the wind'.

'Michael, have you tried the milk and soot?' asks one of the Mayo group. 'Works like a gift from the fairies themselves. My old mother put me on it when I was just a lad and couldn't stop rifting.' None of the others have heard of this cure, so he explains, 'You get a couple of big soup spoons of it, the soot, that is. Make sure it's the fine stuff, the finer the better. Then you mix it wi' a half pint of milk, drink it straight down and it absorbs all the gas in your belly. Cured me,' he said.

'Nae wonder yer teeth are black!' jokes his neighbour. Everyone laughs at that.

They laugh again, in amazement this time, when the subject of baldness comes up once more. One of the them says in all seriousness that he had been going bald until he used the cure of a farmer he had worked for in County Clare. 'You should have seen the head of hair that man had. Like Samson himself, so he was. And d'ye know what he did? He buried a whole jar of worms in the dung midden. Left it for a month, so he did. Then he took it out and rubbed it on his scalp. He had me do it, and youse can see for yerselves.' He bows his head to show his full head of hair.

'Put yer bunnet back on, Dan,' his pals say, 'or that wormy heid of yours will put us aff the drink.'

They go through a variety of their favourite cures before getting on to the subject of piles. It is the man from Rosturk again who has the best cure of all for them. It was handed down to him by his great-granny, no less, and she had told him that she'd got it from her own great-granny. 'She collected the roots of wild buttercups, ground them all up, and after boiling them till they were soft, mixed them with lard and stored the paste away in an old jar. It would last right through the year until the buttercups came again. If it ever ran out and someone had the piles, she had another remedy, and that was a poultice of boiled onions.'

'Bring tears to yer eyes that one,' the Doochary man says and roars with laughter.

'Aye,' adds one of the Mayo boys, 'but that's nothing compared to what it does to yer arse!'

The joke reminds one of them that where he comes from, up in the wilds of Loughsalt Mountain in Donegal, there was an old fellow who swore there was only one cure for piles: 'He would burn this ould bit of tarry rope in a bucket and when the smoke was coming from it like it was a chimney on fire, he would make them sit on it till the bluidy smoke was coming out o' their ears. Nane of them ever complained about the piles after that.'

None of them can come up with a more fanciful tale than that one. Not even Proverbial Pat.

– CHAPTER 15 –

The Glasgow Shinners

They came with all their baggage. Goodfellas and badfellas. And girls and families. It was the full spectrum of an entire population, and they had their own views on things. And being Irish, they also had no hesitation in airing them. They might have left Ireland, but they had not left their Irishness. Nor would they ever.

Men and women in exile feed on dreams of various kinds and one of the fondest desires of the Glasgow Irish was for the independence of the land that they or their ancestors had left. To that end they were to give support to those who campaigned for it, by democratic means or not. In the years before and after the First World War, they included the most virulent of campaigners, the supporters of Sinn Fein and the Irish Republican Brotherhood, a forerunner of the IRA. There was a different ring to such names in those days; they conveyed a romantic image of freedom

311

fighters rather than the vicious and ruthless bombers of recent times. Blowing up innocents in packed pubs, restaurants and department stores, or wee boys in Warrington, was not on the agenda. This partly explains why they gained far more support in Glasgow and central Scotland in earlier years, such as the 1920s, than in later campaigns. In turn, it also partly explains how the sensational events in this chapter came about.

When the Irish immigrants first arrived, their own immediate needs and family priorities were all that mattered. They had to get work, find accommodation and get their children nourished, schooled and try to plan some kind of future. Then, and only then, would there be time to think about other things. They were away from Ireland now, but that didn't make them any less Irish. Of all nations, who is less likely to dispense with their sentiments for the land of their birth, and that of their ancestors, than those from the Emerald Isle?

By the end of the First World War, most of the post-Great Famine wave of immigrants had been in Glasgow for nearly half a century, for most of them those first priorities had been met. There could now, perhaps, be more time for consideration of the state of affairs in that country they still thought of as home and that still held the dearest place in their hearts. They say no man can be a patriot on an empty stomach, but now that the hungriest days were over, the flames of patriotism could be rekindled.

During the latter part of the nineteenth century, when the independence movement in Ireland was going through an active and stormy period, there were bomb attacks in mainland Britain. Scotland was not exempt from these; there was a flurry of minor terrorist activity by members of the Glasgow branch of the Irish Republican Brotherhood. These included bomb attempts on the Tradeston gasworks, the Buchanan Street railway goods station, the Ruchill canal bridge and two gasometers at Dawsholm, resulting in a number of casualties. That turbulent period passed, however, and there was little activity for a number of years afterwards.

In 1920, just three years after the end of the Great War, that most terrible of conflicts, they were talking of war yet again, but not the trench warfare with tanks and wholesale slaughter that had been known in France and Belgium. The struggle that was all the talk now was on a smaller scale, but it was still war and there would be death and destruction, just as there would be great controversy, concern, dispute, debate . . . and taking sides. Just whose side do you take when one of the countries engaged in a war is the land in which you took your very first steps, the birthplace of your parents and your forebears – and the opposing country is your adopted one, albeit one of necessity? The answer may seem obvious, but there would be days of great consternation ahead for the Glasgow Irish.

Ireland in 1920 was as troubled as ever, with talk of impending war and bloodshed. The migrants had left an Ireland that was part – the very oldest part – of the great British Empire. But the chains were slowly (tortuously slowly) being loosened. The aim was independence and support for it had now reached new levels. In the 1918 General Election, the party known as Sinn Fein (which means 'Ourselves') had become the major force in the Irish Assembly, the Dáil. Sinn Fein's cause, its very reason for existence, was independence, and it had won 73 out of the 105 Irish constituencies. The grimmest of showdowns was on the horizon. Recruits, known as Volunteers, were flocking to join the military wing of the party, a collective of potential insurgents unofficially known as the Irish Republican Army (IRA). The British refused to acknowledge the rag-tag Volunteers in this way and would refer to them only as Sinn Feiners or 'Shinners'.

If they were not to be given their independence by democratic means, then the IRA would pursue it by other methods, and they launched a guerrilla campaign against those they saw as their colonial occupiers. Their immediate targets were the British army and the police, whose force was known at the time as the Royal Irish Constabulary (RIC).

The insurgents concentrated their campaign on a series of deadly ambushes of patrolling soldiers and policemen, and there was a horrific spate of these and other killings throughout the country. Ireland was in the ugliest of moods. The scale of guerrilla activity was so bad that the Royal Irish Constabulary couldn't cope with the number of attacks on them and urgently pleaded London for more men. The British responded with the establishment of recruiting offices on the mainland to enlist men for the RIC, their special assignment being to take on this new Irish Republican Army. With post-war unemployment figures soaring, there was no shortage of men willing to become one of this new breed of Irish policemen, some 7,000 joining up in the first few months of recruitment. Most of them were former First World War veterans, many of whom found it difficult to accept the humdrum normality of civilian life after their years on various battlefronts. The Glasgow recruiting office was one of the busiest; hundreds, many of them unemployed ex-soldiers, were attracted by the advertised wage of ten shillings (50p) a day, plus keep and uniform – conditions that were much better than most could find at the time.

Winston Churchill, Colonial Secretary of the day, referred to the new police reinforcements as men who were 'carefully selected from a great press of applicants'. They were carefully selected, all right – for their ability and willingness to be the toughest and most ruthless of combatants, who would be prepared to be the frontline troops to take on the insurgents with matching force. If that meant being savage and brutal, then so be it. The terrorists would be met with terrorism. Prime Minister Lloyd George had spelled that out in no uncertain terms, decreeing that if it was the wish of those participating in this new uprising to wage a ruthless war on the British, then the British in turn would be equally ruthless with them. He determined that the revolutionaries required a short, sharp shock to bring them to order, and these new men in the police force were the ones to do it.

The new division became known as the infamous 'Black and Tans', one of the most aggressive and compassionless police forces of its kind anywhere in the world. Their name lingers to this day in Ireland, and is equated with brutality and murder. They got their nickname because of a lack of official police clothing, as a result of which they were issued with jackets and trousers that were a mixture of military and police uniforms, an ensemble of khaki and dark green with black belts, inspiring one wit to name them after one of the country's most famous pack of hounds, the Black and Tans. The 'Tans' were supplemented by another new wing of the RIC known as the Auxiliary Division, nicknamed the 'Auxies', whose members were all former British officers who had served in the war. The mood of the country grew even uglier as the new Black and Tan and Auxiliary police units toured the countryside in armoured cars, ferociously rooting out everyone and anyone they considered a terrorist. The questioning of suspects was one of their lowest priorities. The shooting of them was not. Ambushes between the Tans and the insurgents became more regular and fierce. Their flying patrols of armoured car columns would roar through the streets of little villages, firing their guns at anyone who had the temerity not to be behind locked doors.

'We are the boys of the RIC, as happy as happy as can be' was their popular anthem, and they'd bawl it lustily after terrorising yet another little community. Houses of suspects were often burned by the roving and heavily armed police patrols. They pinned notices to trees in the worst of the 'bandit' areas, warning that for every policeman or soldier shot, two 'Shinners' would be taken out and shot as a reprisal. Attacks and counter-attacks became more regular and news of the killings filled the newspapers in Scotland and England. They made grim reading, as the following examples demonstrate.

A patrol of 18 British Auxiliaries fell into one of the Sinn Fein traps at Kilmichael, County Cork. The entire unit was wiped out. Auxiliaries set fire to the centre of Cork as a reprisal, allegedly preventing firemen from stopping the spreading of the blaze. Eight Royal Irish Constables were ambushed at Rathmore, County Kerry. None survived. At Balbriggan, about 20 miles north of Dublin (and just a 15-minute drive from the city airport of today), a head constable was shot dead and his brother wounded by IRA Volunteers. The Black and Tans' retaliation included shooting two suspects, burning down four public houses, a factory and 19 private houses, wrecking 30 others and leaving Balbriggan, in the words of a prominent British politician, 'looking like a Belgian town that had been wrecked by the Germans in the war'. Following a massacre on the morning of Sunday, 21 November 1920, in which 14 undercover British intelligence officers were shot in Dublin, Black and Tan police opened fire at a football match in the city's Croke Park, killing 12. It was the first Irish Sunday of the twentieth century to be known as 'Bloody Sunday'. In Dublin, an 18-year-old student member of the IRA was hanged after a street ambush in which a

British soldier was killed. The student's name was Kevin Barry. They were terrible days.

It wasn't just new constables for the Black and Tans that were being recruited in Glasgow. Sinn Fein too was actively enlisting Volunteers from the Glasgow Irish, both Scots- and Irish-born. Sinn Fein and IRA supporters were less furtive in their activities back in the 1920s than in later stages of the Troubles. They had their own Sinn Fein office in the heart of the city, at the top of Renfield Street, and they openly advertised in newspapers for new members. A typical advert of the day read:

> Sinn Fein. Those desiring to form Sinn Fein clubs should write to the undersigned. No club may be opened without permission of the organising Committee. Week nights advisable for open meetings. Applications coming in great numbers.
>
> J. O'Sheehan, Organiser for Scotland, Renfield Street

Michael Collins, the Sinn Fein leader, veteran of the Easter Uprising and one of the most effective revolutionaries in Irish history, appointed O'Sheehan to take command of the movement in Glasgow, one of his first duties being to tour the Sinn Fein clubs already in existence, many of which had been founded even before the Easter Uprising of 1916. By 1921 there were more than 30 Sinn Fein clubs in the country, most of them in central Scotland, with some 22 in Glasgow alone. Until O'Sheehan took over, however, they were badly organised and poorly attended. O'Sheehan, under Collins' instruction, changed all that. He pumped much-needed enthusiasm and drive into the various clubs, ensuring that their members were there for the main purpose of Sinn Fein's existence, the winning of independence for Ireland and not for any other reason, such as treating the clubs like exclusive drinking establishments where you could share the black stuff with old neighbours from Derry, Donegal or Mayo. Those who preferred such social pursuits were shown the door and the Glasgow Sinn Fein members set about supporting their organisation's longstanding and unyielding cause – independence. Funds were required, so they organised evening ceilidhs and weekend fleadhs, the traditional music competitions of the Irish Gaels. They conducted raffles and organised collections around the most concentrated Glasgow Irish areas, including regular ones at Parkhead – although because of police activity those at the football ground were more surreptitious than the others.

The fit and active were encouraged to sign up as Volunteers for their Irish Republican Army. It was reckoned that the Glasgow Irish provided between 4,000 and 5,000 such recruits, a few hundred of them experienced former soldiers who had served in the First World War. From throughout Scotland it was reckoned that they could supply the IRA with some 7,000 such volunteers, that figure coincidentally approximating the numbers recruited from Glasgow and throughout the rest of Britain to serve with the RIC's Black and Tans.

Such was the help and encouragement, both financially and in terms of manpower, made available from Scotland, principally Glasgow, that Eamon de Valera, President of Sinn Fein (later to be Prime Minister and ultimately President of the Republic of Ireland), paid special tribute to the Scots' outstanding contribution to their cause. Victory in the struggle, he said, in reference to the Irish in Scotland, could never have been made possible without 'their sustained efforts in assisting the dreams of independence', adding that the Scots' efforts had even excelled 'the great works of our brothers in America'.

Perhaps the legendary de Valera had a special fondness for

Glasgow. During my research into the biography of that other legend, Benny Lynch, the son of a Donegal man who became Scotland's first-ever world boxing champion in the 1930s, I was in regular touch with an elderly contact in the Gorbals. He knew everything there was to know about the area and told me how he remembered when de Valera had secretly come to the Gorbals after escaping from Lincoln Jail, where, as an active revolutionary, he had been held in the city by some of the parishioners at St John's RC Church in Portugal Street, one of the three chapels in the Gorbals at the time, and guarded by members of the Major John McBride Sinn Fein Club, the bold major being the father of Sean, who was to become chief of staff of the IRA and later a high-ranking politician.

The Sinn Fein collections, the fund-raising ceilidhs and Gaelic song contests continued throughout the first two years of the 1920s. Their activities were to many, of course, a great source of comfort and conviviality, and to others an introduction to the genuine Irish way of life. In their political pursuits, the Glasgow Irish nationalists were given the stoutest support from the various groups of Scottish socialists, a breed of political activists as far removed from today's New Labour as one end of the colour spectrum from the other. The Independent Labour Party supported them, and so did the active Communist Party in Clydeside, as well as the followers of the man who was a household name in Glasgow at the time, the legendary John MacLean, the Marxist Republican who was hailed by the Russians as such a hero that they elected him, together with the celebrated Russian revolutionaries Lenin and Trotsky, as an honorary president of the first All-Russian Congress of Soviets. Not only that, they made him their first Consul in Britain, with offices in the heart of the Glasgow Gorbals! It was certainly something of a historic first. When all the socialists from their miscellaneous parties took part in their annual May Day parades, they would enthusiastically sing the Irishmen's 'The Soldier's Song' as lustily as they did the 'Red Flag' or 'Internationale'. But then, Trotsky himself had made the observation that the most radical elements of the contemporary British Labour movement were mostly 'of the Scotch and Irish race'.

However, there were other, more dubious activities being organised by Sinn Fein, activities which could be viewed as disloyal and treacherous. The ceilidhs, song contests and the like were harmless, but there was nothing harmless about the regular weekend manoeuvres and weapon target practice held in secluded spots such as Cathkin Braes and the Fenwick Moor, the latter because of its isolation being the more popular.

All those Volunteers who were willing to do their bit for the Republican Army in their war across the channel against the British military and those dreaded Black and Tans had to get some experience in the art of warfare. They had to know how to load a Browning without it jamming, how to fire a Colt without allowing its kick-back to knock you off your feet, how to strip and clean rifles and machine-guns, how to run when burdened with heavy magazines and weapons, how to obey orders without question and be, in the words of their anthem, 'soldiers . . . whose lives are pledged to Ireland . . .' To raise and maintain the standards of those recruited and trained in Scotland, there were regular inspections on windswept braes and lonely moors by visiting IRA officers of varying ranks, men who had seen service in real armies before joining the current guerrilla campaign.

The way things were going in the campaign over there, the Volunteers from Scotland might be required sooner than anticipated. The skirmishes and ambushes, reprisals and counter-reprisals were becoming more ferocious, more lethal.

At the start of 1921 the war in Ireland had become even more vicious, 59 police and nine soldiers being killed in the first two months alone. Help from Scotland was essential. Weapons and ammunition had to be obtained, either for use of the Scots Volunteers or to be sent to their comrades in Ireland. As a result, stone quarries, coal mines, railway and construction work stores throughout Scotland became regular targets for the theft of explosives, detonators and the like, as did Territorial Army and other military depots for arms. At Finnieston Quay a shipment of 100 detonators destined for Ireland was seized, and there were raids on suspected houses and church halls in various parts of the city. Police intelligence had been stepped up by 1921, and this was to result in a spate of dawn swoops and arrests throughout the city and other parts of central Scotland. A total of 183 Irish nationals and supporters were detained on a variety of charges, mainly for the illegal possession of arms and explosives.

One of the most successful of these police raids was at the Parochial Halls in Tollcross, in the East End of Glasgow, where a big haul of rifles, revolvers and other arms was seized and 13 Irishmen were taken into custody. The weapons were actually being loaded into packing cases ready for shipping to Ireland when the police stormed into the hall. But just how legitimate were these well-timed raids? That was the question being posed by the main journal of the Irish community in the city, the *Glasgow Catholic Observer*. It had doubts about some of the circumstances behind the Tollcross raid, but that was perhaps predictable, with the paper's stance so firmly on the side of the independence for Ireland movement. The *Observer* was to put forward the theory that the Tollcross raid, and many others, were set-ups, either by agents provocateur or paid informers who tricked unwitting nationalists into such acts. These instigators then claimed rewards for having the Irishmen and their supporters detained. The police raid at Tollcross had been typical of such set-ups, claimed the *Observer*, and an editorial with the strongest of their views on the subject appeared in the paper that week.

> The police were evidently well informed prior to the [Tollcross] raid . . . they always are well informed on these matters! The agents of the government who engineer these ploys and who pose as Irish patriots of the super kind, leave nothing to be desired. The dupes who become their victims are like cattle sent to the slaughter. In every case it has been the same. We are sorry for them. In one case police watching a bridge had captured men with explosives. It was a trap. Spies and agents provocateur set them up. The arms go to the government when arrests are made, money is collected to defend the men but no one knows who gets it and how much. Men are selling out these people in the name of Ireland and liberty. We warn young Irishmen and women to be aware of these evil courses. They are being trapped by traitors and informers who pose as incorruptible extremists. That's their game!

While the level of IRA support and activity in Glasgow and central Scotland was viewed by many as comparatively negligible and of no real concern, the credit for that quite mistaken view belonged to the commander-in-chief himself, Michael Collins. For it had been his specific instructions to O'Sheehan, the organiser in Glasgow, that all such activities should be conducted in as low key a manner as possible. Despite that order, however, events in and around the city were to be highlighted due to the increased activity of the IRA Volunteers, and to a number of swoops and arrests by the police – genuine arrests that were the result of investigation, as opposed to those considered (some probably were) set-ups.

In the early part of 1921 the activities of the Glasgow Sinn Feiners were stepped up, as was the war over in Ireland. In Glasgow two Volunteers were arrested and accused of plotting to blow up bridges in the city. A line of nine telegraph poles carrying the main communications link between Scotland and Ireland was blown up on the Nitshill road, at Darnley, on the outskirts of the city, and there was a spate of other minor incidents.

Britain was still insisting that Ireland be partitioned, with six of Ulster's nine counties being hived off from the other 26 counties which made up the country. Each would have its own ruling body, the southern part of the country was to be known as the Irish Free State, the rest as Northern Ireland. Apart from the fact that the Irish Free State is known as the Republic of Ireland, that is still the physical shape of the country and the continuing source of contention between the nationalists and the British. Although the proposals pleased the Protestants, giving them a corner of the island in which they would form the majority, it infuriated the nationalists. In the last week of April 1921, there was the strongest-yet condemnation of the British insistence on partition, and once again it came from the *Glasgow Catholic Observer*. In those days newspaper front pages were low-key – in fact, most of them carried no news, the page being given over to classified advertisements. The fact that the article was on page one of the *Observer* made it nothing less than sensational. The entire front page was in the biggest type the pages had ever used. The headline read: 'Ireland United Says

No Surrender To Ulster'. The remainder of the page continued delivering a loud message to readers:

> England is endeavouring to mutilate our Motherland by tearing from it six of the fairest counties of the north to form an English Pale in perpetuity. To effect this they shall first pass a Partition Act and the first election of what she calls the Northern Parliament takes place in May.
>
> The Object: to defeat the Partition of Ireland, to maintain Ireland One, Whole and Indivisible as God made it . . . to expose to the world the mockery and sham of English professions that Ireland is a country divided against itself and that Ulster is opposed to Ireland. Now Ireland calls for your help to win the fight. Keep proudly alive the Red Hand of Ulster. Irish Gaels have set out to raise £10,000 as a fighting fund. Rally Irishmen Rally. Ireland will never surrender to the British Empire one inch of that Northern land, the land that St Patrick sleeps in, the land that heard the eloquence of St Columba. Give generously. Give quickly.
>
> [Note: in more recent times the ancient symbol of Ulster, the Red Hand, has become associated with Loyalist Paramilitaries, but that was not the case in earlier days, when it was used as a symbol against the Partition of the country.]

The target of £10,000 was no mean sum for a small paper like the *Observer* to try to raise, being the present-day equivalent of around £210,000. Nevertheless, by the end of the first week they had already raised more than a seventh of that figure, eventually achieving their impressive target.

Elsewhere in the same issue, incidentally, sportswriters did not hold back in expressing their bias against their greatest rivals, Glasgow Rangers. The Ibrox team had apparently been in dismal form that weekend and the paper's sports pages let them know just how poor their performance had been. Rangers played Partick Thistle, who beat them 1–0, that score not indicating that the game had been as bad as the *Observer* sportswriter recounted.

'What Again,' began the headline of the report, 'Another Rangers' Failure! Should the Light Blues try for the Qualifying Cup?' The report continued in a similar vein:

> The result was due to Rangers' woeful ineptitude and the never-say-die resistance put up by the Firhill defence. They saw chance after chance slip away and became uneasy, rattled, panicky and definitely hopeless! Ibrox had no great men, but it had many weaklings. The crowd were so quiet you could hear the shouts of the players throughout the game, attended by a small crowd. A splendid Thistle victory!

That dismal performance by Rangers, the blowing up of the telegraph poles at Darnley and the various raids and arrests in the city were, in reality, the last things on most people's minds during the first week of May 1921. The city had just come out of a long and miserable winter, and the month began with a full week of the most brilliant, summer-like weather. It had started on the Saturday of that weekend, the last day of April, continued on the Sunday and went on for the rest of the week. Although motor traffic was only a fraction of what it is today, the roads had been so incredibly busy during the weekend that it was one of the main news stories in the papers on the Monday. The crowds, in buses and cars, on bikes and motorbikes, had been flocking to all the coastal and rural resorts, said the three Glasgow evening papers, the *Evening News* describing the weekend's holiday-mood traffic as a 'phenomenal scene in the city as a wholesale exodus took place to seaside and country'. The big favourite for the Glasgow crowds, according to all three papers, had been Largs. Some things never change!

Despite their continued popularity, the Glasgow parks were a considerably bigger attraction in the early 1920s than they are today. Thousands of families spent entire days in them as a substitute for an outing to the seaside, which was beyond their means. With bandstands all providing some form of entertainment, a day in the park could be every bit as good as a trip down the coast. In fact, such were the crowds that had been heading to the Rouken Glen Park, on the southernmost edge of the city, in order to get on a tramcar going there, thousands had to first of all take a tram going in the opposite direction, to the city and beyond even, in order to pick up a southbound tram not already filled with passengers. Apparently, the return journey was even worse, with a wild scramble at the Rouken Glen tram terminus. Hundreds were left stranded and had to hike back home on foot. Incidentally, it was reported that the city trams had that week carried the staggering total of some nine million passengers.

It had been brilliant weather up at Fort William too; though a pair of climbers reported on their return from scaling Ben Nevis that they had encountered eight-foot snowdrifts, and that the winter gales had been so severe that they had blown down the observatory and other buildings, which had included a tearoom.

That weekend had also seen one of the biggest-ever turnouts for the marchers in the May Day Labour Parade. More than 300 organisations were represented, gathering first of all in George Square before marching off to Glasgow Green. They were escorted through the city by dozens of silver, brass and pipe bands with hundreds of children from the socialist Sunday schools, dressed mainly in white with big red rosettes, many of them carrying colourful banners and all of them, at intervals, singing their favourite socialist anthems, among them 'The Soldier's Song'.

When the marchers and day-trippers returned home at night, they could continue the holiday mood with a visit to one of the theatres. Those in town featured as good a selection of stage entertainment as could be found anywhere in Europe. The huge crowds who went 'up town' in the evenings (the main streets were packed with them every night) enjoyed the privilege of living in one of the liveliest cities, where, in those pre-TV days, the entertainment was as varied as it was plentiful. Plays, dramas, comedies, burlesque, music-hall variety shows and circuses at theatres and other venues, which, it seemed, were on almost every corner. There was the Coliseum, the Lyceum and the Athenaeum, the King's and the Queen's and the Princess's too, as well as the Theatre Royal, the Pavilion, Olympia, Empress, Gaiety and Hengler's Cirque. And there were many more in the suburbs. There was what they called 'A Joy Night' at the Empire in Clydebank, appropriately featuring the Full Joy Chorus. At the Empire in Sauchiehall Street, the top of the bill was a duo called Scott and Whalley, a sort of Morecambe and Wise of their day, in a show simply called *As Per Usual.* And for the Glasgow Irish who wanted a special laugh, there was a unique show at the waxworks near Glasgow Cross (which hailed itself as 'The Waxworks – Trongate-by-the-Sea') called *A Genuine Irish Freak of Nature!*

The Great War of 1914–18 was behind them, and for the

majority of Glasgow people there were now other things to get on with. Going out at night and enjoying yourself was one of them.

Despite the command of their leader Michael Collins to the Sinn Fein units in Scotland to keep matters low key, events in the city would project these Irish nationalists to a pitch that has never been reached before or since. The culmination of these events was a quite remarkable happening in the city's High Street on a pleasant and warm Wednesday morning, 4 May 1921.

The story of the sensational gunfight in the Glasgow High Street has been told before – it is, in fact, covered in one of my previous books on the city (*Great Glasgow Stories*). Nevertheless, this extraordinary occurrence was of such a scale and had so many ramifications that it cannot be overlooked in any historical review of the story of the Glasgow Irish. When I looked into the consequences of that event more deeply, I discovered some rather intriguing fresh information, which adds a completely new aspect to this quite exceptional episode in the history of the Glasgow Irish. Some of these consequences were as bitterly ironic as they were tragically bizarre and they have never been revealed in this fashion before.

The basic outline of the story is that a dramatic rescue of an IRA prisoner from a police van was attempted in the heart of the city. A police officer was killed in the ensuing gun battle, which raged just yards from the Royal Infirmary. The event is usually referred to as 'The Glasgow Outrage', that being the description given to it by the newspapers of the day. But as I was to find out, there's much more to the story than that single incident. While the main events took place in the months of May, June and July 1921, it gives the story a whole new aspect if events are taken forward by one year.

The Black and Tan War, as it was known, is over, the young patriots of the Irish Republican Army having won something of a moral victory over the British government. But there are only a few weeks of relative peace before war breaks out again. This time it's the worst kind of war – a 'civil war', with brother against brother, sister against sister, family against family. It is another terrible Irish calamity which is to see more than twice the number of Irishmen slain by fellow Irishmen than had been killed by the British in the preceding war against the ruthless Black and Tans.

In April 1922, the civil war erupts between the opposing factions and there are battles for supremacy in many parts of the island. On one side are those who accept the offered treaty with the British – agreement to the Partition of Ireland, with six of Ulster's nine counties in the north and the remaining 26 in the south to be known as the Free State. On the other side, bitterly opposed to the Partition of the country, are the staunchest of Republicans, whose IRA are prepared to fight against their own countrymen, many of them their former comrades, for their cause. A variety of names are given to each of the opposing armies. Those fighting in support of the treaty are referred to as the National Forces, or sometimes the Regular or Free Staters. Those against them are called the Rebels, Mutineers, Die-Hards or Republicans. Some of the fiercest action is to be in and around Sligo, over in the west. And two men who had been the central characters in that sensational Glasgow incident the year before are in the forefront of the fighting there.

In the early part of July 1922, the battles around Sligo reached a new pitch, with a series of ambushes, attacks on barracks and other strongholds, and even hand-to-hand fighting. In one particular battle between the two sides, the pro-treaty men had the use of one of the best-equipped armoured cars in the country. Armoured cars like this one were to be a feature of this civil war, just as the tank was a feature of the First World War. They were huge vehicles known as ARRs, Armoured Rolls-Royces, usually built around the chassis of the most élite of Rolls models, the Silver Ghost. Just like tanks, they had revolving turrets complete with a Vickers .303 water-cooled machine-gun, and such was their formidable prestige with the pro-treaty forces and their value in fighting the Rebels that the nationalist troops gave each of them a name, as if they were warships, which in a way they were – warships of the countryside. Some of the names were predictable, like the Danny Boy and the Big Fellow. The High Chief and the Manager were another two. Perhaps the best known of them all for its outstanding record was the one they called the Ballinalee, named after a hamlet in County Longford. The Ballinalee had featured in a number of successive actions against the Rebels in the early part of July 1922, being used in the town of Sligo to root out Rebel posts and patrol the streets. It was also the principal weapon used in the routing of Republicans who had taken over the town's Wine Street Barracks. Such was its reputation among the nationalist forces, the Republicans made it their prime target in the area and were determined to either capture or destroy it at all costs.

On Monday, 10 July 1922, while patrolling country roads near Sligo, the Republicans attempted to seize the Ballinalee in an ambush, but were easily beaten off. Next time, they vowed, they would be much better prepared and it would be completely different. The same night, the Rebels met and made new plans to capture and destroy the Ballinalee. The following morning, Tuesday, 11 July, a 50-strong force set up another ambush, this time near Collooney, on the road which goes from Sligo deep into the country towards the lovely and lonely Curlew

Mountains. In order to maintain the secrecy of their ambush, the Rebels had first of all put a guard on all the houses in Collooney to make sure none of the villagers leaked their presence to the pro-treaty men. In civil wars you can never really tell which of your fellow countrymen is on your side, and in Collooney they were taking no chances. This was to be the ambush that would not fail and they would wait there, hiding in roadside ditches and behind outcrops of rock, for 24 hours before the Ballinalee appeared, as they knew it eventually would. It was being used at this time as an escort for a truckload of pro-treaty soldiers searching for Rebel outposts.

As the two vehicles approached a spot known as Dooney Rock they were stopped by a road block. Nervously some soldiers jumped from the truck to clear the obstacles from the roadway. They were met by the most fearsome hail of gunfire, volley after volley of rifle and machine-gun bullets riddling the truck and ricocheting off the thick armour-plating of the Ballinalee. The concentrated fire caused more soldiers to spill from the personnel vehicle, a number of them were hit, some dying and others left wounded.

Some of the crew from the Ballinalee also came out, presumably intending to help out the beleaguered soldiers they had been escorting. Two of them were killed within seconds, one of them being the unit's quartermaster, a man by the name of Sean Adair. The Republican Volunteers who ambushed and killed him were under the orders of a man called Frank Carty. Sean Adair and Frank Carty – these names are to be noted, names with a very special Glasgow connection. They are the focal point of one of the bitterest ironies in this chapter of the Glasgow Irish story. For just a year before that attack on the Ballinalee armoured car, both men had been in Glasgow. Then they had been brothers in arms, one so dedicated to the other

331

that he had risked his own life to try and free his comrade from the custody of the Glasgow police. For Sean Adair and Frank Carty were the central figures in the Glasgow Outrage. They had come to the city as a result of their roles in that long campaign against the British in the vicious Black and Tan War. After that, however, when the civil war flared up, there was a parting of the ways, experienced by so many. Carty thought the fight should continue against the British until they got everything they wanted. Adair had sided with those who considered it was time to do a deal with the London government and agree to their treaty proposals. So strongly did each of them feel about their respective views, that they were willing to do battle against their brother in the cause. Sean Adair died for those views . . . and it was Frank Carty's men who fired the guns that killed him. It may even have been bullets from Carty's own gun that shot down his old friend.

So what were the circumstances that had brought the two men to Glasgow in the early part of the previous year? Frank Carty had been forced to flee from Sligo to Scotland because of his role in fighting the British. Carty had been one of the most active Volunteers in the Sligo Brigade of the IRA, a man with a big reputation as a dedicated and fearless revolutionary, holding the rank of Officer Commanding No. 4 Brigade, 3rd Western division, Irish Republican Army. He had been in and out of prison for his activities against the British; it was for escaping from prison that the authorities were once again looking for him. Carty had broken out of Sligo Prison and after that had been captured and held in custody in the jail at Derry before escaping from there also. He was on the wanted list specifically for these two offences, as well as for having stolen a revolver. But more than anything else it was the senior rank he held in the IRA that made the authorities keen to get him securely behind bars again.

Soon after his breakout from Derry in January 1921 it became known to Special Branch officers that he was in the Glasgow area; going there was considered the most prudent thing to do because of his high ranking on the wanted list. There were ample places in Glasgow for a man like Carty to hide. Others like him had also taken the night boat over and were quickly taken to one of the safe houses in areas like the Gorbals, which at that time had the biggest concentration of Irish in Glasgow.

Special Branch police had been active in the city because of the number of men thought to be hiding in various suburbs, and Carty figured prominently. On Friday, 29 April 1921, three months after his escape from Derry Prison, Frank Carty was arrested by Special Branch officers in Glasgow. He was held in custody in the cells of the building immediately behind the Central Police Court, not far from Glasgow Cross.

Carty made an appearance before the magistrate there the following Wednesday, 4 May, and was ordered to be detained in custody at the nearby Duke Street Prison until arrangements could be made for his return to Ireland.

There had been word that in view of Carty's reputation there might be a rescue attempt at some point during his stay in Glasgow, particularly as it was understood he had come to Glasgow in the company of other Republicans also on the run from the authorities. One of these was Carty's friend from the Sligo Brigade, Sean Adair. It was in the narrow route called the Drygate, which leads from the High Street to the doors of the Duke Street Prison, that the police were to discover just how accurate the information about the rescue attempt had been. Adair was there, together with around 30 Republicans, in three groups of ten. Some of them had come over from Ireland, the others were Glasgow residents. Most were armed with revolvers and ready for the biggest shoot-out Glasgow was to know that century.

It was to be the classic ambush, similar to others that some of the Rebels had experienced either in real combat or in training. The van was repeatedly hit with bullets from their guns, many of them ricocheting off the high buttressed wall on one side of the road, a wall which still bears the scars of those bullets to this day. Despite the scale of the onslaught and the large number of assailants involved in the attack, they were unable to free Carty, the locked doors of the van resisting all their attempts, including being pumped with bullets. Tragically, the officer in charge of the police escort, Inspector Robert Johnston, who lived in Shettleston, was killed, and Detective Sergeant George Stirton, from Petershill Road, Springburn, was badly wounded in the spectacular shoot-out.

When they eventually realised that it would be impossible to free Carty from the police van, the IRA men quickly evaporated into the morning shopping crowds of Townhead, none of them being immediately arrested, leaving behind the ghastly spectacle of the bullet-sprayed police van, steam cascading from its punctured radiator, and the dead and injured policemen sprawled on the street. Those earlier orders from Michael Collins that Republican activities in Glasgow should be as low key as possible were irrevocably shattered. The attack just off the High Street heralded the fact that the IRA were in Glasgow in a very big way and were capable of anything that might be asked of them.

Every available policeman was called out on duty that night, when there were some of the ugliest scenes of crowd disorder witnessed in the city since the Partick riot. The authorities became so alarmed that they even requested help from the military, a detachment of Gordon Highlanders being rushed to the Central Police Station and Court, on standby in case matters deteriorated beyond what the police could handle. The worst of the trouble was in the East End, in and around St Mary's in Abercrombie Street, where 32 years before the parochial hall had witnessed that historic night when a group of Glasgow Irishmen formed a club called Celtic FC. The crowds had immediately flocked to St Mary's because of the considerable police activity there had been there following the shootings, early details of which were sensationally splashed in the three city newspapers of the time, the *Evening Times*, *Evening News* and *Evening Citizen*. Stories circulating among the large crowds spoke of swoops by Special Branch officers, detectives and uniformed police on the houses of Glasgow Irish in the area, but it was the events at St Mary's that caused the greatest concern. Word had gone round that the most sacrilegious of deeds had taken place there. A policeman, they were saying, had gone into the church while confessions were being heard and arrested one of the priests.

Then there were rumours that it was two priests who had been taken away by the police, one of them being the parish priest himself, Fr Fitzgerald. It was on hearing such news that the worst violence erupted. The uniformed police were the first targets, bottles, stones and other missiles being hurled at them. Then a passing tramcar was attacked, its windows smashed. As news spread about the invasion of the chapel, the confession-box sacrilege and the detention of the clerics, the crowds grew bigger and the mood uglier. Hundreds flocked towards the city and the Central Police Station, to which others being arrested were taken.

Meanwhile, the crowd continued to swell outside St Mary's and it was only as a result of the intervention of the parish priest himself, Fr Fitzgerald, that matters cooled down. The senior priest reassured the crowd that the story about the break-in during confession was untrue, that he himself had not been arrested and would be remaining free, and that in the good name of the community they should peacefully disperse. It was confirmed, however, that an assistant priest had not only been detained but had been charged with the raid on the van. He was a young Irish curate called Fr Patrick McRory, one of around 20 prisoners, including six women, arrested in a series of police swoops which had gone on through the night, most of them in the East End of the city. One of the female prisoners, a Margaret Dehan, charged with the murder of the police officer, appeared in the well of the court with a baby in her arms.

Extraordinary precautions were taken at the Central Police Station to exclude the public; the corridors and the courtroom itself were patrolled and guarded by squads of constables. Those arrested and held were all charged with offences in connection with the ambush and shootings in the High Street, Fr McRory appearing in court dressed in clerical garb, holding his wide-brimmed hat and described as looking 'extremely pale and obviously nervous'. Eight men and four women were also arrested for their part in the disturbance in and around Abercrombie Street and Gallowgate in which stones, bottles and other missiles were thrown, and they appeared on separate charges at the Eastern Police Court in the Calton.

There were further arrests on the Saturday following the shootings, when police went to the Parkhead stadium looking for a number of suspects. There had been a crowd of over 20,000 there to see the home team play Partick Thistle in the Glasgow Charity Cup and in order not to exacerbate the already hostile feelings towards the uniformed police, it was made out by the officers that the two men they had plucked from the crowd were being taken away as suspected pickpockets. These and others held during the week, including occupants from a house in Thistle Street, the Gorbals, in which ammunition had been stored, brought the total number of arrests to 37.

The fact that the priest McRory was still in custody a week after the incident was a source of considerable concern to the Glasgow Irish of the East End. There was no way a young man such as he could have been connected with that terrible affair, they maintained. What had an innocent man like him got to do with it? He was a priest of the church, and priests didn't do things like that, did they? The *Glasgow Catholic Observer*, predictably, took a similar line in its first publication following the shootings. Fr McRory's arrest and detention, it asserted, was causing 'an unprecedented feeling in eastern Glasgow'. Its editorial went on to say that the utmost sympathy had been manifested by the people of St Mary's 'in the best possible way by intercession to the Almighty for the young priest's speedy release'.

The Church swung into action in support of the detained clergyman, organising various spiritual functions for the faithful in times of such crisis. An all-night vigil was begun at St Mary's in support of the incarcerated priest which, according to the *Observer*, 'was one of the most remarkable religious services in the record of the Church in Scotland'. News of it, it said, 'went around the district like wildfire and before midnight, the church was packed to the door'. Special services were also conducted every hour and confessions were heard throughout the night by the priests of the parish, assisted by other priests from neighbouring missions. 'The number of communicants at the morning mass,' said the *Observer*, 'was enormous. The fervour of the congregation surpassed anything ever witnessed before in the parish.'

After a week in custody, the police were still refusing visitors to the detained prisoners and a solicitor on behalf of St Mary's made an application to the court that Fr Fitzgerald be granted permission to make a visit to Fr McRory in order to discuss 'parochial and ecclesiastical matters'. Stipendiary Magistrate Neilson, however, refused any special facilities for the St Mary's curate.

The *Catholic Observer* continued to take issue with what it considered the overreaction of the police in the number and manner of arrests they continued to make, considering the allegations against some to be minor charges:

> The Scottish police appear to be making wholesale arrests of Irish Catholics on various charges of non-registration of firearms and complicity in furthering movements against the interests of the British Empire. There are cases of men on minor charges of possessing Irish literature and their homes being searched.

A month after the raid on the police van, despite continued protests from the Catholic press, Fr McRory was still being held in custody. The *Observer* considered it time for a special feature article on behalf of the young man, who by now had been lionised to such dimensions he was probably the best-known Catholic cleric in the country. He was idealised to such an extent that when the *Catholic Observer* eventually published its special tribute to him, the headline read: '*Soggarth aroon* – an appreciation of Glasgow's hero priest'.

'*Soggarth aroon*', incidentally, is an expression apparently understood by more of its readers in the 1920s than it is today. In Irish it means 'our dear priest'. Although he was being held on the gravest of charges, including taking part in the actual attack on the police van, the *Observer* eulogised the priest as its very own hero. The article began:

If a vote were held to see who was the city's most

popular clergyman, there would be no doubt it would go to Fr McRory and the warmest advocates of the vote would be his fellow clergymen. Until a few weeks ago he was practically unknown. Today his name is on everyone's lips and his welfare the burden of thousands of prayers offered on his behalf.

The newspaper continued:

> Who is Father McRory? Why has he obtained such unparalleled popularity? His fame was not his seeking. He is a quiet, modest, retiring, pious and hard-working young man. But like the overwhelming majority of Glasgow Irish people he has Sinn Fein sympathies. Also he assiduously visits the Glasgow Catholic families of the East End. Now he is a prisoner in Duke Street.
>
> A guilds' parade [guilds being various Catholic associations] with bands, their instruments decorated in green, after their meeting at the St Andrew's Halls, paraded then went to the East End via Duke Street to let the prisoners hear the bands. It shows how deeply the Irish people love their priests and the marching of the bands past the prison was a glorious idea and grandly carried out.
>
> Fr McRory is from Omagh, the youngest priest in the mission, and came to Glasgow two years previously after being ordained at Maynooth.

The feature then went on with lengthy and detailed descriptions of the all-night vigil service which continued to be held in his support.

Two weeks later there was a story that the detainees being held at the old Duke Street Prison for the van ambush, including Fr McRory, were being kept in their cells for 23 hours a day. Duke Street, as it was simply referred to, which was long ago demolished, was a grim collection of soot-blackened buildings surrounded by a forbiddingly high stone wall, and was the city's oldest prison at the time. It was notorious for its primitive conditions: the inmates' only exercise was what they termed the daily 'airing', a half-hour walking period in an outdoor area they called the 'cage'. It was given that name because that was precisely what it appeared to be; in order to prevent prisoners having contact with one another, the 'cage' was divided into small corrals, or pens, a bit like a cattle stockyard. When the *Catholic Observer* heard about the prisoners' long periods of confinement, it made an immediate representation on their behalf to the Prison Commission, requesting them to conduct an inquiry into the claim. The commission's reply was prompt, curt and unyielding:

> None of the prisoners suffered any ill health as a result of lack of exercise. However, prisoners shall take the exercise it is deemed necessary for their health on medical grounds. The length and time of the exercise is regulated by the medical officer. The Irish prisoners are treated in no way differently from the other prisoners.

Another month and a half passed before there was any further detailed news about the St Mary's priest. It was on Thursday, 21 July, almost three months after the sensational Wednesday in early May 1921, that there was the first news leak, if only a rumour, that an announcement was pending about the curate McRory. The strength of the rumour had grown so much by the

Friday that once more huge crowds began milling around the chapel in Abercrombie Street. Early in the afternoon a window of the chapel house was suddenly raised and the parish priest, Fr Fitzgerald, gave them the news for which they had been so dedicatedly praying. There had been a phone call to him from the governor at Duke Street Prison, he announced to the huge crowd: 'Your Father McRory is being released from prison today, I was told. All charges against him have been dropped.'

They couldn't have cheered louder had Celtic just won the Scottish Cup. There was no better news. That part of the East End of Glasgow prepared for the celebration of a lifetime. They stretched flags, bunting and ribbons along the buildings and across the streets from one side to the other. Tenement windows were draped with them, gas lamp standards were bedecked, close mouths and public-house entrances festooned, and vendors' barrows were trimmed with them. Children wrapped themselves in them and so too did many adults. It was a flaunting of the green like never before, even in that part of Glasgow, and it spectacularly transformed the drab, serried rows of soot-blackened tenement houses as though they were colourful backdrops for some splendid festival.

An enormous cheer greeted Fr McRory as he walked out of the main door at Duke Street Prison, and he was then carried shoulder high through the huge crowds after reaching St Mary's in Abercrombie Street, not far from the jail. The bandsmen were out in force, their instruments decorated with green ribbons, and if they weren't playing and singing 'God Save Ireland', they were lustily giving yet another rendition of 'The Soldier's Song'. His parishioners had been told that their all-night vigils and prayers of intercession during McRory's 11 weeks in custody would be answered and, sure enough, it had all come to pass!

The *Catholic Observer*, which had campaigned so vociferously for the man it called their 'brave young priest', was scathing in its comments on his long detention, and demanded to know why he had been held in the first place. 'The total absence of any reason is now acknowledged by the young priest's release,' it said. Apart from that, the *Observer* was as triumphant as the wildly cheering crowds, urging its readers that in their celebration they should: 'Unroll Erin's flag, flying its folds to the breeze, let it wave o'er the land, let it float over the seas.'

Just 11 days before Fr McRory's release from custody, the 30-month war against the British in Ireland had come to an end. Sean Adair and Frank Carty were both back in Ireland, the latter being eventually released from prison. Six months later, Adair and Carty were back in action once more, only this time they were on opposing sides in their own tragic civil war. Not many months after it had begun, the two men who had come to Glasgow in such varying circumstances would be involved in that bizarre confrontation on the road from Sligo to the Curlew Mountains, in which one of them would be shot dead by men under the direct command of his old comrade.

There was never again to be such prolific Sinn Fein or IRA activity in Glasgow as there was in the early part of that century. Two Volunteers were sent to Glasgow in 1938 to set up one of the five British centres for the bombing campaign just prior to the outbreak of the Second World War. Throughout the long period of the more recent Troubles, which erupted in the late 1960s, the Glasgow Irish, both Republican and Orange, participated in various ways in aiding their brothers-in-arms in Ireland. Funds were raised, weapons were procured, and safe houses were made available. Glasgow police made arrests from both communities, mainly of those involved in arranging weapons, ammunition and explosives for shipment over the water. But there were never to be any bombings or any serious involvement with such activities as drill meetings, target practice, shootings and the like. Such involvement in a Scottish context was a bridge, it appeared, they had no wish to cross. Thankfully, it was a bridge too far.

Following his return to Ireland, and at the conclusion of the civil war, Frank Carty, the man who had been at the centre of the Glasgow Outrage, became a politician and was elected as TD (Teach na Daile, a Member of the Irish House of Parliament), in which he served until his death in 1942. There is, alas, one final twist in the remarkable story of these two men, Carty and Adair. It relates to that location, Collooney, near Sligo, where Carty's men erected the roadblock and staged the ambush on the armoured car in which Adair was killed. How the bones of the soldiers' graves of another century must have rattled that day, how the ghosts of the valiant departed must have wailed and wept. At that very spot at the end of the eighteenth century a similar ambush had taken place in which men fought against each other and were killed in the cause of Ireland.

It was in the days of the United Irishmen's Uprising, a singularly momentous time in Irish history, when Wolfe Tone, the Protestant, inspired a rebellion of all Irishmen – Catholic, Protestant, Dissenter, whatever – to rise together against, and to break for ever all connection with, the English. Tone enlisted the aid of the French to help his United Irishmen in their rebellion. On 5 September 1798, an army of the two allies, the Irish and the French, had joined forces just off the main Sligo to Dublin road, outside the little town of Collooney. The English garrison at Sligo mustered and came out to do battle with the advancing French–Irish force, setting up a blockade in the form of a cannon. The cannon was placed at a strategic spot and commanded by their most experienced gunner. The English had established their blockade on virtually the very same site at Collooney where Carty's men set up their ambush.

One of the United Irishmen, a young soldier called Bartholomew Teeling, saved the day by galloping off on his own and shooting dead the cannon's operator. The blockade was breeched, the Irish and the French advanced and the English soldiers fled back to Sligo, leaving behind 60 dead, 100 others being taken prisoner. Teeling is the great hero of Collooney and a statue in his honour near the little town recalls that singular act of daring bravery and the fact that he was later to be taken prisoner by the English and sentenced to death. Thanks to Teeling, however, those in rebellion had been the victors that day, but the war was not to be theirs and the cause of Catholic, Protestant and Dissenter, United Irishmen together, was eventually lost.

So there they were, from the eighteenth to the twentieth century, Carty, Adair and Bartholomew Teeling, all having fought in the name of Ireland at a place known as Collooney. If only those United Irishmen had won all their battles as they did that day at Collooney! If only their insurrection had not ended in the failure it did. Indeed, if only!

– CHAPTER 16 –

Billy Boys and Tim Malloys

Perhaps it was inevitable that the young males would have their wars. Forming gangs and warring with rivals was their active and aggressive response to times of crisis. And many of the young lives of the first and later generations of Irish immigrants had been about crisis. They were born into the most dreadful of slums. There were times of great unemployment, and what jobs were available paid breadline wages. They felt trapped in their tenement ghettoes, ill-prepared because of their background and environment to compete with their counterparts in better parts of the city for jobs which offered some scope other than that of the tradesmen or labourer. The gangs gave them a sense of belonging that was absent from other aspects of their lives. The gangs were their very own clubs, where the only formality was your expression of courage and daring. It was also the finest way, if you were a Catholic, to show these

Protestants just how good you really were, and for those Protestants to relive all those victorious battles against that other religion they so often sang about.

The Glasgow street gangs were not entirely sectarian, but the majority of them were in some way allied to one of the religious camps. They were to endure for several decades and would have continued even longer had not the authorities decided they should be curbed and brought in Britain's most famous policeman to do the job.

There would have been street gangs battling it out in Glasgow, just as there were in other major British cities, even had there been no Irish immigrants. The slums, poverty and unemployment were the causes of the hooliganism. Nevertheless, the presence of the Irish was certainly a factor in their existence, particularly during the 1920s and '30s, when they plagued the city, giving it a most unenviable and notorious reputation. It was in 1931, therefore, that Glasgow Corporation decided something very positive had to be done about the street gangs, the most famous of them being the Irish Catholic and Protestant ones, who were capturing headline after headline for their bitter battles in various parts of the city. These regular and deadly skirmishes could at times witness hundreds taking part in the most vicious of encounters, flourishing knives, swords, bicycle chains, open razors, knuckledusters, hammers, hatchets and clubs. They were a bit like their counterparts in New York at the time, who were caught up in perpetual warfare over imagined territorial disputes. That's right, *West Side Story* was happening right here in Glasgow. Without the music and dancing, that is.

The Sharks and Jets of Glasgow had the added dimension of their warfare being inspired by their diverse views of Christianity, the teachings of which neither side really knew much about, let alone practised, apart from token appearances in chapel and church. On one side were those who, in the main, would have been the first or second generation of the main wave of Catholic Irish immigrants who had fled the Great Famine and the continuing impoverishment of their country. On the other side were the same generation of descendants of those other incomers to the city, mainly from the Highlands and other rural parts, as well as Ulster – Protestants all. Irish Catholics and Protestants in the city at the time generally viewed each other with a range of similar feelings, from ambiguity to dubiety, trepidation to suspicion – or plain, outright malice and hostility, as the gangs did.

Many people saw the gang members simply as a bunch of aggressive and dangerous thugs with nothing better to do with their time than burn off their testosterone in all-too-frequent and vicious gang battles. In these fights they murdered and mutilated each other, and anyone who got in their way. Others saw them as unfortunate victims of the mass immigration of two rival religious communities, whose bitterly opposed views of one another appeared to be more about contention than about being Christian. Trying to find a remedy to the root causes of their problems would obviously have been the solution to their warfare. Such a course would take years – generations. Something other than that had to be done much more immediately. Someone had to get them to stop, make the streets of Glasgow a safer place. The city was the talk of Europe for its street violence. *No Mean City*, it had been labelled, that expression really meaning the city was something special, quite a place. But that's not the way it was seen after people read the book and heard all the news about the city. Al Capone and his gangsters had done it for Chicago. The street gangs of Glasgow did for this *No Mean City.*

A new chief constable was to be appointed in the hope that he could rid the city of its street scourge. He had to be someone rather special – a crusader with foresight and determination in cleaning up one of the biggest social problems with which the city had been faced, the toughest and most fearless of men. Someone with a hard image, the very sight of whom would put the fear of death into those who persistently slashed, stabbed, kicked and clubbed their way around the streets of Glasgow. The advertisement for the post made it quite clear that this was one of the biggest posts of its kind in the British police service. The Glasgow force was second only in scale to the London Metropolitan and the wage being offered reflected that – the position offered a yearly salary of between £1,500 and £2,000 – between £30 and £40 a week for being a top cop! But let's get it in context: that sum is today's equivalent of between £48,000 and £64,000, still well below the current going rate for such a post – the salary is about double that now – but for the day a most handsome wage.

Following a scrupulous and painstaking background inquiry, and the most probing and thorough of interviews, out of the final list of candidates came the man who was to become known as the toughest and most feared cop in all of Britain. When they lifted the curtains on who he was, and what was his background, the latter was the most surprising thing of all. For the new chief was a mild-mannered Englishman whose Christian name was Percy, and who as a youngster had been an angel-faced boy soprano, good enough to qualify as a boarding pupil at St Paul's Cathedral Choir School in London. In fact, he was such an accomplished chorister that he had been chosen to sing at the memorial service for Queen Victoria and at the coronation ceremony of King Edward VII. What! An English bloke called Percy who had been a boy soprano! Hardly the kind of upfront credentials you'd expect for someone expected to be the most feared cop in Britain. But Percy Sillitoe was to demonstrate just how misleading such details could be.

Glasgow's new chief constable made his mark in enforcing law and order in the city by being one of the greatest-ever innovators in police work and tactics. Police forces throughout the world are still influenced by the imaginative new methods he introduced. You can see evidence of his work in dozens of police forces, in almost every continent. For instance, zero tolerance; everyone thinks it began in New York, but Percy Sillitoe was enforcing it right here in Glasgow with huge success all those years ago. Those recognisable chequered bands round policemen's caps – you can see them everywhere, throughout England, on the continent, in the States, in South Africa and a variety of other countries. They're on the most fashionable headgear of policewomen, and Australian police even have them round their bush hats. The bands were another Sillitoe idea – Sillitoe's tartan they nicknamed it – and were introduced to the uniforms of the men on Glasgow police-car patrols after complaints from motorists having difficulty during the hours of darkness in distinguishing policemen from civilians. Sillitoe decided to copy the chequered pattern on the hats of soldiers in the Guards' division.

Cars with radio communication are another conception of Sillitoe's. Glasgow had Britain's very first police patrol cars with radio links to their stations. The idea quickly spread to every force in Britain. The extensive use of police boxes, the small cabins used for years by constables as mini-police stations everywhere in Britain in the days before mobile phones, was yet another of this remarkable policeman's innovations. He was also to modernise the Glasgow force's fingerprint department, at the time a one-man operation in a small, out-of-the-way office run by an elderly sergeant overdue for retirement, as well as to encourage the use of forensic science in solving crimes. Sillitoe, ahead of his time, was convinced that it was the way of the future for criminal detection work.

There was a lot more to Percy's background than singing soprano in church. His CV included decades of confrontation at the sharp end of police work in some of the most dangerous corners of the world. He spent time in Africa, first of all as a frontline police trooper in action against a variety of dissidents, a record which would be read and appreciated in those days of Empire preservation. He had taken up boxing in an African frontier town in order to defend himself against some of its rough and tough itinerants. As a young trooper he had been sent into the bush to track down a dangerous criminal and for days, single-handed and on horseback, he doggedly followed the fugitive's trail before catching up, overpowering and bringing the man back to town, manacled to his horse. Glasgow, it seemed, wasn't just getting another chief constable, it was getting Wyatt Earp into the bargain.

Prior to his appointment, Sillitoe had been the Chief Constable of Chesterfield and Sheffield, making his mark in both cities by cleaning up their gang problems, said to be the worst in England at the time. The two cities had previously tried a variety of initiatives but all had failed. Sheffield's city magistrates had openly confessed to being intimidated by the viciousness of the gangs who roamed and ruled the streets. When Sillitoe took charge of the city's 700 policemen, one of his first missions was forming a special task force composed of the biggest, toughest and most fearless of men. They were then enlisted into crash courses in a variety of forms of unarmed combat, one of the most popular being ju-jitsu, the traditional Japanese self-defence perfected by samurai warriors. If the boys on the streets want to fight, here's some partners for them, was Sillitoe's philosophy. Platoons of his frontline constables were speedily rushed to the scene of any bully-boy operations or skirmishes between the gangs, who were very quickly to discover that they were now having battles in which they always ended up the losers. It didn't take the gangs long to get their new chief cop's message.

There were still some in Glasgow, however, who were apprehensive about Sillitoe's ability to tackle the city's gangs. There was also the little problem of the man being English. The Glasgow Establishment didn't quite put it that way, the chattering among even the highest of officials taking the line of 'Surely there were lots of Scots who could do the job?' Sillitoe got the measure of such feelings at the annual police ball not long after he had taken over. The chairman of the Glasgow Corporation Police Committee, the millionaire Sir John Cargill, had been against his appointment, making that painfully clear with a variety of loaded innuendo in his 'welcoming' speech at the ball.

The somewhat sour reception he received from Cargill and others connected with the City Corporation included the news from Lord Provost Sir Thomas Kelly that the Corporation would be cutting his contract salary by a somewhat massive 12½ per cent. Welcome to Glasgow! However, he wasn't being singled out – the Corporation had had to implement drastic spending cuts imposed by a cash-strapped government, and the Lord Provost announced that would apply to all the police, not just the chief constable.

Long before coming to Glasgow, Sillitoe had done his homework on the major problems with which he would be confronted there. The suburban gangs and their continual street warfare, corruption in the council, and lack of morale and efficiency in the police force were his immediate priorities when he took up the post. After tackling and effectively dealing with the latter two, Sillitoe concentrated on ridding the city of its dreadful reputation of gang culture.

Gang problems were not confined to Glasgow, of course, just as big-time crime in America was not confined to Chicago. As the street gangs obviously didn't keep enrolment registers or any other kind of record, research on the scale of them from city to city has always been difficult. There were street gangs in Liverpool, Manchester, Birmingham, London and, notoriously, in Sheffield, but Glasgow had the worst reputation for gangs, just as it had the worst social conditions in Britain. As crime and poverty go hand in hand, it may be assumed that the scale of the gang violence reflects that.

The city's congestion and poor housing conditions in the years after the First World War and into the 1930s were unparalleled anywhere in Britain, just as they had been before the turn of the century. By now there were nearly three-quarters of a million people living in the centre of the city, an area of 7.7 kilometres with an average density of over 900 people per hectare. Housing standards were still appalling and, viewed from today's perspective, unbelievably basic. The statistics are shocking, particularly those highlighting the differences between conditions in Glasgow and major cities south of the border. More than 40 per cent of all houses in Glasgow at the time consisted of just one or two rooms: lounge, bedroom, dining-room and kitchen were all confined to those two. Compare that with conditions in London in the same period, where only 5 per cent were living in such overcrowded conditions. It was even less in Merseyside, where the figure was

2.5 per cent. Almost a third of all Glasgow's families had to share common toilets with their neighbours, compared with a mere 2.6 per cent in London and 1.1 per cent on Merseyside. And 175,000 of these so-called houses in Glasgow had no baths. Little wonder the infant mortality rate was about double that of London and Birmingham. Little wonder there were young men out in the streets waging war.

Unemployment was endemic, much worse than at any time since the Second World War. There was a time in the 1930s when a third of the city's adult population were without jobs. Just as prevalent was the problem of alcoholism, the rate of alcohol dependence being two or three times as high as in equivalent cities in England. Glasgow had around a tenth of all the alcoholics in the United Kingdom. While drink wasn't a factor in the existence of the gangs, it was certainly a complexity in their presence, much of the street violence being fuelled by alcohol. More pointedly, however, society had turned its back on the young people of the city, and they were in the forefront – and the losers – in the class struggle, and so they were also to turn their backs on society.

The cultural and ethnic mix that had over the generations formed the character of the young Glasgow male meant that when expressing their masculinity they revealed a rebellious independence, a reaction against authority. They also demonstrated an active, even aggressive, response in times of crisis – and crisis was part of daily existence in those years of deprivation, which had few parallels anywhere in Europe.

The Glasgow gangs mainly originated around the 1880s, although there are records of much earlier skirmishes between rival groupings from opposite sides of the river, who would meet at the shallow fords to stone each other in the days before the Clyde was bridged. It was with the growth of the slum tenement areas that the real street gangs were born, gangs who were to carve up areas and claim them as their own, and give themselves names. Their descendants made up that unsavoury part of the Glasgow scene Percy Sillitoe was employed to clean up in the 1930s. Some of the earliest of these street warriors appear to be the ones known as 'penny mob gangs'. This was probably a generic title taken on by gangs in more than one area of the city, simply meaning that there was a penny levy on members as a sort of 'fighting fund' (forgive the pun) to help pay regular fines imposed on members. The penny mobsters apparently weren't averse to supplementing their funds by asking for contributions from local shopkeepers, the small businessmen being assured that moneys received from them was a form of 'insurance' to keep their shop windows intact. And this was years before Al Capone got up to his nasty tricks in Chicago!

Sillitoe was aware of the problems of those caught up in the gangs and expressed some understanding of them in his autobiography, *Cloak Without Dagger!*, published in 1955, by saying he appreciated that when they began they were not composed of what would be termed true criminals, nor were they even in any sense organised teams of experienced lawbreakers who grouped themselves around a 'mastermind'. In the main they were merely unemployed youths who had lived through the awful years of the First World War without being old enough to take part in it.

The authors of *No Mean City*, the all-time bestseller about Glasgow and the gangs of the 1930s, also recognised that, describing gang members: 'Broadly speaking, the Glasgow gangster is not a criminal, he is just a hooligan and a fighter, battling for excitement and adventure and not for profit.' But irrespective of just why they existed and flourished, civilised society could not tolerate them and they had to be curbed. The biggest and most active gangs in the 1930s operated in areas close to the city centre, such as Calton, Bridgeton and the Gorbals and were Irish-inspired – that is, their members would either be Catholics of Irish descent, Protestants of Irish descent, or just plain anti-Catholic Protestants. The principal gangs were identified to Sillitoe in intelligence reports, giving their areas and names: the San Toy Boys from Calton and Tradeston, mainly Protestant, and their great local rivals, the Baltic Fleet, mainly Catholic, from Bridgeton; and the Tim Malloys, who were obviously Catholic-Irish. South of the river in the Gorbals there was the South Side Stickers, Catholic-Irish who had had continuous warfare with the Calton San Toy since the early 1920s, as well as the other mainly Irish gangs of the district, such as the Cumbies and the Beehive. There were plenty more, like the Redskins, the Calton Tongs and the Calton Entry Mob, again associated with Calton as well as Tollcross, the Shamrock from Townhead, the Kelly Boys from Govan, the Cross Boys from Partick, and another similarly named group from St George's Cross, the Butney Boys from Maryhill. There were also the Black Star, Liberty Boys, Parlour Boys, the Sticket Boys, Kent Star, the Briggait Boys, Wee Cumbies and, perhaps the most notorious rivals of all, the Norman Conks and the Billy Boys, both of Bridgeton, the name of the latter the loudest proclamation of any of just what side of the sectarian fence they were on. Some gangs, such as the Redskins and the Tongs, sprang up in different areas with the same name. In all, police intelligence at the time estimated there were around 50 known and recognised gangs, their members totalling many hundreds, vaguely reminiscent of Chinese secret societies. But such comparisons should only be confined to their esoteric titles, their membership exclusivity and their proclivity for fighting.

Some of those gang names may sound like the cast list for our own version of *West Side Story* – many have a touch of the bizarre about them – but this is not the result of any ingenuity from those who thought them up. Subtlety and originality were not exactly the strong point of the gang members, many of whose academic levels of education had barely reached that of joined-up thinking. Many of the names they flaunted were simply geographical, like the Beehive gang, taken from the Gorbals store on whose street corner (of Cumberland and Hospital Streets) they would congregate; or the Baltic Fleet, from Baltic Street, where many of their members lived. The San Toy was the name of a popular small cheroot at the time and for some reason known only to them – probably a touch of the exotic appealed – the gang thought it was appropriate. The name of the Catholic-Irish Tim Malloys originated from the slang, 'Malloys' for the Boys, and the use of the word 'Tim' by Protestants when referring to Catholics.

Because of the gangs' complexity and numbers, they were to be no small problem in controlling, suppressing and eliminating, as Sillitoe was to realise. One of the main concerns about the gang warfare was the amount of weapons they deployed, anything from swords to bayonets to sharpened bicycle chains, scissors, screwdrivers, knuckledusters and razors. The latter, of course, was the weapon with which Glasgow gangs were to be identified, Johnnie Stark, the Razor King himself, being the central character of *No Mean City*. Yet Sillitoe was to find in his studies of them that despite all that had been written about the gangs and their razors, that weapon was by no means the principal means of combat. It was more likely to be the commonplace beer bottle, followed by the knife, bicycle chain, and so on. As Sillitoe himself wrote: 'It was easier to stun an opponent with a beer bottle, knock him down, and then kick him in the face.'

Even though it happened years before Sillitoe came to Glasgow, they were still talking about one of the most memorable of gang battles, the night the man known as Razzle Dazzle was killed. His very name demonstrates the almost mythical dimensions this Gorbals character assumed. Razzle's real name was James Dalziel and he worked as the chief runner and collector for Pat Donnachy, one of the many Gorbals bookmakers of Irish extraction, whose business was operated from an illegal pitch in Herbertson Street, the small street at the rear of the old Coliseum cinema. Dalziel was known as one of the best dancers at the nearby Parlour dance hall, a small venue situated behind the old Bedford cinema. A man who was as good with his feet as he was with his fists was something special in those days, especially in places like the Gorbals. Dalziel also happened to be the leader of the local Parlour Boys gang, mainly Irish Catholic, the gang taking their title from the name of the local dance hall where Dalziel was the star dancer. One Saturday night at the Parlour, a mob of the Briggait Boys from the Gallowgate, an offshoot of the mainly Protestant San Toy gang and deadly enemies of the Parlour mob, invaded the dance hall. The ensuring battle was one of the bloodiest and most vicious of its kind ever witnessed in the city.

It was Donnybrook at the dancing, ambulances hauling away the worst of the wounded with injuries reminiscent of something that might happen in a real war. Being the leader of the Parlour Boys, Dalziel had been the main target of the invading gang and he was to die as a result of the horrific wounds he received in the battle. That gory night at the Parlour was sufficiently notable for Sillitoe to make mention of it in his autobiography as an example of the kind of violence with which he was confronted.

The Razzle Dazzle murder was typical of such affrays. There were similar occurrences in public places, mainly dance halls, cinemas and football matches. Typical newspaper headlines of the day announced: riot in city picture house, gang warfare erupts, warning on night of fear, amazing story of gang attack, and so on.

Sillitoe's arrival in Glasgow coincided with the flourishing of two of the most legendary of all Glasgow gangs, the Brig'ton Billy Boys and their bitterest rivals, the Norman Conks, whose names alone tell most of their story. The song of the former is still part of the ritual of Rangers football fans. The two gangs had originated in the East End in the mid-1920s, the Billy Boys coming first. Their emergence, so the story goes, came about as a result of an attack during a junior football match on a player known as Billy Fullerton. Alas, from such humble events! By the early 1930s, however, both gangs had grown in such stature that by then they were the two biggest and most formidable gangs in the country.

As anyone with any connections with the East End can testify, Billy Fullerton was one of the most legendary of all the great Glasgow street battlers. Rangers fans still sing about him whenever their team play, chanting 'We are the Brig'ton Billy Boys'. For those Brig'ton Billy Boys were the creation of Fullerton and were the biggest and most widely respected (by other gangs, that is) of all the Glasgow gangs. Fullerton spent much of his time in boxing circles, working at various periods with one of Bridgeton's best-known characters of that era, Tommy Gilmour, bookmaker, boxing promoter and manager, the son of a famous boxer and promoter and father of today's promoter of the same name. One of the many ironies in the gang leader's life is that his gaffer, Gilmour, was a Catholic, while Fullerton himself was the truest, bluest of Protestants. Fullerton was often used by Gilmour in the erection of boxing rings, an occupation in which he was known as something of a specialist.

The gang that formed around Fullerton was just like himself, Bridgeton Protestants, that meaning very true, very blue Protestants. It's likely that the name of the gang didn't actually originate from Fullerton's own, but from that of the other Billy, the man on the prancing white charger, King William of Orange. Nevertheless, Fullerton was the King Billy of Brig'ton, and you didn't even pause to think otherwise, let alone argue about it.

Being a gang with a cause, as it were, the Billy Boys had branches in other areas, even as far out as in rural Lanarkshire and Ayrshire, and were so well organised that they even had their own officials, a secretary and a treasurer. Membership cards were issued to remind the ranks of the basic rules of their existence, those being to support King and Country and defend all other Protestants. These cards weren't merely a vanity token to prove you were really one of the Boys – they were issued for the efficient collection of the weekly membership fee of tuppence, the moneys going to a fines' fund. At one time the gang was said to have something like £1,500 in the bank, a sum which would approximate to today's £49,500, handy money when cash was an option to prison.

Considering what they stood for, and it being Glasgow, the Billy Boys' great adversaries, the Norman Conquerors (usually just the Norman Conks) were as Catholic as the Billy Boys were Protestant. Their gang title, incidentally, was only a play on those original conquerors. Their name was merely geographical – many of its followers living in and around the Norman Street area of Bridgeton. The Billy Boys had their champion in Billy Fullerton, and the Conks had their own hero too, the redoubtable 'Bull' Bowman, who was to 'star' in numerous conflicts with the Fullerton boys. The Conks were also identified with their own favourite weapon, heavy pick shafts said to weigh around 3 lb and measuring more than 40 inches in length. The Billy Boys, on the other hand, defended themselves with more than membership cards. Their weaponry included the usual gang range: First World War bayonets, swords, daggers, bottles and chains. Thus armed, the East End for much of the 1930s was to have its own version of *Oh, What a Lovely War*! It takes on the aspect of a seemingly endless tragicomedy when viewed in the retrospect of more than half a century, making it difficult to fully appreciate the true feelings and animosity which inspired those wild and lawless days between the two world wars in that part of Glasgow.

The Billy Boys, being King Billy's Boys, had their own band, which would accompany them to their Sunday morning church services. At least that's where they appeared to be going. But the route they normally chose to get them to church invariably went by the most circuitous course, taking them, surprise, surprise, along all the tenement streets which they knew were mainly populated by Irish Catholics, the main ones being Poplin and French Streets. Both were adjacent to little Norman Street, from where the Conks would clearly hear the lilting flutes and beating drums, especially the gargantuan Lambeg, the biggest, loudest and most fearsome of all marching drums, thumped by their drummer who had the somewhat magnificent name of Elijah Cooper. The various Catholic saints and holy days of the Roman Church were particular favourites for the Billy Boys to go out on their marches, and on such days they were even more exuberant, their band even more impassioned, as they let that part of the East End know they were once again 'Marching Through Georgia' and 'Guarding Old Derry's Wall', the thumps from

Elijah's monstrous Lambeg (the name comes from a wee village just outside Lisburn in Ulster) reverberating through the district like terrifying thunder claps.

One such march, about which both sides would talk for years, was on a celebrated 12th of July – the Protestant day marking the anniversary of the 1690 Battle of the Boyne. After their customary assembly at Bridgeton Cross, the Billy Boys had marched down Main Street. On this occasion, however, the bandsmen, though carrying their instruments, were not playing them. The only sound was the beat of a solitary kettledrum, tapping out the left, left; left, left, left of the silent march of band and Boys. It was only when they got to the Poplin and Norman Street intersection that the band struck up. And how! BOOM! BOOM! BOOM, BOOM, BOOM went the cue from the mighty Lambeg, the flautists, drummers and other musicians following with their most rumbustious-ever rendition of that hallowed anthem, a tune that might be said to bring out the best and the worst in people on both sides of the divide – 'The Sash'! In order to make sure their appearance and music had the most devastating effect (which it did), they staged the surprise street march at just after seven o'clock in the morning! If you know certain parts of Glasgow, you will have something of an idea about what happened next, although it must be added that any speculation at the reaction to that morning's musical reveille would most certainly underestimate the events that occurred.

Such demonstrations by the Billy Boys and their band would never go without some form of retribution. They were regularly welcomed, especially on the occasions they walked right up Norman Street itself, with anything the householders wanted to be rid of – ideally jetsam which might cause some damage to the musical rabble below. Bottles, bricks and items hauled out the previous night from the midgie (the backcourt waste bins);

anything that was heavy or messy. Invariably the contents of the previous night's bedpan, kept especially for the occasion, would be included. The marchers received all these things that morning in July, with a passion that bordered on the perverse, a relish brimming with rancour and savage spite. But then 'The Sash' can have that kind of effect!

For almost two decades the battles between the Billy Boys and the Norman Conks, as well as the two gangs' own conflicts with other groups, were to be a continuing saga of mythic dimensions. If one lot were agitating, the other would be retaliating. They provoked and evoked, they irritated and instigated. They incited and they inflamed. And they revelled in revenge, as they battled their years away for no purpose other than to defend their causes, express their masculinity and demonstrate that they were most macho of macho men, seemingly uncaring about the consequences: the bloodied and scarred faces, the battered and bruised bodies, and the lives that were lost.

They were so entrenched in their warfare that not even the great police tactician Sillitoe could entirely cleanse the city of them, although he was to go a good way towards subduing them in a series of epic encounters which, like those band parades, would become part of the mythology of that part of Glasgow. Like he had done in Sheffield, Sillitoe formed teams of his biggest, fittest and toughest constables and, with the use of furniture lorries as transport for his men, would station them at likely trouble spots, where, with drawn batons (the riot versions, like the ones the New York cops call night-sticks), they would battle it out with the gang members, then fill the big vans with as many prisoners as possible. Well, if the Trojans could have their wooden horse, Sillitoe reckoned he could have his furniture lorries! He would use too, with great effect, his mounted troopers – Sillitoe's Cossacks they called them – wielding their long batons to charge in among rioters.

Both police-filled furniture lorries and the 'Cossacks' were to do this most effectively on one of the occasions when the Billy Boys (Lambeg, flutes and drums blasting from the street) were this time heading for the Norman Street area via Celtic Park for one of their 'spectaculars'. As they approached the Celtic football ground, they had been ordered by the police to go no further but had predictably ignored the command, marching straight past the officers who tried to stop them with outstretched arms. That was as far as the police tolerance was to go on that occasion, the order being given for the lorries to disgorge their 'special forces' and the horses to charge.

The battle that followed was to be gone over in minute detail for years to come, each version of the story including the tale of Elijah Cooper, the corpulent Lambeg lambaster. Even Sillitoe remembered that particular confrontation as something out of the ordinary and included the story of it in his autobiography. The battle between the police, the gang members and their bandsmen had been of true riot dimensions, and apparently one of the very few not to be injured in the fray was the legendary Elijah. The dedicated drummer had saved himself by jumping through the torn skin of his huge drum to escape the flying police batons.

Prison sentences were doled out to the chief protagonists of this memorable riot, the Billy Boys' leader Fullerton being arrested at the height of the battle by a constable who had something of a reputation in the East End. He was known as Big Tommy from the Toll – his full name was Tommy Morrison and the Toll was local jargon for the East End's best-known landmark, Bridgeton Cross. Big Tommy was big all right. He was an impressively huge man and one of the stalwarts of the furniture-van squad, and his arrest of the battling Fullerton was very Hollywood: holding King Billy with one arm, he carried on fighting, knocking out numerous would-be rescuers with his other arm. Fullerton received a year's imprisonment for his part in the action. This virtually marked the end of the career that had made him a legend in his own lifetime in the streets of Glasgow's East End. When he died at the age of 57, just over a quarter of a century after that most remembered of street battles, there was practically nothing to show for the fame and idolatry he had once enjoyed. But that was the way of such careers; princes on the streets, paupers in their lives. The asphalt monarchies over which they presided were the most impoverished of kingdoms. Fullerton ended his days in poverty and was found dead in the bed recess of the humble single-roomed house in which he lived in Brook Street, near Bridgeton Cross. It was noted by one morning newspaper that such living conditions were almost identical to those in which he had been born all those years previously.

The East End was not to forget him, however, for the King of the Billy Boys was seen off in a style that he would have cherished. Massed flute bands were at the head of some 600 marchers who accompanied his hearse all the way from Bridgeton to the cemetery at Riddrie, playing along the route such airs as 'Onward Christian Soldiers', 'Imperial Echoes' and 'Melrose'. The true and loyal colours of red, white and blue predominated in the swathes of wreaths that went with his coffin, one card simply saying 'To our former leader'. Such was the respect for Fullerton, there were those among the marchers who were anything but Billy Boys, including the greatest boxer of the day, Peter Keenan, one of the city's Irish Catholics; his own great-grandfather was one of the multitude who had fled to Scotland during the Great Famine.

Billy Boys and Tim Malloys

The team of those Irish immigrants, Celtic Football Club, and their great rivals, Rangers, were also to come under Sillitoe's law. The big Englishman created one of the greatest sporting sensations when he threatened to stop them playing each other. Really – Sillitoe warned that this would happen unless the two sides took some action to curb the violence that, at the time, accompanied their every meeting. No Rangers versus Celtic football matches! Just imagine the sensation if that was in today's news! Sillitoe was deadly serious about the threat, which to fans seemed inconceivable. He summoned both team managers to his office and warned them that unless the current waves of rowdiness at their games were cleaned up, that was it. There would be no more games between the two teams. Being the kind of man he was – he had by now demonstrated his strength very positively – they knew it could actually happen. Sillitoe's threat led to him receiving a death threat from one irate fan, his team affiliation unknown. It was the first time in his long career that he had ever received such a warning and police officials took it so seriously that they put a guard on the family home at Kilmacolm, with all mail carefully scrutinised; the house was even evacuated on one occasion, when a suspicious parcel was delivered.

In the meantime, Sillitoe set about his own plan of campaign for the terracing thugs, establishing the foundations for the kind of law enforcement which is still used by the city police at Old Firm and other big matches. He had a ring of uniformed men on the track circling the pitch, each man scrutinising the crowd for troublemakers, other uniformed and plainclothes men mingling with spectators, plus a large number of men held in reserve, out of sight and ready at a second's notice to swoop on any disorder. The 'Cossacks' would be there in force. Sillitoe himself made sure he attended all major fixtures with potential trouble, dressed in his smartest uniform and taking a prominent place in the stadium. It was clear to everyone that this chief cop feared no one. One of his favourite punishments (because it worked!) for those he considered to have hooligan potential, but so far had merely made a nuisance of themselves at a game, was to make them report to a local police station for the following four Saturdays. They would have to check in at kick-off time and stay within the station's precincts until the games were over. He considered that missing their beloved football for a month was the absolute worst punishment that could be doled out. Percy Sillitoe didn't have to worry about European human rights law! And crowd behaviour improved sufficiently for him not to enforce his Rangers versus Celtic ban.

It was by such tactics, along with his furniture lorries, his 'Cossacks' and other ploys, that Sillitoe drummed home to the sectarian gangs that Glasgow would not tolerate them. As a result, he did curb their activities, although the more minor ones continued until the outbreak of the Second World War, when both sides suddenly found they had a common cause against another enemy.

When he left Glasgow, Percy Sillitoe went on to be appointed by the Prime Minister as head of MI5 and was knighted for his varied and most notable police career. He died at his home in Eastbourne in 1962, aged 73.

– CHAPTER 17 –

More than Championés

Some might dispute that it has been their greatest achievement. Few would argue, however, that it is their best known, most envied, most talked about and most symbolic. It is also their most loved achievement, at least by their Catholic supporters.

The creation of Celtic Football Club was the fulfilment of a dream. One reason for its existence was to feed the poor children of the East End. Another which wasn't talked about so much but which was felt very strongly about, was to keep those of the faith together and prevent any defection to those in whose midst they had arrived – the other team, as it were. It was somewhere for young local lads to go, keeping them off the streets on a Saturday. The creation of Celtic Football Club achieved all of those things and more, many of them rather splendidly. But the real dream that Celtic attained was showing those who so often looked down on the Irish immigrants that they could achieve the best; they could form a club with the finest of stadiums, and the sportsmen who played for them could be the very best in the new country. Not only that, Celtic would show the world that while this Glasgow Irish community might have originated from the poorest of the poor (and many of them were still struggling to be free of deprivation), they could do anything they put their heart and souls into. That was the dream that Celtic was to achieve for the Glasgow Irish. It was the greatest single demonstration of the community that, although they were down, they were never out; that dreams of being the best really could come true and be an inspiration to them all. That is the real story of Celtic Football Club.

There is no other single manifestation of the two communities who migrated from Ireland than that of the support of the two football teams which represent them, Celtic and Rangers. While the latter may loudly profess its Scottishness, in many ways it ironically owes its existence to its Irishness – to the influence its support derived from the Orangemen among the immigrants from Ireland who settled in Glasgow.

Keeping the flock together had been one of the major concerns of the Catholic Church authorities in and around Glasgow during the years of the post-Great Famine migration. It had been easy enough maintaining the faith back in Ireland, where they were surrounded by their own kind. Some, of course, lived in closer proximity to Protestant communities, but even then they all lived in enclaves of their own. It was different in Scotland. There were no separate Irish communities, no ghettos, no special settlement areas, no Harlems, no Sowetos. Of course, there were clearly delineated areas of the city in which they congregated, districts with the lowest rents, where kinsmen were already housed. Large communities of Catholic Irish settled in areas such as the Gorbals, Calton, Bridgeton, Townhead and Anderston. In these places they lived cheek by jowl with other immigrants: Highlanders cleared from their glens to make way for sheep and cattle and bigger profits for their lairds, Lithuanians, Poles and Jews, fleeing various forms of persecution, as well as other incomers from different parts of Scotland. Not everyone around the Irish immigrants was of their faith, and it was the same at their places of work. It was a matter of concern to the minders of their flock, the priests, whose problem was compounded by the fact that there just wasn't enough of them to go around.

The enormous inflow of Irish who had come and settled had not done so all at once and were not accompanied by the proportionate Catholic hierarchical infrastructure, the backbone of their community. There was reluctance among some priests in Ireland to follow their departing flocks. Some considered that their presence was more vital in Ireland; others took a harder attitude and viewed emigration as a form of desertion. Whatever their reasons, in the early years of the post-Great Famine migration, the huge community of Irish Catholics in Glasgow had a drastic deficiency of priests and churches as well as of ancillary institutions such as orphanages, schools, seminaries, various religious orders and the like, and even their own newspapers, all of which are vital in the constitution of the complete Catholic way of life. Much of what they had known and expected to provide a dynamic religious life was absent. The shortage of clerics in Glasgow was such that hard-pressed priests in the city had to serve other parishes, often miles away. St

Mary's in Abercrombie Street, in the East End, had to look after Hamilton and Rutherglen, while such disparate localities as Milngavie and Dunfermline were cared for by a priest based at Stirling.

The first priority of the Catholic authorities in Glasgow in the late nineteenth century had been to tackle a major church-building programme, and this was achieved with what must surely be considered quite spectacular results. In 1860 there were only five Roman Catholic churches in the west of Scotland; by 1884 there were 54, with 18 extensions having been completed. As well as being faced with this major building programme, the Church's great challenge was to retain its own youth within the fold, confronted as the young people were with what they saw as the great evils of their Church – indifference, radicalism and, perhaps worst of all, Protestantism. The Irish priests were well aware of the danger facing their young people, none more so than one of their most tireless and devoted servants, Andrew Kerins, a man in his late 40s, who had come over from Ballymote in County Sligo as a younger man.

Kerins was better known in the East End of Glasgow as Brother Walfrid, a member of the Marist teaching order, and for ten years as headmaster of the Sacred Heart School. He was well aware that the youth of St Mary's in the East End, the biggest parish in Glasgow, with which he had been closely connected for years, came into regular contact with Protestants, both in the workplace and where they lived. In the priest's eyes, such regular contact was a problem, particularly since Catholics might be affected by the more relaxed attitudes of that reformed branch of Christianity.

Then there were the Protestant soup kitchens, which were now flourishing, following in the footsteps of that very first one, opened all those years earlier by members of the Protestant faith right on the doorstep of their very own cathedral in Clyde Street. Soup kitchens were one thing, but flaunting them like that under their very noses was another. Like others, Brother Walfrid was not without a deep and inherent Irish distrust of charity from those who were non-Irish, especially by those who were Protestant and non-Irish. He would have known of, and probably even experienced back in Sligo in those dreadful post-Famine days, the worst of the 'soupers', as they were known, who only gave handouts to those willing to convert to their religion. Were the ones in Glasgow likewise trying to proselytise with their philanthropy, get converts with their charity? Were they really as open-hearted as they appeared to be, or was it a conspiracy to subvert those of their faith . . . the faith? Whatever, they had to be wary if their flock was to remain intact, never to let down their guard and always be on the lookout for ways and means of inspiring them and keeping them all together.

To Brother Walfrid, who was perpetually on the lookout for such opportunities, it was like a gift of inspiration one evening in 1887 when he enthusiastically attended a historic reception at St Mary's church hall in East Rose Street (now known as Forbes Street), just off Abercrombie Street in the Calton. It was in honour of the newly crowned champions of Scottish football, Hibernian of Edinburgh. There they were, the first Scots–Irish football club to win the Scottish Cup, the most coveted trophy in the country. Although they were from Edinburgh, they had thousands of supporters throughout Scotland, and some of the most enthusiastic were in Glasgow. Many of them, with green cards in their hats with the slogan 'Hurry Up Hibs' (that was as far as fan identification went), had been at Hampden Park earlier in the day when a crowd of around 10,000 had seen Hibs beat Dumbarton 2–1 to win the cup, only the fourteenth time the tournament had been staged.

It had been a much-awaited victory for Hibs, who had three times in previous years got as far as the semi-finals. At last it had been their day, and what a great night for the Irish that was. Weren't Hibernian the most Irish of clubs? Started up by the Irish-born Canon Edward Hannan, they were run as a strictly Catholic team, all players having to be practising Catholics. One was even rejected from team selection because he had missed mass too often. Their all-Catholic team policy was eventually dropped, but nevertheless they were so Irish that when they were first formed 12 years previously and applied to join the Scottish Football Association, sending off their entry fee to them, it had been rejected on the grounds that they weren't a Scottish football team! That problem was eventually ironed out, however, and they were finally accepted as a Scottish club, albeit with an Irish orientation. Now they were the champions of Scotland, and wasn't that something for St Mary's to be celebrating on that historic night . . . historic not only because Hibs had won that championship, but because of other events that happened that evening.

It was a thought-provoking evening for Brother Walfrid. If only the Church had the money that the football club was generating then the St Vincent de Paul Society wouldn't have such a struggle to provide money for the Poor Children's Dinner Table movement. Not only that, if the Glasgow Irish had a club of their own like Hibs, and they became champions too, it would be the greatest thing for the people of the East End. Wouldn't it put an end to all those other influences: the radical, the indifferent and, the most pervasive, the Protestant?

There were representatives there that night from the other two Glasgow parishes as well, St Andrew's and St Alphonsus. When Brother Walfrid and the others spoke together during the celebratory dinner, one thing was uppermost in their minds.

Why couldn't they have their own 'Hibernian', their own team that could inspire the community? If they could have their own championship-winning team it would show those who so often castigated them for their religion and lack of education, said they were second rate, made constant barbs about them and joked about them that they were wrong. It could be the very thing that would change all that, give their own communities the sense of achievement they so badly needed, and restore their pride in themselves. A dream was born that night in a little hall in the East End of Glasgow. Now they had to make it a reality.

There followed meetings throughout the summer of 1887 on the pros and cons of creating a football club of their own. Right from the start, in all their conversations they were unanimous and determined about one thing: the future team would be no mere suburban club providing a kickabout for the lads. It would be the best – champions, an inspiration to every Irish person and their descendants in Glasgow. They would do everything the great Hibernian had done. And the more they talked, the more they became enthused about the project that dominated their minds right through the summer. St Mary's was the most forceful and dominant of parishes in its pursuit of the idea, perhaps even to the extent of being overbearing at times, so much so that St Andrew's pulled out as it felt 'sidetracked'.

Having been given the blessing of Archbishop Eyre of Glasgow to pursue their great sporting plan, a mass meeting was convened on a Sunday afternoon in early November of that year, 1887, once more at St Mary's hall. All the talking had been done; now was the time for decision-making, which was the purpose of the meeting that day. The city's new football team was to be launched and not only were they out to emulate the great Hibernian of Edinburgh, it would also carry the same ancient Roman name for Ireland and be known as Hibernian of

Glasgow. (Despite the fact that the year 1888 is boldly displayed at the entrance to what is now their magnificent stadium at Parkhead, the Celtic Football and Athletic Club was actually launched at that meeting on 6 November 1887.) That, however, was the only point on which Brother Walfrid was in disagreement with his confreres. Right from the inception of his idea about having a football team, he had spoken of it in terms of having but one name – Celtic. It was a name, he told the meeting that day in the most impassioned of tones, which more identified with and would be representative of their peculiarly immigrant community. His vision was that the very word encapsulated the concept of a club around which he believed the kindred but religiously divided Celtic peoples of Ireland and Scotland could rally and be united. It could even be a name, he told them, which would one day become a Scottish institution, while at the same time cherishing its Irish heritage.

His persuasion carried the day, and Celtic it was to be, with just one minor difference. It would be Celtic with a soft 'c' and not 'keltic', the way Brother Walfrid always pronounced it. And so their new team and sporting movement would be known by the full title of Celtic Football and Athletic Club, and it mattered to none of them that the man who had worked so hard to get it started would for the rest of his long life (Brother Walfrid died in 1915 at the age of 75) continue to call it 'Keltic'. The remaining details were finalised that Sunday, with the drawing up of the basic principles for the club, the formation of a committee and the election of its first office-bearers. Celtic were in business.

Three weeks later, on 29 November, a news item of no great significance appeared on the pages of the *Scottish Umpire*, making it the first-ever story about Celtic Football Club. It read:

> We learn that the efforts which have lately been made
> to organise in Glasgow a first-class Catholic football
> club have been successfully consummated by the
> formation of the Glasgow Celtic Football and Athletic
> Club under influential auspices. They have secured a
> six-acre ground in the East End which they mean to put
> in fine order. We wish the 'Celts' all success.

In order of their priorities, the first thing the club did was raise funds and get themselves a playing ground, which was a different way of going about such things; it was usually the case that first of all you got your team and then the ground came later. But that was how it was to be. From the date of the meeting, 6 November 1887, they moved with an impressive display of determination and objectivity. Within a week they had obtained a rented site for what would be known as Celtic Park. It didn't look much, being a rough, uneven piece of spare ground, situated at the junction of what was then known as Dalmarnock Street (now Springfield Road) and Janefield Street, bounded on one side by the Janefield cemetery (Eastern Necropolis) and just a couple of hundred yards from the present Parkhead Stadium. The site, incidentally, is now occupied by that great Scottish institution, the Barr's Irn Bru factory. Mr R.F. Barr, an early member of the soft drinks family, was one of the original subscribers to the club. Despite their newly acquired ground being a rather scruffy patch of land, the committee saw its great potential and agreed to the landlord's terms of £50 for the yearly rental.

Two months later, in January 1888, the club was to distribute its first fund-raising circular for the purpose of enlisting subscriptions as well as revealing what plans they had made so far and proclaiming their future intentions:

The main object of the club is to supply the East End conferences of the St Vincent De Paul Society with funds for the maintenance of the 'Dinner Tables' of our needy children in the Missions of St Mary's, Sacred Heart and St Michael's. Many cases of sheer poverty are left unaided through lack of means. It is therefore with this principal object that we have set afloat the 'Celtic', and we invite you as one of our ever-ready friends to assist in putting our new park in proper working order for the coming football season.

We have already several of the leading Catholic football players of the West of Scotland on our membership list. They have most thoughtfully offered to assist in the good work.

We are fully aware that the 'élite' of football players belong to this city and suburbs, and we know that from there we can select a team which will be able to do credit to the Catholics of the West of Scotland as the Hibernians have been doing in the east.

Again there is also the desire to have a large recreation ground where our Catholic young men will be able to enjoy the various sports which will build them up physically, and we feel sure we will have many supporters with us in this laudable object.

While they canvassed for financial support throughout the city during that winter of 1887–88, hundreds of volunteers donated the most valuable commodity they could to the club – their labour. It was vital in converting what had been a rough tract of ground into a trim and level playing field, together with a spectators' stand, into which were built dressing-rooms for two teams, shower baths, a small office, a trainer's room and storage facilities. All those Irishmen and their sons with their close links in the building trade had never been so useful – and appreciated – to the local community.

The fledgling Celtic, still minus a full playing team, had created such a wave of enthusiasm for their cause that Hibernian returned to Glasgow to play a special charity match for St Mary's in aid of the Children's Dinner Table, Clyde Football Club freely offering their home ground at Barrowfield Park, on French Street, for the game, billed as the East End Charity Cup. The match attracted over 12,000 spectators, an even bigger crowd than there had been at Hampden to see Hibs win the Scottish Cup. One of the big draws was that the team taking part against Hibs was the famous Renton FC, one of Scotland's top clubs of that era. Renton were so good, in fact, they were even billed as the 'world champions' and, while that term might surprise, it was not used loosely. After having won the 1888 Scottish Cup by beating Cambuslang 6–1, Renton had been invited to meet West Bromwich Albion, the English Cup holders, in a special challenge match billed as the 'World championship'. By beating the English team 4–1, the Scottish club took their proud place in soccer history as the world's first-ever world club champions.

By the spring of 1888, Celtic were concentrating on getting a team together and were in the concluding stages of finalising an impressive squad of top-calibre players, six of the best members of the Hibs team who lived in the west leaving the Edinburgh club to join them. This caused, as it might be imagined, a calamitous affect on the Edinburgh Irish club's playing strength, not to be easily forgotten by the Edinburgh supporters. The new Celtic team still had to be finalised and accepted by the Scottish Football Association, however, and it was decided that in order to publicise the fact that a new Glasgow football club would shortly be making their debut and that the city's newest football ground had been completed and was ready for use, a Celtic Park opening game was staged in early May of that year. Once more it was Hibs (their star players' defection to Celtic not having happened yet) who journeyed through to do the honours, a crowd of 3,000 seeing them draw 0–0 against Cowlairs. Rangers had been invited to take part in the match and although, unfortunately, they couldn't attend, to make amends they agreed to be the team in opposition in an even more important match – the new Celtic team's first-ever game.

Just under three weeks after that early bit of Glasgow Irish sporting history, the opening of their ground, that even more historic event was to take place: Celtic's very first public outing on their own pitch. At last the dream had become a reality, the organising committee of the club having pulled off no small miracle by starting from scratch and turning a few acres of rough land into a regulation standard football park with the best of playing turf, building a spectators' stand complete with all the necessary facilities, and having got together enough players to field a first-eleven team, with enough men in reserve for emergencies, all in a period of six months. If this quite remarkable achievement was to be a benchmark of what they were about, maybe all those other dreams that Brother Walfrid and those pioneering officials had for their sporting enterprise might just come true after all.

So on 27 May 1888, the new Celtic team took to the field for their very first game against the team they called the Light Blues, who would become their greatest rivals. The traditional hoops of the Celtic team weren't on display for that first game, incidentally. The club's colours were registered with the SFA as white and green, but for their first few games they played in white shirts donated by local drapers, Penman's of Bridgeton Cross, only the collars being green, with the club badge of the shamrock in red. Later they changed to a strip of green-and-white vertical stripes, and it wasn't until some years afterwards that those hoops were introduced. It is perhaps only with hindsight that the significance of that very first game of Celtic FC – and its final score – on that night in May 1888 can be appreciated. The game was a friendly and, as if to enhance the great occasion, Glasgow Rangers, the team who were to become their legendary rivals of the future, were in opposition. At the time, however, the fact that it was Rangers had little or no meaning other than that they were the first team to take on this brand-new Glasgow club, the first-ever Irish Catholic team in the city. There were no other connotations. Rangers were not known as a Protestant side. There were no Orange connections. Their fans were not anti-Catholic. There were no Irish banners or symbols on display, nor were any fans waving Union Jacks or Saltire flags. No one chanted anything about the Pope, nor did anyone from the opposition terracing say anything about the Queen – it was Victoria at the time and she still had another 13 years to reign. There was no animosity between the fans, apart from the usual, over the match itself. These were all to be unfortunate developments of the future, and sadly a not-too-distant future. Why, it might be asked, were Rangers chosen to be the very first club to play against this new team of Glasgow Irish? The choice, it appears, was not Celtic's. According to manager Willie Maley, speaking some years later, it was 'our good Light Blue friends' who desired it be recorded that they were Celtic's first opponents.

Rangers had been in existence for some 16 years, having begun life in something of *Boys' Own* fashion, a story that any devoted Rangers fan knows by heart, although it does tend to vary according to who is telling the story. What doesn't vary is the fact that while Celtic's equally romantic beginning kicked off with a Brother Walfrid, Rangers got theirs from a brother called Moses. This was the memorably named Moses McNeil, one of a family of six brothers from Gareloch. Moses was a student in Glasgow and, along with one of his brothers, Peter, and a group of fellow students from his village, was a keen athlete. Rowing was the group's speciality. One day, so the story goes, they were romantically skimming over the rippling waters of the Clyde. As they passed the part of Glasgow Green where there were the first football pitches, the oarsmen were fascinated by the various teams at play. One writer gaily includes the colourful scenario of them upping their oars and heading for the riverbank in order to have a closer look at those ball games. The new sport appealed so much that Moses and his friends decided to found a team of their own, at a park in the West End of the city.

What about a name for their new team? Back to Moses again. The young man from Gareloch had been thumbing through a sports book one day when he came across an English Rugby team whose name appealed. They were called Rangers. Moses liked the name so much that he suggested to his friends that it would be a good title for the new club they were forming. They unanimously agreed, and Rangers FC was born. Rangers played their first three seasons on Fleshers' Haugh, where they had first seen those footballers while rowing on the Clyde and also the historic part of the Glasgow Green where O'Connell celebrants had planned to meet. After playing regularly for three years there, Rangers moved pitches, this time to Burnbank Park, just off Great Western Road in the West End. Their next move was to another field known as Ibrox Park, although it was not on the exact site of the present Ibrox Stadium, which came later. Within two years of being founded, the new club were good enough to do well in the Scottish Cup, and the very first goal scored by them in the competition was by none other than

Moses McNeil. Scriptwriting it may seem, but the story is all apparently true.

The first game of the new Catholic football team on that spring night of 1888 was to be a dream debut for Celtic, the final score being 5–2 in their favour. Their victory over Rangers came at a time when the Ibrox team were emerging as one of the rising stars of Scottish football; their first ten years saw them twice reach the final of the Scottish Cup and by now they were rivalling Queen's Park as the most popular team in the city, holding their own with the best teams, not only in Scotland but also in England. Despite the fact there was only a meagre crowd of around 2,000, mostly local fans, there were ecstatic scenes at the end of the game and boundless jubilation from the founding fathers of the St Mary's committee who were there. Maybe all the dreams they had about the club making its mark not only for the Irish people in Glasgow and Scotland, but also in its fund-raising efforts, would come true a lot sooner than they ever imagined. Incidentally, that humble attendance figure of around 2,000 was to mark the game as a doubly historic event. It was not only Celtic's first-ever game, but the smallest-ever crowd to see the two teams play. It would never – ever – be like that again.

After the match, the two teams, with their helpers and officials, walked back together to St Mary's hall, where they were given a slap-up supper and entertained by a concert, which included solo singers and musicians. The proceedings were described in one of the sports papers as 'of the happiest character'.

Relations between the two teams were to continue along such lines for several years following that historic night. There was nothing about Rangers at the time to make them any different from the many other teams with whom Celtic were in regular contact. Even after 15 years they were reported to be travelling together on one occasion when both teams were meeting rival Edinburgh clubs. The sporting press recorded that they had gone through to Edinburgh on the 1.15 p.m. express on the Saturday afternoon. Each club had its own saloon carriage, and it was noted that Celtic had the foremost of the two carriages, one wag suggesting that the coaches had been arranged according to merit. The two teams also returned together in similar coaches, with the players mixing freely and the *Scottish Sport* newspaper noted in its gossip column that 'both teams were reported to be very pally . . . and why not?' But in the Scottish/Protestant–Irish/Catholic context, something, somewhere had to give. Perhaps it was inevitable that it would happen right there in Glasgow, the heartland of the two disparate communities.

Many in the Orange and other ultra-Protestant groupings were of the opinion that it was bad enough having all those Catholic Irish pouring into and settling in the city, but now things had taken a turn for the worse. They were not only a formidable presence in the country's major sporting scene and on the playing field, but were also emerging as a business entity in the East End of Glasgow. While Celtic would evolve to become the great and outstanding Scottish club it is today, in those early days it was viewed in no other context than that of 'Irish' and 'Catholic'. You only had to look at the committee running the club, composed as it was of either Irishmen or the sons of Irishmen, to appreciate just how Irish the club was. And they were Irishmen who in general were closely connected with a variety of active Irish movements of the time, such as the Home Rule movement, the Young Ireland Society and the Irish National League among others. As one of their directors put it, 'Celtic is the pride of the Irish race in England, Ireland and Scotland.' One of the founding Irish committeemen, Patrick

Welsh, had been an active rebel and Fenian and had fled for his life to Glasgow from Ireland during one of the uprisings. His connection with the legendary Maley family is one of the great sagas of those formative days of Celtic. The Maleys included Tom and Willie, both members of the first team. Willie became one of the outstanding figures in Scottish football, having an awesome career with Celtic. He was one of its first players as well as the club's first match secretary, before becoming the most legendary of managers in a remarkable 52-year association with the club. Although their opponents wouldn't see it that way, the Welsh–Maley connection is one of legend and always figured largely whenever Maley recounted his life story.

The story has its beginnings in Ireland in 1867, a notable year in the calendar of turbulent Irish history, the date of the Fenian Uprising. The Fenians had emerged from the thousands of Irishmen who fought on both sides of the American Civil War, and from whose traditions the Irish Republican Army is derived. Their experience in the bloody battles of the Civil War had made trained and hardy soldiers out of thousands of them and, when it was over, almost a quarter of a million of them were sworn in as Fenians, taking the name from the Fianna, a legendary band of warriors from the ancient and mysterious world of Gaelic mythology. It was also the same Civil War veterans, who decided to celebrate their Irish heritage by inaugurating New York's first official St Patrick's Day parade in 1766. In 1867, the Fenians decided it was time for them to mount a military insurrection in Ireland, an event that was to have the bloodiest of consequences. Patrick Welsh, then just a lad, was one of those young Fenians but he wanted no more of the bloodshed. He was on the run from the authorities and hoped to get over the water, to that place of refuge of so many of his countrymen – Glasgow.

He was hiding from the police and soldiers around the

docklands of Dublin, hoping to spot a ship heading for Scotland and, like others had done, get a passage there by stowing away. One night as he was lurking around the docks in the vicinity of Pigeon House Fort on the banks of the Liffey, he was suddenly confronted by a man with a rifle. This was the end for him, he thought, as he recognised the man as a British soldier. The soldier was on patrol with his regiment, the North British Fusiliers, later to be known as the Royal Scots Fusiliers. He barked the customary command at the slim youth: 'Halt, who goes there?' Although the man's accent had softened, it was still sufficiently Irish for Welsh to spot. He pleaded with the soldier, Irishman to Irishman, to hear him out and the soldier patiently listened to his story. He was up to no evil, he told the soldier. All he wanted was to be away from all the Troubles and the killing, and go somewhere he could get on with his life in peace and freedom. He had been told that Glasgow could be that place and if only he could get there, he pleaded, then he could live out his dreams.

The soldier, it turned out, not only had patience but understanding for the young fellow Irishman before him and went out of his way, at some considerable risk to himself should he be caught by one of his officers, to guide him towards a ship and ensure that Patrick Welsh got safely on board. After wishing the lad the best of luck for a safe voyage, the pair exchanged their names. The soldier's name was Tom Maley and he was from Ennis in County Clare. He too had run away from home, in his case to join the British Army and had fought for years for them in various wars. He had been to Sebastopol and Balaclava, no less, in the bloody Crimean War.

The soldier and the runaway Fenian kept in touch over the years and when he reached the rank of sergeant and completed his 21 years' service with the British Army, Tom Maley too thought that Glasgow had much better prospects for his young family than those terrible times in post-Great Famine Ireland. Patrick Welsh by this time had carved out a successful career for himself in Glasgow, having served an apprenticeship as a tailor and become skilled and successful enough to be in charge of his own business in Buchanan Street. Of course he was delighted to be of assistance when Tom Maley asked if he could help him and his family of young sons when they arrived in the city.

Two of the former sergeant's sons, Tom and William (the latter was born in Ireland while his father was stationed at the barracks in Newry, Co. Down), became keen and active sportsmen after the family settled in Glasgow. Their father continued his military career, this time as a drill instructor with the Volunteers, first of all at Thornliebank and later at Cathcart. The two boys became active footballers, William playing with Netherlee then going on to Third Lanark. He was also keen on athletics and was good enough to become the Scottish 100 yards sprint champion.

At one of the inaugural meetings of the St Mary's committee, who established the Celtic club, the Maley brothers were mentioned by one of their scouts. Patrick Welsh, the successful businessman tailor, was on that committee and on hearing of the boys' soccer prowess was able to give them the recommendation that they were from a very respectable family, which he knew well, and would be ideal players for the club. On the strength of that it was decided that Patrick Welsh, accompanied by Brother Walfrid and another committeeman, should pay the Maley household a visit, with a view to signing the boys for the club. And so the sons of the man who had helped Welsh get away from the Troubles and come to Glasgow became two of the first-ever Celtic players.

Others on that early committee were every bit as Irish as

Patrick Welsh. John Glass, the first president, was active in Irish Nationalist circles such as the Glasgow Amnesty Association, the Young Ireland Society and the Irish National League and made speeches on behalf of Home Rule and other such causes. William McKillop, the son of an immigrant family, became the MP for North Sligo and also regularly campaigned on nationalist ideals. When he died, he was given a papal blessing from Rome. Tom Colgan often spoke at Amnesty for the Prisoners' meetings, and the four Maley brothers took active roles in similar activities, as did virtually all of the founding members of the club.

Airing their Irishness and their attitudes was often a feature of events where speeches were required, such as half-yearly or annual general meetings as well as supporters clubs' festivals. It was at one of these in the National Halls in the Gorbals, the same venue where the fictional Hannah attended the Cavan Reunion Gala, that John Ferguson, the Protestant who had been called Glasgow's Greatest Irishman and was by then a bailie in Glasgow Corporation, wondered if the young men might be as true to Ireland as their fathers had been. 'There was a time in Scotland when Catholics were not what they are now but that they now stood on equality with any church or people in the land. If they were at times disloyal it was not because of the constitution of Scotland. It was because of the plundering of their native land.' His words were met with rousing cheers.

Celtic aired their own feelings vociferously just after their third year in existence, when the landlord for the ground on which they had established the first Celtic Park confronted them with an enormous rent hike. He had closely monitored the club's progress and was aware of the fact that the team they called Celtic were most certainly going places and on the way were making themselves some nice money. He wanted a bigger share of it. Celtic were having none of his demands and at their half-yearly meeting in 1891 in the Caledonian Halls in London Road, committeeman John McLaughlin let fly at their landlord when moving the motion to adopt the report of the meeting.

Being an Irish club, he said with no little bitterness, it was but natural that they should have a greedy landlord and that they had one who was working to take a high place among the rack-renters (extortionate landlords) in Ireland. In the old country, those gentlemen were satisfied with doubling or, at worst, trebling the rent, but the bright genius who boasted to possess Celtic Park wanted nine times the present rent, from £50 to £400. They would be having none of it, he said, which was why they had to look around for another ground.

Seconding the motion, Stephen Henry took up the theme, saying that the splendid report was proof of the ability of Irishmen to manage any concern in which they took an interest. They had in their team and club membership men who were fit to compete favourably with those of any similar institutions in the country.

In moving the adoption of the report, Thomas Flood added to this. He said that Irishmen in Scotland years had been made little of in the past because very few of their number were in business or positions of responsibility. He believed they had demonstrated they could be successful, not only in commercial life. They had proved to possess pluck and perseverance by the manner in which they had risen to the top of the ladder in the football world.

Sites in Springburn and Possilpark were considered as an alternative to their Parkhead ground; there were good bargains available in spare acreage in these areas at the time. However, with some luck, they were able to secure a much closer site, almost adjacent to the original park and, obtaining it on a ten-year lease, immediately set about converting it into one of the finest football grounds in the country. It was just across the road from their first Celtic Park and is the present site of Parkhead Stadium.

The owner of the new Parkhead site, incidentally, on which they had taken the long lease, was eventually persuaded to sell the ground to them. It has to be noted that this transaction must be one of the most interesting of the club's deals over the years, for the owner of the ground was none other than the wealthy estate owner of the day, Lord Newlands. It so happened that his lordship was one of the most senior Freemasons in Britain, being described in *Who's Who* in Glasgow, 1909, as 'an enthusiastic Freemason'. He was so enthusiastic, in fact, that he was Grand Master of the Masons for a number of years at the turn of the century and one of the great establishment figures of the day in Glasgow and central Scotland. His titles and connections included that of Vice-Lieutenant of Lanarkshire, president of the Lanarkshire Territorial Force Association, former Scots Greys officer, ex-Eton and Oxford, and, to boot, a generous benefactor. One of his bequests was the building of a convalescent home in Lanark as a memorial to his late wife. Just along London Road and virtually in the shade of the present-day Parkhead super-stadium there's a small street named Mauldslie Street. It was named after the home of Lord Newlands at the time, Mauldslie Castle, and is perhaps the only existing reminder of the great Freemason who sold Celtic their Parkhead ground. Celtic moved to the new ground on the south side of Janefield Street the following year. It was designed as a multi-sports ground, complete with cycling and athletics tracks, and was of such a standard that it was even to become the venue for the world cycling championships (cycling was going through a phase of great popularity in Scotland at the time). When they had moved to the new ground, one wag commented that it was like leaving the graveyard to enter into paradise. His comment was repeated in the newspapers and was for evermore to be the fans' favourite name for their beloved Parkhead.

The inauguration of the new ground was again a reflection of the ultra-Irishness of the club. The man chosen as Celtic patron at the club's AGM in 1889 was Michael Davitt, founder of the Irish National Land League, a former Fenian who had served a 15-year penal servitude sentence in Dartmoor for 'Fenian agitation'. To help appreciate the significance of Davitt's presence in Glasgow, to British-Protestant-Loyalist-Royalists of the day, he would have been viewed with similar feelings to the likes of Gerry Adams or Martin McGuinness today. That aside, it was still a memorable day for Celtic, getting their new ground launched and having someone considered such a great Irishman on hand to lay the first sod of the superb new park. It was no ordinary sod at that, for this one was composed entirely of genuine Irish shamrocks, so that even their very laying field would be for ever more a little part of Ireland. Shamrocks mean much more to the Irish than merely being pieces of three- or four-leafed clover. The shamrock is steeped in Irish legend, and is particularly associated with St Patrick himself. He used the shamrock, so it is said, to illustrate the doctrine of the Trinity: one leaf for the Father, one for the Son, and one for the Holy Ghost. But what about when there's a fourth leaf? The story goes that it represents God's Grace. And there's something else about the little shamrock. It's also said to have mystical powers: Eve carried one with her for good luck when she was forced to leave the Garden of Eden. And the shamrock's leaves, they say, when standing upright, give warning of impending storms. One Glasgow Catholic newspaper of the time was so enraptured with the whole idea of planting that first sod of turf (imported all the way from Donegal, no less) that it was to dedicate a pre-ceremony poem to the occasion, a piece of mock-McGonagall doggerel written as though it's the turf itself speaking the words:

> On alien soil like yourself I am here,
> And although I will be crossed sore and oft by the foes
> You will find me as hardy as the Thistle or Rose,
> If metal is needed on your own pitch, you will have it
> Let your play honour me and my friend Michael Davitt.

After that sort of poetic dedication, those little shamrock leaves may well have been standing firmly upright in mystic prescience, knowing what was to happen after Michael Davitt firmly put that very special square of Hibernian turf in its hallowed place. But you might have guessed it, especially if you know Glasgow! That precious sod of shamrocks wasn't even to last the night. It mysteriously vanished just hours after the hero Davitt had ceremoniously dug it into the centre of the playing pitch. And the culprit? He was never found, although it is probable that it was either someone who disliked such a man having planted such a symbol right there on Scottish soil, or else an ultra-fan who was so in love with that sod he just had to have it for himself. The bookies' bet, I think, would have been the former.

Celtic in those early years had its critics, but it also had dissenters within its own ranks. One of the earliest signs of such discord came when the club had been in existence for just two years. There had been talk, more than likely mere chit-chat, about the drinking habits of some of the players. While drink in Glasgow was every bit as prevalent then as it is now – although many more in those days were regularly arrested for drunkenness – the temperance movement was much more active. At one time as many as 50,000 were registered members of the various temperance societies in the city and the biggest number of them were Irish. It was even a source of bonding between the two communities, Irish Catholics and Irish Protestants marching together in the name of alcohol denial. There were branches of male and female Rechabites, abstinence societies of varied descriptions and temperance movements. They marched with their banners behind the best of brass bands, and their demonstrations on Glasgow Green were some of the biggest gatherings ever seen there. They were never more vigorous with those marches or the flaunting of their banners, or more vocal in their proclamations than when holidays approached, such as the Glasgow Fair, Easter and especially New Year. This perhaps accounts for some of the sensitivity at the time over the stories, whether true or not, about the players and their drink.

Some members of the Celtic Football Club, so the talk went, were only in it for the drink and not only that, it was also whispered, this sport they called soccer was infringing on the moral rectitude of young East Enders. That was to be the tenor of a letter to the editor of the *Glasgow Catholic Observer* newspaper from a Mr Owen McGerrigan, living in Butterbiggins Road, Govanhill. His long letter of outrage, at what he considered such terrible goings on, said that football was not only 'sapping the morality of the youth of St Mary's', it was also keeping people from their religious duties. He said he agreed with the priest who had said 'Would to God that the Celtics [*sic*] had never been started!' The question had to be asked, he went on, if after two years of Celtic being in existence, whether St Mary's had the size of congregation it should.

Mr McGerrigan had obviously been paying close attention to the activities at the East End parish, noting what he termed 'the long procession' which took place between St Mary's Hall between eight and eleven o'clock at night to the public house at the corner of the street. He said it was a well-known fact that a number of Celtic players were on the lookout to buy a bar, 'and if St Mary's are not encouraging them they are not preventing them'. St Mary's would be guilty of a grave dereliction of duty if they did not do more to stop the 'insidious evil of intemperance'. Clearly, Mr McGerrigan was a very concerned man.

The following week, Fr Carroll of Calder Street, also in Govanhill, was also to write to the *Observer,* taking great umbrage to the claims in McGerrigan's letter. Accusing him of 'a cowardly attack on the Celtic Football Club and St Mary's parishioners in general', and asking what authority the man had to dictate his line of morality to the Celts or the Catholics of St Mary's. There were some of the Celts first XI, he said, whose morals and religious attendance would equal that of the letter-writer, 'but when he says that many of the Celts are just now looking out for whisky bars of their own, then I say this is a deliberate untruth and I challenge him to prove it. One has certainly taken to the spirit line, but does that affect the whole of them?' Fr Carroll also protested that no one from St Mary's League of the Cross took part in the 'procession from the hall to the public house in East Rose Street'.

A week later there was a farewell presentation to Fr Van der Hyde, a curate at St Mary's who was leaving to take up a position in New Orleans. The allegations that had been made about Celtic were mentioned in the priest's farewell address. Rather than having any ill effect on the parishioners of the East End, he said, the advent of Celtic had resulted in the very opposite. There had been an increase in membership of the League of the Cross at St Mary's and the morality of the parish had actually improved since the advent of Celtic FC. 'At least 200 members per half year have joined,' said Fr Van der Hyde, 'and not because they have a liking for total abstinence but because Celtic FC are in some manner connected with St Mary's.' That remark was greeted with loud cheers. When he had arrived in the parish, he said, there had been a debt of £300 but now they were in credit by £26 8s 9½d. That news was met with louder cheers.

A strange reaction to the existence of Celtic from some of the Catholic Irish in Glasgow was the efforts made by one group to start a club of their own, a second Irish football team. This came about within a couple of years of the foundation of Celtic. The group were not happy with the present officials of the club and, realising the business potential of a successful football team, just as Celtic was shaping up to be, wanted an Irish team of their own. They began negotiations with Hibernian of Edinburgh in a bid to resettle that club in Glasgow. The talk of such a move made the fans of the Edinburgh Irish team furious. They remembered with some bitterness how the club had inspired the foundation of the Glasgow club and also how they had been one of the very first teams to support them by so willingly taking part in the club's opening meeting. The very hand that had fed them, they said, was now to be severely mauled, that being a reference to Celtic persuading six of the star Hibernian players to join them.

The Hibernian fans had already demonstrated their disgust at that, showing Celtic just how badly they thought of them when the Parkhead team went to the Easter Road ground in Edinburgh for their first game against Hibernian. The Glasgow club was met with a hostile crowd. It had been too much for the jeering Hibs fans when the score got to 3–0 for Celtic, clearly the better side on the day. That was it, and over the rails they went for a pitch invasion. Matters looked so fearsome for the Celtic players from the threatening fans (one report labelled the home supporters 'the navvies') that the Hibs team members gallantly surrounded their rivals on the pitch in order to protect them from the angry invaders. The referee had no such protection and was so terrified he turned and ran for his life, and had to be persuaded to return to the pitch from the dressing-room, where he had gone into hiding. Even at that, on his return to the pitch he still felt so intimidated that he blew the final whistle ten minutes early in order to quickly return to the safety of the rooms under the stand.

In order to silence the rumoured move of the Edinburgh side to Glasgow, Michael Whelahan, of the Catholic Young Men's Society attached to St Patrick's in Edinburgh, and one of the co-founders of the club, issued a special statement on the subject. It was forcefully worded in the clearest of terms that the Edinburgh Hibs would be staying where they belonged. 'Hibernian are the Edinburgh Irishmen,' Whelahan's statement began, 'and will carry on as the Edinburgh Irishmen. There will be no move to Glasgow or anywhere else.' One sporting newspaper interpreted the non-move in a slightly different fashion, saying that 'the men in the west had not been able to come to an agreement with the men in the east'.

Undeterred, the men from the west decided to go it alone and their next move was to hold a meeting in the Public Halls in Bridgeton, at which they revealed their plans to the sizeable crowd who turned up. Their objective, they said, was the creation of another club of Glasgow Irishmen in the city on similar lines to that of Celtic. Following the meeting it was announced they were hopeful of completing their arrangements in time for the first round of SFA matches for the forthcoming season, 1889–90, and they had applied and been accepted as members of the Glasgow Association as well as the Scottish Football Association. They had also secured a six-acre site in the vicinity of the Oatlands district, on the south bank of the Clyde directly opposite Fleshers' Haugh with an entry point in Rutherglen Road. They reported that their new ground, to be known as Hibernian Park, was a splendid site and ideal for their requirements in that it was level, drained and well turfed, and in every way ready for an athletic enclosure with a grandstand to be erected complete with a surrounding cinder athletics track. A club secretary, Hugh McGuigan, a member of Clyde Football Club, had been appointed. As a demonstration of how deadly serious they were, the group announced they were assured of financial backing, 'a considerable sum having been put forward to cover immediate expenses' and that they would be proceeding immediately with work on the stand; the track was to be completed sometime later in the year. 'And when the time comes,' said the organisers, they would be announcing a wonderful 'surprise packet'.

The new team, Glasgow Hibernian, were eventually launched in opposition to Celtic with the prediction from the twice-weekly *Scottish Sport* newspaper that their existence could have an effect on the gate money of the Parkhead club. This would have happened, if the new Glasgow Hibs had been a good team. For one of their early games in 1889 they invited the Edinburgh Hibernian to come through and play them, but the original Hibs team couldn't make it on the proposed date and Shettleston took their place. The new Glasgow side won 3–1, but that was a rare victory for them and the team in general were a lacklustre bunch. They failed to muster a solid fan base, were quickly disposed of in the Scottish Cup and with crowds of around only 500, compared to Celtic drawing in 20,000 upwards at the time, the writing was on the wall. As the fans might have chanted, 'There's only one Glasgow Irish', and that was how it was to be.

But that was not to be the last of such threats of establishing a Glasgow Irish team to rival Celtic. Some years later other dissenters threatened to establish another club unless the Celtic officials 'mend their ways'. The new threat came just after Celtic had become a limited company in 1897, and the directors, it was claimed, had not kept some of the promises made to their brake club supporters about season and other ticket prices. The brake clubs were the equivalent of today's supporters' clubs, the name coming from the horse-drawn buses, or brakes, which transported them around the country to support their teams. They were supporters in the best sense of the word, raising money for their clubs with raffles, lotteries, dances, sports meetings, sales and other events. Celtic's brake club members were furious over what they termed the 'high-handed attitude' of their team's directors for reneging on promises over the sales of tickets to them.

At the annual rally of the brake clubs in 1897 in the National Halls in the Gorbals, speaker after speaker hit out at the club directors, who were obviously no one's favourites that night. The rally was told that the letter they had sent to these directors on the subject had been ignored, despite the brake clubs having been of such help and such a good advertisement for Celtic. One speaker was to say that the club had departed from the purpose for which it was originally promoted and that 'the press knew about it'.

What had happened to Celtic, claimed another speaker, was that a lot of 'moneybags' had got hold of them and it seemed that the working men who had spent time and money supporting the club were to have nothing to do with it in the future. They had not cared for the 'moneybags' and the working men would take their sympathy and support in another direction. It was for the meeting to say whether they would tamely submit to such treatment. The same speaker went on to point out that the club had been started for charitable reasons, but these objects were now being ignored. 'If they can do without the working man, then the working man can do without them.'

The subject of drink came up again; this time allegations were made about it and the directors of the club. The delegate for St Patrick's said the directors should keep out of public houses and out of the club as well. This warning was met with a rumble of approbation. Another delegate said he had been in touch with some men who had as much money as the Celtic directors and if they were not satisfied there would be plenty of money from them to start a new club.

Just as they had in the past, such threats subsided after the club and its supporters came to a better accommodation with one another, and Celtic got on with the task for which it had been set up: to raise money for the poor and, in the words of Brother Walfrid, to be a symbol of Irish accomplishment.

Within those first few years, they were well on their way to achieving both of these goals, having handed over £5 a week for free dinners for children and given over £500 to various charities – considerable sums in both cases, considering their present-day respective equivalents are £275 and £27,500. One can only speculate, however, what might have happened had there not been a settlement between the club and those at loggerheads with the board. If Glasgow had two Irish Catholic clubs, would that have inspired two Protestant clubs? It only requires a few moments of contemplation to realise what some of the ramifications might have been.

Although it was not till their fifth year in existence that Rangers beat Celtic, there was a certain relevance about the two teams meeting each other which brought wide smiles to both clubs' boardrooms. What brought those satisfied grins was the fact that Rangers and Celtic meant good business. Very good business. Fans of both teams complain today that the game is all about business, but the bosses were well aware of that more than 100 years ago. In fact, by the 1893–94 season they had given up the team's annual jaunt to England for short tours during the festive season. As far as the boardroom of both teams were concerned, there was a lot more financial festivity to be had right here in Glasgow when these two teams played each other and, as a result, the annual Ne'erday game was to be born. Rangers' income for that 1893–94 season had been a record of more than £5,000; five years previously it had been just over £1,000. Between the two clubs, total gate receipts for the year were more than £12,000, over £600,000 in today's terms. By 1898, just ten years after that humble attendance of 2,000 who had watched the first-ever Celtic–Rangers game, there was a crowd of more than 50,000 there to see the 1898 game. Rangers and Celtic were in business all right – very big business.

Ten years after that first Ne'erday match between the two clubs, when they were regularly attracting the biggest crowds in Britain, Rangers and Celtic had become so substantially established as big money-spinners that they were to be given the everlasting title of the Old Firm. The term came from a cartoon in one of the sporting newspapers on the eve of the 1904 Cup final, reading: 'Patronise The Old Firm. Rangers, Celtic, Ltd.'

There were numerous cartoons in a similar vein, depicting the two managers grasping big bags of cash, players carrying sacks of money to the bank (for their clubs, that is) and others, making a variety of aspersions about the money now being generated by the two clubs.

But other factors were beginning to emerge between the two sides, disturbing and sinister factors which would for ever change the face of football as it had been previously known in

Scotland. First Hibernian and then Celtic had introduced the sectarian aspect of soccer by the creation of an Irish Catholic team and it was inevitable that anything they could do, others in another cause would want to do better. Unlike Hibs, who had initially barred non-Catholics from their side when it came to players and workers, Celtic was free of sectarian discrimination within the club. Nevertheless, there had been moves in that direction, the first of them an attempt to limit the team to only three non-Catholic players. Then there was another attempt for 'only the right sort' of player to be signed. Both moves were immediately thwarted, but that didn't stop the cynics from commenting that the only reason they didn't go for their 'right sort' was because there weren't sufficient of them good enough to make up a team.

Celtic were proving to be doubly upsetting for those who were not fans. Not only did they now have an Irish-Catholic team in their midst, it was a team that was as good as – and proving they could be better than – any other team in Scotland. There they were after just a year, having already won their first trophy, the NE Cup, proudly publicising their very impressive playing record for that first complete season. It reads: games played 56, won 42, drawn 11, lost 3, goals scored 109. Enough was enough, they were muttering in the pubs and other meeting places. They had to be shown they weren't that good. They would have to be put in their place. A good team of Protestants should be teaching them a lesson. And in Glasgow, the choice of team for those opposing fans was Rangers, and so the Protestants and Orangemen became more and more identified with the Ibrox club. They were in effect a Protestant club, but only because every other football club (without an Irish name that is) was a predominantly Protestant club. They were not created as Protestant clubs. They were not out to advance the fact that they were Protestants. They were not known or accepted as Protestant clubs. None of them had a rule about the religion or ethics of their team players by virtue of their religion. But Rangers were to evolve that way. Protestants and Orangemen gradually dominated among their officials, just as they did with their fans. Also, their home was in the proximity of Govan and the shipyards, and many of those who worked and lived in and around those yards were predominantly Protestant. When it came to choosing a team to support, Rangers were the obvious choice for them.

By something of a coincidence, at the time there was an influx of Orangemen among the shipyard men who had come from Northern Ireland to settle in Glasgow. A considerable number came when the most famous of the Belfast yards, Harland and Wolff, expanded to the Clyde. The relevance of that particular yard on the Clyde figures notably in the story, a story of considerable legend as well as considerable myth.

Harland and Wolff originated on the Lagan in Belfast. They built the biggest, the best, the most talked about ships in the world. Among them was the tragic and legendary *Titanic*. The Belfast company was founded by Edward James Harland, a young Englishman who had done his shipbuilding apprenticeship on the Clyde. He left there to go to Belfast, where he was made manager of a yard at Queen's Island, on the city's River Lagan. Ambitious and highly regarded, Harland eventually took control of the yard, teaming up with a Liverpool-trained German engineer called Gustav Wilhelm Wolff. Their company became world renowned for the succession of magnificent ocean liners it produced.

'Harland and Wolff' in Ulster terms also equated with Protestantism, although not uniquely so in that society, in a shipbuilding or engineering sense. Catholics had traditionally been associated with the rural trades, the Protestants with higher skilled occupations: jobs which they zealously guarded as their own, locking out, whenever they could, all those who were not Protestants. That discrimination was brought about by a chronic fear of what they saw as the Catholic menace. At Harland and Wolff, which at times had a huge workforce of up to 20,000, the Catholic proportion of workers never exceeded a mere 5 per cent, and they were employed in the most menial of jobs.

Stories abound about Catholics and Protestants, and Harland and Wolff, many of a 'hit or myth' character. A typical tale originated around that time in the early part of the last century when the company was making its move to expand to Glasgow, purchasing three adjacent sites at Govan. The story, which those who told it swore was the gospel truth, was about the ominous hull number which had been allocated to the ill-fated *Titanic*. Ships are given a hull number as soon as building commences and are known by it, and it alone, until the launch-day naming ceremony. The story was (and it is still talked about to this day) that the hull number given to the Titanic was '390904'. There is nothing strange or sinister about that, until the next bit of the story, that is. Apparently, if you held that number to a mirror, coupled with a bit of imagination, it would read 'No Pope'! Such was the foreboding of Catholic workers at the yard, they were said to be convinced that this was some kind of ominous warning for the future of the great ship and had to be reassured by the management that it was all coincidence and not design. Even that latter twist of the tale is all part of the great myth; the actual hull number of the ship resembled nothing like '390904' and anyway the few Catholic workers at the yard would have known better than to send delegations to meet the management.

A true story about Harland and Wolff and Protestants, however, is one from much more recent times, when Aristotle Onassis, the billionaire Greek shipowner, and his new wife, Jackie, widow of the assassinated President John F. Kennedy, visited Belfast in the 1970s. Onassis had a 25 per cent stake in the company and was negotiating a takeover. It was in the early days of the recent Troubles and to Belfast Catholics, Harland and Wolff was a continuing reminder of the low esteem in which they were held in Protestant eyes and of British rule, harbouring as it did bitter memories of the seven occasions in the history of the yard when they had been the victims of severe rioting there. The rivets they used to bombard each other were labelled 'Belfast confetti'.

It was just after Aristotle and Jackie had left on their private jet, to return to somewhere slightly more salubrious than the Belfast shipyards, that one of the yard's Protestant shop stewards in conversation with a journalist told him how worried they all were about 'that Greek'. He went on: 'If he ever takes over, in no time Jackie will have the yard full of papist foremen.' But he didn't take over, and that news was yet another reminder of what the yard meant to them, a local preacher offering up his gratitude with the words: 'We give thee thanks, O Lord, that the hand of the foreigner has been taken from the throat of Ulster and that our shipyard will remain always Protestant. Amen.'

While they may not have constituted a sizeable input in numbers, the new supporters at Ibrox from the Belfast Harland and Wolff certainly gave the Protestant backbone of the fans' base a whole new dimension. The very first signs of religious discord among the Celtic and Rangers fans appears to have coincided with the latter team at last having come to terms with, and gaining a series of victories over, their new adversaries. It had taken Rangers five years to get their first victory over Celtic, in February 1893, and they were to repeat that outcome on several occasions. They had begun the following season well and that September in the league tournament, Rangers won 5–0. Two weeks later they met again, this time in the semi-final of the Glasgow Cup, Rangers winning by a goal.

Such was the scale of interest and devotion that both clubs now had among their following, it was decided by the two managements to stage the annual Ne'erday friendly, Rangers winning the first and completing a hat-trick of victories over Celtic. They were to meet yet again in the Scottish Cup final at Hampden Park, where Rangers won once more, this time by 3–1 before a huge crowd of 30,000, at last gaining their first-ever Scottish Cup after having failed for 22 years. Celtic had already won their first Scottish Cup the previous year, just four years after they had begun playing.

The supporters so far appeared to have been rather mild-mannered towards each other: Celtic fans were reported as saying that 'the boys in Light Blue are favourites when they come to Parkhead'. They were all such jolly good chaps, in fact, that when a Celtic fan loudly made the sarcastic point at the end of the Cup final, which Rangers won, that it had taken them 22 years to do so, manager Maley answered that it was 'rather cruel and unkind' of the fan to have made such a point. Alas, it was not always to be so. In the ensuing seasons there were the first rumblings of the emergence in the sport of the great west of Scotland divide, fans becoming more antagonistic towards each other. The shouts and taunts between the two sides had begun, although it was still tame stuff compared with what was to come in the ensuing seasons. At one of their matches in 1896, it was uneventful enough for *Scottish Sport* to comment that there was 'none of the bad blood which unfortunately disgraced more than one of their recent meetings ... although a handful of fools took part in an outbreak of disorder at the end of the match. But they took on the wrong people – the police, who were well capable of dealing with them.'

Contrast that rebuke of Mr Maley to the sarcastic fan with his reaction just a few seasons later when he hit out at what he obviously considered a principal source of bad feeling against his club, the sporting press. They were the subject of his wrath when he castigated them for what he called the 'bigotry and anti-Celtic feelings of the alleged fair-minded athletic press of Glasgow'. Maley claimed that ever since the club had been formed they had been against them, taking every chance they could to belittle them and their followers 'and to gloat over its defeats'. In their last game at home, Celtic had been host to Hearts and the Glasgow crowd apparently hadn't been the best of sports, cheering when Hearts scored and remaining silent when Celtic put the ball in the net. It was not usual at the time to cheer when the opposition scored and the response of the crowd at the Celtic–Hearts game was a real insult.

'This spirit of anti-Catholic feeling has been so drummed into the Glasgow public by these Saturday afternoon reporters that the public can't see any good in Celtic at any time,' went on Mr Maley. 'This, however, does not concern the club or its following. What does concern us are the great misstatements regarding the club's management and the security of Celtic Park.' This comment was prompted by criticisms about Parkhead not having sufficient turnstiles, and about an incident when a barricade gave way and three spectators were injured.

Those first disturbing signs of sectarian crowd disorder, noted by the sporting press within the first few years of the creation of Celtic, were to continue throughout the turn of the century and be an increasing source of consternation for the two clubs as the years went on. Hooligans had infiltrated the brake clubs, which in the beginning had consisted of the best of supporters. Mr Maley rounded on them, just as he had the sporting press, labelling the clubs 'a happy hunting ground for that breed termed gangster which has become such a disgrace to our city'. He also noted that 'religion has become the common battlefield for these supposed sports'. Hooligans, he said, disgraced the sport and city, and were tarnishing the game's good name.

Despite those early condemnations of sectarianism and hooliganism, relations between the two sets of fans continued their downward spiral and over the years both have been involved in a catalogue of the most deplorable behaviour. Rangers and Celtic matches have witnessed the worst disorders Scotland has known in this century. Scenes in and outside both clubs' stadiums during and following their meetings have been witness to murder and mayhem, riot and rumpus. Old Firm matches, as sporting occasions, are simply unique, a sort of Glasgow version of the Passion Play as might be staged at Nuremberg is as close as you'll get to the intensity of the sentiments expressed by the supporters of the opposing teams. The fervour and emotional fury of the fans is such that one can only assume that those who aren't experiencing apoplexy have an accentuated form of Tourette's syndrome. As recently as 1980, following a Cup final between the two teams at Hampden Park, mounted police were used in the first massed charge of its kind to be seen in Scotland since the General Strike of 1926. Even more recently, a survey by Unison, the public health workers' trade union, showed that in the hours following an Old Firm game there was a dramatic increase in assault victims requiring hospital treatment throughout central Scotland.

Still the fans continued to taunt, provoke, deride, insult and torment, the voice of one side proclaiming their Irishness, the voice of the other their Scottishness, while, bizarrely, both sets of supporters sing Irish songs at each other, Rangers' fans have 'The Sash' and 'Old Derry's Walls', Celtic 'Fields of Athenry' and 'The Soldier's Song'. None of the songs have anything to do with football, but are about historical events in which one side either scored or suffered against the other. At no other football game in Britain, or indeed anywhere, is there such sheer hatred from such a number of nominal Christians, with not a Christian word to be heard. The apoplectic shouts and screams of poisonous bigotry from around the stadium are such that when the editor of the *Belfast Telegraph* recently attended his first Old Firm game, he was to say it was the most overtly sectarian sporting event he had ever witnessed. If they were to be judged by such vocal obscenities, such hateful obsessions, then it could easily be concluded that the behavioural standards of the two sides are as bad as ever, maybe even worse. But yet Glasgow is no Belfast. The city has no barricades, no dividing walls called peace lines, no ghettos, no street rioting, no petrol bombs, no patrolling soldiers, no armour-plated police Land Rovers, no flak-jacketed constables toting baton-round shotguns. While post-match assault figures may still be alarming, the overall violence during and after matches is considerably less now than in previous years. There is certainly nothing like the constant scenes of crowd violence which occurred at virtually every meeting of the two in the inter-war years.

There may be something in the observation that Old Firm games act as a sort of safety valve between the two communities. It is notable that only at Ibrox and Parkhead, and the occasional meeting at Hampden, are the worst of these base feelings between the two communities displayed. They are not manifested as such in any other aspect of Glaswegian and Scottish life, apart from the odd skirmish following Orange Walks. Glasgow's two communities do tolerate each other, the irony of these regular 90-minute deviations being that it is done in the name of sport.

Meanwhile, the descendants of those two historical brothers, Walfrid and Moses, are in charge of two of Scotland's most thriving companies, their combined turnover being in the region of £100 million. They are in the lists of Scotland's top 500 companies, their annual reports, reviews, summaries, balance sheets and so on are delivered with all the aplomb of the best of boardrooms. Their chairmen's statements are mahogany-table stuff and are couched in the kind of terms that sombre, directorial gentlemen best understand, like gross investment, sector strategy, diversification of revenue base, infrastructure strengthening, corporate governance and the development of additional income streams. Where once their dealing with players would centre on what kind of day job the club might be able to secure for them with a construction company or shipyard, today's dealings are done with all the formality and strictures of an industrial company contracting their new fuel supplies. It's almost casually mentioned in the 2001 Celtic Plc annual report that in the year just ended, the club 'made a gross investment of £21 million in players'. Elsewhere in the report, everything comes in millions. Tangible assets £46 million; intangible assets £24 million; net assets £30 million; turnover £42 million; staff wages and salaries £22 million; shares in issue £47 million.

For the Glasgow Catholic Irish, however, Celtic is about much more than all these millions. Celtic Football Club is their greatest triumph, achieving everything their Brother Walfrid dreamt it might, and that too was not about those millions. It was about showing what a deprived and impoverished community in a new country could, with determination, accomplish; and it in no small way showed the way for those who were to follow that example in so many other avenues of Glasgow and Scottish life.

– CHAPTER 18 –

AnÐ CupiÐ HelpeÐ, Too!

They don't come sailing up the Clyde any more,
except for a holiday. The days of the little boats
and their pathetic cargoes of impoverished
humans looking for a country to take them in are
long over. The Irish no longer live in a poor land,
and no longer have to desperately seek out
another country in which to survive. They still
come over, of course, perhaps to meet relatives
who might live here, have a few drinks with them,
do some shopping and then head back home
again. Lots of them do it; there are even regular
bus services between Ulster and Glasgow. It's a
casual sort of run, picking up passengers more or
less on demand, in places like Clydebank, Paisley,
Eastwood Toll, Glasgow city centre and, naturally,
the Gorbals – at one time the city's biggest Irish
enclave – before heading south to the Stranraer
ferry, Belfast, and on to the most popular of
destinations, places like Donegal, Dunlow, Lifford,

Innishowen, Buncrana and Gweedore, on a single
fare of around £30. Of course, they come over for
every Old Firm game too. Ibrox and Parkhead are
still their nearest, their biggest, their best and their
most beloved soccer stadiums.

The coming of the Irish to Glasgow and Scotland hasn't all been
sweetness and light, but neither has it been the tragedy
doomsayers were predicting when those woefully overcrowded
little ships, the boats of heads and faces, were puffing up the
Clyde with yet another cargo of immigrants. There's probably no
other city anywhere that has proportionately taken in the
number of single-country migrants as Glasgow. Melbourne in
Australia might be the biggest Greek city outside of Athens, New
York has more Jews than Jerusalem, more Irish than Dublin,
more Italians than Palermo, but like so many other New World
cities they are creations of recent times and their populations are
composed entirely of migrants from other countries. None of
them had such a singular community arrive in their midst, to
live alongside a native population as did Glasgow. The sheer
volume of the immigrants was the exceptional and biggest
problem of the Irish coming to Glasgow. Had they been an army
of enemy invaders, the Scots would have been overrun. This was
an armada of Spanish dimensions, a nation in lemming-like
flight, escaping the clutches of the nightmare monster which
plagued its land – starvation. Among them were those stricken
with disease, so ill they could barely walk from the ships and on
landing would head to the nearest infirmary. All the city's
medical centres were swamped with the victims of such
outbreaks that they had to erect huge outdoor marquees to
house the sick.

That was Glasgow, a city besieged at the height of the exodus from Ireland in the years during and in the wake of the Great Famine. Little wonder that the city's population was to more than quadruple in the first half of that century, only New York rivalling it as the fastest-growing city in the world. Little wonder Glaswegians of the day found it difficult to look on the bright side, with so many telling them their city had become one of plague, paupers and popery. And while at times it certainly appeared to be heading that way, in the fiercely Protestant Scotland of the day, it was probably the fact that most of those arriving were Roman Catholic that was the most difficult to accept.

Glasgow changed dramatically as a result of the Irish invasion. It became as much a part of them as they became part of it. Over the years the 'alien race', as the Catholic sections of the migrants had been labelled by the Church of Scotland, was to prove that they were not so alien after all. But there were times when even the most reasonable must have wondered how it would all turn out. The riot in Partick wasn't the only occasion when the two communities were at each other's throats. There were regular attacks on Catholic chapels throughout the nineteenth century, communicants coming and going to mass were frequently stoned. They were treated with disdain because of their poverty, detested because of their Catholic religion and, perhaps worst of all among labouring men, despised because numbers of them had resorted to being strike-breakers. This had come about through circumstances in which the migrant workers had found themselves, initially in the coal-mining industry. Among those circumstances which forced the Irishmen to become strike-breakers was the fact that because of the religious bigotry they faced, they had been prevented from joining workers' campaigns for better conditions. The Scottish employees wanted nothing to do with them, even as comrades in their fight against the masters. This left them with little alternative when those masters asked them not only to take over the jobs of men who were striking but to allow themselves to be hired at lower rates of pay. It was circumstances such as these which did more than anything to compel the Irish Catholic immigrants into almost siege-community attitudes. They developed a ghetto mentality without living in ghettos. It strengthened their desire to remain Irish rather than to become Scots, and such attitudes would remain with them and their immediate descendants, some more fiercely than others.

It was to be an attitude which was to affect much of the community's way of life, becoming almost inbuilt in some succeeding generations, and was doubtless one of the factors in the formation of their own clubs and organisations. These included dance and music clubs, Irish-speaking groups and classes, political movements like Sinn Fein, and soccer teams, among them, of course, the one which was to be the most famous of all, Celtic Football Club.

While some were forced into acts such as strike-breaking, others achieved distinction among the employees of various industries, principally weaving, as tireless campaigners on behalf of the workers and became highly respected among all sections of the workforce. Eventually there was to be a large and notable Irish presence among the trade union activists who did so much for the betterment of working men and women.

There was discrimination against the employment of Catholics in many industries, the most notorious of them the Protestant-dominated sections of the skilled trades and crafts in the Clydeside shipyards and engineering plants. There was discrimination too in a variety of white-collar occupations.

'What school did you go to?' was the Glasgow version of the 'NINA' notices they at one time attached to the vacancy signs of the most select New York apartment houses – 'No Irish Need Apply'! Only a few short generations ago it was unheard-of for Catholics to be employed in Scottish banking, as well as several other establishment professions, whose employees thought of themselves as 'professional gentlemen'. Sadly, the 'professional gentlemen' of the day didn't wish to mix with these Irish types.

In other city workplaces and industries, there was a two-way cut in operation: various departments within particular companies were mainly staffed by those with the same religion as the section boss. It was like that in more than one of the Glasgow newspaper offices in which I worked back in the 1940s and 1950s. In one there was little chance of getting a toehold in the financial department unless you were Catholic. In another it was the circulation and despatch departments that had their command, the editorial departments of a further two being establishment Protestant. And it was much the same in many other city offices and institutions. It was the way of it. Thankfully, it's not the way of it now. Although there is little proof of it, and I have none to offer, discrimination undoubtedly still exists, albeit in a more subtle form. However, it is generally accepted by those who have made the closest scrutiny of the subject that it is nowhere near the extent to which either community were deprived of entry into specific areas of Scottish work life just a generation or two ago.

For years there was a considerable variation in the social class profiles of Catholics and Protestants, the former being more associated with lower wage scales and less job enhancement than the latter. The occupational statuses of younger Catholic and non-Catholic men and women are now closer than they have ever been. At one time there was a huge divide between school leavers from non-denominational schools whose fathers were in non-manual jobs and those from Catholic schools whose parents were manual workers. A survey conducted in 1980 showed the gulf to be narrowing, although there was still a considerable gap. It revealed that there was twice the percentage of school leavers from non-denominational schools with fathers in non-manual occupations than those leaving Catholic schools. Fourteen years later, in a similar survey, the gap had narrowed considerably. The number of Catholic students going to university has soared. At Glasgow University they went up by almost a third from 1967 to 1974. By the beginning of the 1990s more Catholics were recorded to have obtained university degrees than adherents of the Church of Scotland. Nevertheless, it is still felt by some that religious discrimination still exists in the country, despite the fact that Scotland can no longer be justifiably called a Protestant country with just 12 per cent of the population now regularly attending the national Church. According to the Scottish Election Study in 1999, the largest group in the country is now those with no religious affiliation at all. Not long after that finding was made public, however, one of Scotland's brightest young creative talents, the composer James MacMillan, made some surprisingly outspoken comments on the subject. MacMillan, who composed the fanfare for the opening of the new Scottish Parliament, made an address at the Edinburgh Festival, an address entitled 'Scotland's Shame'. In it he described Scotland as an 'Ulster without the guns and bullets' and claimed that the country was riddled with bigotry. It was his view, he said, that while religious bigotry did not impinge on the lives of the majority of Scots, most Scottish Catholics learned at an early age that the best self-defence was to keep their heads down and avoid attracting attention to the fact that they were of that faith.

While Mr MacMillan's address might not have been one of his better compositions, there was nevertheless considerable support for what he had to say. A newspaper survey found that about a third of those interviewed felt there was a deep-rooted anti-Catholic attitude throughout Scottish society – although the results of that poll mean that two-thirds would have felt no support for MacMillan's views. There was a similar conclusion in a 1997 survey, which found that most Scots either thought that any conflict between the two communities was not very serious or that there was none at all.

The accomplished musician's airing of his controversial opinions had come at a time when the sectarian issue had created other sensational news, in a somewhat lighter vein. Not long before Macmillan's address, another Scot, a man with a household name, had been airing his own musical sentiments on the subject. The leading criminal lawyer, Donald Findlay QC, had been caught up to his knees in it, as it were, when a sneaky video was shot of him singing his heart out with the most virulent of sectarian songs at a post-match celebration of his cherished football club, Glasgow Rangers. The disclosures of the video brought considerable disgrace on Mr Findlay and cost him a £3,500 fine imposed by his fellow associates of the Faculty of Advocates for 'professional misconduct and behaviour unbecoming to his role'. He resigned his esteemed post as vice-chairman of Rangers FC and issued an 'unreserved apology' for his behaviour. It was interesting to note that in making his apology, Mr Findlay paid tribute to the 'many hundreds' of Celtic supporters who had gone out of their way to express their sympathies with his embarrassing situation. One can only speculate at the number of them who were men of a similar professional standing to the distinguished Queen's Counsel and whose generous and open-minded understanding of the situation went along the lines of 'There but for the grace of God . . .'

The disgusting manifestation of bigotry at Rangers–Celtic meetings, of course, cannot be ignored. Nor can the fact that it is only when those teams are in opposition to each other that such a level of bigotry is exercised, leaving one to ponder why such eminent and powerful institutions as these two clubs can so effectively eliminate smoking and alcohol consumption at their grounds, yet make no incisive moves on the ridding of the one remaining blot on the relations between the two communities. At the same time, it must not be ignored that the rift in which the two communities seem so inextricably locked wasn't created at the football parks, but by the stalwarts of their religion, and therefore any lasting solution must come from such a source.

The words and deeds, and the reaction to them of Messrs MacMillan and Findlay at least proved beyond any doubt that sectarianism and bigotry remain contentious subjects in Glasgow and throughout Scotland. Of course, it stems from those thousands of settlers from both communities, Protestant and Catholic. As it has been shown, there were undoubtedly years when religious discrimination was rife, particularly in Glasgow and central Scotland. Those who have made serious studies of such attitudes no longer consider that to be the case today. As the Lord Provost of Glasgow commented about the fiery and fervent Irish nationalist John Ferguson, the man who was said to be the greatest Glasgow Irishman, 'Glasgow had toned him down.'

There is little doubt that the Irish who came and stayed and made Glasgow what it is, were most certainly affected, just as John Ferguson appears to have been, by the experience. They became part of a unique social fusion which took place between community and city as a result of their coming. One accommodated, the other mitigated. Both native and migrant communities were to be changed in a variety of ways, not least by Cupid himself. Mixed marriages between Protestant and Catholic were at one time rare in Scotland. When I was growing up in the South Side of Glasgow, they were spoken of in the sort of disapproving whispers that should only be heard by one of your own kind. It's still that way in much of Northern Ireland. In Armagh, for instance, they represent a scanty 4 per cent of marriages. But as far back as 1966, more than a third of Scots were intermarrying. Now Catholic–Protestant partnerships represent about half of all marriages.

Perhaps even more dramatically, the attitudes of Catholics towards Catholic schools have changed. At one time the subject was without question, every Catholic staunchly supporting the right to have separate schools and insisting that those schools be provided by the state, just as they are for non-denominational pupils. Various studies have shown a withering of this stance, the most recent one indicating that just over 50 per cent of Catholics wished to retain the separate schools that they were granted under the Education Act of 1918 while 45 per cent of them believed separate schools should be phased out. At the same time, one must be wary about such polls; another similar one commissioned by the Catholic Church registered more support for the right of Catholic parents to send their children to Catholic schools.

While a quarter, or even more, of the immigrants from Ireland were Protestant, it is those of the opposing religion who manifest themselves most as being some part of the Irish tradition, whether by sporting, cultural, family or some other allegiance. The Protestant Irish who came to Scotland proportionately contributed every bit as much as did the Catholic Irish, but they integrated to such an extent that they virtually vanished as an entity. Their acceptance and assimilation was, of course, due to their religion matching that of the native; they were not subjected to the suspicion and hostility which prevailed in the strictly Presbyterian Scotland at the time to those of the other faith. So well did these Protestant Irish become absorbed into the Scottish culture that when I discussed the subject with senior officials of the Orange Order, they found it well nigh impossible to name prominent Protestant Scots with an Irish background. Conversely, ask that question of any Catholic and the names of countless Glasgow Irish who are household names in sport, business, politics and the arts will be reeled off. Three such well-known names spoke to me of their own feelings about coming from the Glasgow Irish, their own ancestors all having undergone some of the dreadful experiences described in earlier chapters. Their responses and conclusions are probably symbolic of three prevailing attitudes among the community today: that they continue to consider themselves Irish; that they think of themselves as being completely Scottish; or that they are so proud of both they will answer only to being Irish-Scottish. To aid understanding of why these three people think as they do, I thought it vital to include some background to their own Glasgow Irish story.

Pat Crerand is one of the legends of Scottish football, having played with Celtic for six years before going south in 1963 to join Manchester United and become a member of their sensational European Cup-winning team. Pat has lived in the Manchester area since leaving Scotland nearly 40 years ago. However, the accent is still Glaswegian and there is no hesitation when he is asked how he considers himself. 'Irish,' he says, proudly, defiantly, but without a hint of the aggressive nationalist, although his firm beliefs are that a united Ireland should exist.

Pat had the kind of Glasgow Irish upbringing normally associated with earlier generations in the city. By the 1940s and 1950s, most in the community were of second- and third-generation Irish descent, but Pat, his brother and his two sisters were all first generation. They lived at 129 Thistle Street in the heart of the Gorbals, his father Michael having been born in Kilmacrennan, just outside Letterkenny, his mother Sarah in Gweedore, both in Donegal. Coming from a Gaeltacht region of Ireland where Irish was the vernacular language, they both spoke it fluently. So did their friends and neighbours, who were regular visitors to their house in the old soot-begrimed tenement in which the Crerands lived, the six of them sharing the standard room and kitchen, their communal toilet a tiny closet on the stairhead landing. Most of the family friends were also from Donegal and it seemed that so were most of those living around them in that part of the Gorbals. Everyone and everything about the Crerands had the flavour of Ireland. With his pals, Pat would go to Hampden for any international football matches involving the Irish team, whom they supported rather than the home side. Scotland's greatest hero of the day, the boxing legend Benny Lynch, another with a Donegal background, had been born just a couple of streets away, and other great sporting heroes and characters of the time who lived in the district also had roots in the Irish community.

Summer holidays, when they could afford them, saw the Crerands back in Donegal, where they enjoyed days at play with what seemed like countless Irish cousins, days that vividly live on in Pat Crerand's memory as some of the happiest times of his life. When it came time for Pat Crerand, the young man, to get married, there was Noreen Ferry, a young girl who was also from the Gorbals; her family lived above Joe Dodds' pub in Norfolk Street and her parents were both from Donegal: her dad from Gweedore, her mum from Creeslough. All of which helps explain that quick retort of 'Irish' when Pat is asked how he thinks of his nationality.

There was to be a sad and abrupt ending to the happy childhood days of the young Pat Crerand when his father, Michael, who worked in the giant Singer's plant at Clydebank, was tragically killed in the German blitz on the town, leaving his mother Sarah without a wage earner in the house to bring up her four children. The ensuing years of hardship his mother endured lives on with Pat in a variety of ways, one of them his memory of the family diet which was, as he says, for ever soup and potatoes. 'It was the same every day – soup and potatoes, soup and potatoes. It was all we could afford. But, on the other hand, as a kid you didn't really know about poverty. You didn't have the worries your parents had trying to make ends meet.'

Pat Crerand was to become one of the great stars of football in the years when Scotland was so prodigiously producing such people. He had started an apprenticeship in Fairfields shipyard as a caulker, his job being to seal new vessels' plates, joints and deckings. The caulkers were not at the top end of the tradesmen's hierarchy. 'The yards were notorious for the sectarian thing,' Pat recalls. 'You just knew you would be going nowhere because of the name you carried. The trades were carved up and the best ones, like the engineers, were ruled by Protestants, who made sure none of us Catholics were accepted into their jobs. It was terrible, really. You wanted to better yourself, but you couldn't. They were the ones in charge.' Thankfully, football came along, and after he signed a £3-a-week professional contract with Duntocher Hibs, scouts from the major clubs took notice.

They didn't ask what school he'd gone to in his new profession. They knew. Everyone knew who you were, what you were. They made it their business, like the day one of the principal talent scouts for Glasgow Rangers had words with him. 'He was Jimmy Smith and he took me aside to say he would love to sign me for Rangers, but couldn't. Of course, I didn't need to ask why.' Anyway, Celtic were also interested and he signed with them, aged 18.

The discrimination Pat faced as a Catholic footballer was slightly subtler than it had been in the shipyards, but it still existed, one example being the Scottish team selection. 'It went on all the time with them,' he remembers with a resigned shrug. 'That was why people like Jimmy Johnstone, Billy McNeill and myself didn't get the caps we should have. There was always a certain Rangers player who would be chosen in preference to us. It was much easier if you were a Rangers player.'

The great Jock Stein was to find that out too, says Pat. 'I remember the time just prior to the 1966 World Cup when Jock became manager of the Scottish team, but couldn't pick the players! Imagine that, the man in charge couldn't choose the team. The men on the committee did that. And you would always know who they would go for, and it would be as few Celtic players as possible. Of the 22-player team pool Jock was presented with, 12 of them were from Rangers.'

Yet amidst the blatant bigotry of the day, such as the attitude of the Scottish Football Association selectors, and the war cries, insults and songs of hate from the terraces, Pat never experienced it on the field of play. 'You want to know something, the Rangers teams I played against were all great guys. Every one of them. Players like Shearer and Wilson, I'm telling you, they were the very best of guys. D'you know, I was only called a Fenian bastard once by an opposing player. I'm not telling you his name, but he was from Hearts.'

With a surname like Kelly and a Christian name like Michael, there's no doubting the ethnic background of one of the city's best-known and distinguished of Glasgow Irish citizens. His collection of celebrated posts and honours include having been Lord Provost of his native city, a Commander of the British Empire, a Deputy County Lieutenant, and officer of the Most Venerable Order of the Hospital of St John of Jerusalem and a Fellow of the Chartered Institute of Marketing; various university degrees, including one in economics and another in law, a doctorate in philosophy, lectureships at Aberdeen and Strathclyde Universities and the Rectorship of Glasgow University; being named Scot of the Year; a string of honorary citizenships from towns and cities across North America, ranging from San José to St Petersburg, Kansas City to Fort Worth, Winnipeg; and an honorary mayorship of Tombstone, Arizona.

But say the name Michael Kelly to most, and it's not rectorships, lectureships, lordships or even Tombstone that comes to mind. Instead it's Celtic Football Club. His entire family history is steeped in the club, beginning with the son of the first of the family to settle in Scotland from Ireland, James Kelly, a blacksmith in Alexandria in the Vale of Leven, in 1840. His son James, born in 1865, was to become a talented footballer, good enough to be signed by the local sports team, Renton Football Club. He was a member of their historic world championship side, then became Celtic's first signing, helping them win their first historic game against Rangers.

While no one in those days got rich on players' wages alone, those with commercial savvy could easily capitalise on their names. James Kelly established a small chain of pubs and hotels, and with his expertise in the trade, an engineering works. He rounded off by becoming a stockbroker, making enough in the process to move the family from James Street, Bridgeton, to a house described as a 'country residence' in Blantyre.

When James died, aged 67 in 1935, he left his flourishing commercial empire to his sons, David taking over the engineering enterprise. David Kelly had a family of two, a daughter Maureen and a son Michael, the man Glasgow knows today as its former Lord Provost and one-time Celtic director.

Wealthy Glasgow Irish from the Catholic community were no different from other sections of society when it came to using their money. Michael Kelly, born in 1940, was raised in one of the fine houses of Hamilton and when he was old enough was packed off to the best Catholic boarding school of the day in Scotland, St Joseph's in Dumfries. It is a classic Glasgow Irish story, in a way – the son of the impoverished immigrant who fled the looming famine, finding fame and fortune, and his successive generations becoming proud Irish Scots. But unlike Pat Crerand, the Michael Kelly script takes a different course when it comes to national attitude. He considers himself thoroughly and entirely Scottish.

'We were a wholly integrated Scottish family even before I came on the scene. My father never took the view of himself as being Irish. His father had played centre-half for Scotland and was wholly integrated into the Scottish sporting establishment. Look at the Scottish medals and caps he had [five against England, three against Ireland, one against Wales plus another seven against English and Irish League teams]. Of course, there was that Irish connection which was recognised and acknowledged. We went to Ireland on holiday, just like Italian-Americans do in going back on vacation to the land of their ancestors. But we never thought of it as home and were always very conscious of being Scottish. There was never any Irish memorabilia about the house, or anything like that. Oh yes, we did celebrate St Patrick's Day, but purely the holiday aspect of it.'

Michael also disagrees with the composer James MacMillan's outspoken views on sectarianism in Scotland. 'Oh, I know it existed, all right. My parents were always aware of the discrimination against Roman Catholics and would often tell stories of people they knew who didn't get jobs they were after because of it. I refuse to believe it still happens now to any great extent. Look at the number of Catholic councillors there are, for instance, in the Glasgow City Council. And there's been a Catholic Lord Provost for the past 25 years. If you go around advertising the fact that you are Irish or Catholic then you are asking for it. I am really very surprised at Mr MacMillan's views on sectarianism here. In my experience I have not seen it in operation. While not considering myself as Irish, I suppose if looking at the Northern Ireland situation, it could be said I would take a nationalist viewpoint. So I suppose there is that side of influence on my views. Other than that, I never have felt in any other way Irish. I identify myself very strongly with Scotland and things Scottish. I think that is the way all migrants should behave. They must give the country to which they come their loyalty.'

An example of the third prevailing attitude I have identified comes from a man who was one of Scotland's greatest sports characters. He was at his peak when the champions in his sport were superstars, some of them, it seemed, having walked hand in hand with the very gods themselves. John McCormack was one of them. John was a boxer; they knew him as 'Cowboy'. John 'Cowboy' McCormack – the very name has a great ring to it, even though it was the local kids in the Butney in Maryhill who had christened him that because of his bow legs. But they always said it with a smile on their faces, for young John McCormack was bigger than most of them and when it came to having a scrap, there was none better.

John 'Cowboy' McCormack, retired boxing champion, is Glasgow Irish, and with a broad smile he'll tell you it's 'to the very core'. His ancestral background is by the book. His grandparents came over in the hard old days, hunted from their country by the spectre of starvation, or at best a lifetime of poverty. Glasgow was their only salvation. In John's case both sets of grandparents arrived from Donegal in the latter years of the nineteenth century. They settled in old Maryhill and John was born and reared in Bantaskin Street, in the heart of the area they called the Butney. The Butney was the kind of place where the view from your tenement included sights such as gasworks, iron works, steel works, rubber works and chemical works, with all their accompanying stenches, and a stretch of the Forth and Clyde Canal. The Butney also abounded with all sorts of characters.

The area got its name from (so the story goes) the time back in the early nineteenth century when convicts were given the choice of either going to Botany Bay in New South Wales or to Maryhill to dig the canal. More factual and less fanciful, however, is that when the first divisions were being made of the area, that particular location was known as the Botany Feus. Whatever the origin of its name, the Butney at times seemed part of another world. And according to John McCormack it really was.

'It was full of Irish like myself,' he says. No small part of why so many of them lived there was due to John's granny, Kate. Old Kate Cusick was the only remaining grandparent to have come over from Letterkenny, Donegal. She was an archetypal Donegal Irish granny, small and wiry and always in a long black dress, her grey hair permanently tied in a neat bun. She enjoyed her clay pipe stuffed with the blackest of plug tobacco as much as she did the occasional dram. And she ruled the McCormack clan with matriarchal dominance. If any of the grandchildren, and they had lost count of how many there were, stepped out of line, it was Granny who whacked them. 'A scud on the ear you would get, or if she thought it warranted it, then she would use her old cane carpet beater,' John remembers.

When another family back in Donegal needed a vital helping hand to get to Glasgow, it was Granny Kate they would contact. She organised everything required to get them over, arranging their fares and housing for when they arrived. She saw to it that the others rallied round to help, and had them looked after till they found their feet in the new country. She helped the McBrides, the Cusicks, the Shanleys, the McCormacks and others, all part of their extended clan. 'I'm telling you, she brought hundreds over,' says John.

Just like Granny Kate, the Butney has a special place in the memories of John McCormack. It didn't have a lot to boast about, at least not visually considering the industrial surroundings. There was a pub, a bookie, a grocer and a boxing club. That was all that was apparent in the Butney, but there was a lot more than that. 'You know,' remembers John, 'we had these three brothers. Right tough boys, they were, but characters. And they were Orangemen. I don't know how it came about, but when it was time for their big Walk, it was my mother who collected their sashes, washed and ironed them and fixed them up so they looked like new. When they marched out of the Butney for their big day, we would all gather, all us Irish-Catholic ones, and clap and cheer them off. I never remember any animosity, any sectarianism. That was the Butney.'

John took up boxing and became a champion, travelling the world to win titles: a medal at the Olympic Games in Australia, then victory at the British, European and Commonwealth championships. He made more money than he ever could at his trade as a scaffolder. He was one of the biggest names in Scottish sport, a name to be equated with the likes of Jim Baxter. That is no loose parallel, for Baxter and McCormack were the best of mates in the days when both of them were idolised by a huge section of the Scottish public; one the Irish-Catholic hero, the other the darling of the Protestant Rangers supporters.

John McCormack lives happily retired in a Paisley suburb and unswervingly opposes any form of sectarianism. The answer comes quickly when the question comes up on how he views himself in a nationalistic context. He says it as one word, 'Irish-Scottish'. Not purely Irish. Not purely Scottish. In a sense, Glasgow's very own blend, Irish-Scottish.

When the migrants from Ireland were flooding into Scotland, they said the city of Glasgow would become one of paupers, plague and popery. The paupers have gone. There hasn't been a deadly plague in the city since that last outbreak in 1900 that began in old Mrs Bogie's single-end house in Florence Street in the Gorbals. And as for popery, meaning (insultingly) Roman Catholicism, neither was that to come about in the way they had feared and predicted it would. The Pope has even been welcomed in Glasgow.

The story of the Glasgow Irish is a subject which is literally crawling with historians, academics and social scientists of varying degrees, all of them studying, surveying, scrutinising and searching for answers to the acceptance or otherwise of that huge community with which Glasgow and Scotland was deluged in the nineteenth and early twentieth centuries. Pitted against such undoubted experts, writers such as myself can only offer the most unscientific of conclusions on the subject that has been something of a lifelong fascination and, for the purposes of this book, has occupied my entire life for the past two years. What happened in Glasgow, and precisely why it turned out the way it has, can only be considered to be a most admirable piece of social engineering. In demonstrating how commendable it has been, some will point self-righteously to countries where there have been similar migrations or mixing of opposing religions with drastic results, places such as the Balkans, or north-west India, where in recent times they have experienced the most dreadful of massacres. They will talk of what is still happening in Northern Ireland, where, despite the Peace Process, fear and trepidation still exists in areas like East Belfast, where skirmishes and rioting are commonplace and the murals of hooded gunmen with cocked rifles continue to demonstrate the attitude of hate and hostility which still exists among many. In equally self-satisfied terms they will suggest a scenario of the catastrophe there might have been had the Great Famine occurred in Scotland, and it had been an equivalent number of Protestant Scots who had fled to Dublin for refuge.

Let the speculators speculate. Comparisons are really not necessary when considering what has taken place in Glasgow these past two centuries. That the coming and the acceptance of the Irish was not to produce such eventualities as others may suggest is a tribute to both native and newcomer who, among other things, have over the years, despite the occasional blemishes and eruptions and the lunacy displayed at two football grounds, demonstrated the most commendable scale of tolerance towards one another. That, more than anything, is the celebration of the Glasgow Irish story.

Selected Bibliography

The Anglo-Irish Tradition, J.C. Beckett (Faber & Faber)

Aristotle Onassis, N. Fraser, P. Jacobson, M. Ottaway, L. Chester (Weidenfeld & Nicolson)

The Billy Boys: A Concise History of Orangeism in Scotland, William S. Marshall (Mercat Press)

The Black and Tans, Richard Bennett (Four Square Books)

British Coalminers in the 19th Century, John Benson (Gill & MacMillan)

Bygone Days of Yore: The Story of Orangeism in Glasgow, Bro. Rev. Gordon A. McCracken (Orange Heritage)

Carleton's Traits and Stories of the Irish Peasantry, William Carleton (William Tegg & Co.)

Celtic Football Club 1887–1967, Tom Campbell and Pat Woods (Tempus)

The Celtic Story, John C. Traynor (Grange Lomond Books)

Celebrating Columba: Irish-Scottish Connections 597–1997, edited by T.M. Devine and J.F. McMillan (John Donald)

A Century of the Scottish People, 1830–1950, Professor T.C. Smout (Fontana Press)

431

Cloak Without Dagger, Sir Percy Sillitoe (Cassell & Co.)

The Decline and Fall of the Roman Empire, Edward Gibbon (Penguin Books)

The Faithful Tribe, Ruth Dudley Edwards (HarperCollins)

Farewell to Mayo, Sean O'Ciarain (Brookside, Dublin)

Forth Bridge, Wilhelm Westhofen (Moubray House Publishing)

A Gathering of Eagles, Gordon Maxwell (Canongate Books)

Glasgow: The Uneasy Peace, Tom Gallagher (Manchester University Press)

The Glory and the Dream, Tom Campbell and Pat Woods (Mainstream Publishing)

The Great Irish Potato Famine, James S. Donnelly, Jr (Sutton Publishing)

Great Pit Disasters, Helen and Baron Duckdam (David & Charles, Newton Abbot)

The Ha'penny Help: A Record of Social Improvement, Colin Harvey (Heatherbank Press)

The Health of Glasgow, 1818–1850, A.K. Chalmers (Bell & Bain for Glasgow Corporation)

Ireland: A History, Robert Kee (Weidenfeld & Nicolson)

The Irish, Robert E. Kennedy, Jr (University of California Press)

Irish-born Secular Priests in Scotland, 1829–1979, Rev. Bernard J. Canning (Canning)

The Irish in Britain, Kevin O'Connor (Sidgwick & Jackson)

Irish Family Names, Brian de Breffny (Gill & MacMillan)

The Irish Famine: A Documentary, Colm Toibin and Diarmaid Ferriter (Profile Books Ltd)

The Irish Famine, Peter Gray (Thames & Hudson)

Irish Immigrants and Scottish Society in the 19th and 20th Centuries, edited by T.M. Devine, Professor of Scottish History, University of Strathclyde (John Donald)

Selected Bibliography

The Irish in Modern Scotland, James E. Handley (Cork University Press)

Irish Names and Surnames, Rev. Patrick Woulfe (Gill & Son, Dublin)

The Irish Peasant, edited from the original papers, 'A Guardian of the Poor' (author's pseudonym) (Swan Sonnenschain)

The Irish in the West of Scotland, 1797–1848, Martin J. Mitchell (John Donald)

The Making of Hibernian, Alan Lugton (John Donald)

The Navvy in Scotland, James E. Handley (Cork University Press)

The Newspaper in Scotland, 1815–1860, R.M.W. Cowan (George Outram & Co.)

Old Reminiscences of Glasgow, Vol. III, Peter Mackenzie of the Old Reformers' Gazette (James P. Forrester, 1865)

Philosophical Society of Glasgow, President's Address, 1889

The Prehistoric Peoples of Scotland, edited by Stuart Piggott (Routledge & Kegan Paul)

The Rangers, John Fairgrieve (Robert Hale Ltd)

Recollections of a Donegal Man, Packie Manus Byrne, compiled and edited by Stephen Jones (Roger Millington, Lampeter, Wales)

The Romans in Scotland, Richard Dargie (Wayland Publishers Ltd)

Scotland in Roman Times, Antony Kamm (Scottish Children's Press)

Sir Percy Sillitoe, A.W. Cockerell (W.H. Allen & Co.)

The Story of Celtic, W. Maley (author's publication)

Tacitus on Agricola (The Loeh Classical Library)

Terror in Ireland, Edgar O'Ballance (Presidio Press)

Tiberius Claudius Maximus: The Legionary, Peter Connolly (Oxford University Press)

Irish

Who's Who in Glasgow, 1909, George Eyre-Todd (Gowans and Gray)

The Working Class in Glasgow, 1750–1914, editor R.A. Cage (Croom Helm)

The *Glasgow Herald, The Scotsman, (North British) Daily Mail, Glasgow Catholic Observer/Scottish Observer, Evening Citizen, Evening Times, Cork Examiner, Glasgow Scrap Book, Scottish Sport, Scottish Athletic Journal, Scottish Referee, Glasgow Argus, Glasgow Courier, The Constitutional, Daily Record*, Scottish Brewing Archives, The Pat Woods Collection, Mitchell Library.

Index